CO

AROUND THE WORLD IN
65 YEARS

101 STORIES & EXPERIENCES
FROM THE ROAD LESS TRAVELLED

AROUND THE WORLD IN
65 YEARS

101 STORIES & EXPERIENCES
FROM THE ROAD LESS TRAVELLED

BRITISH GUILD OF TRAVEL WRITERS
EDITED BY MARY ANNE EVANS

First published in the UK in November 2025 by
Journey Books, an imprint of Bradt Travel Guides Ltd
31a High Street, Chesham, Buckinghamshire, HP5 1BW, England

www.bradtguides.com

Most of the articles have originally appeared in other publications. We attribute the original publication at the top of the article. The editors have amended and updated some articles where necessary.

Editor: Mary Anne Evans
Experiences Editor: Daniel James Clarke
Assistant Editor: Roger Bray
Copy-edited by Ross Dickinson; project managed by Anna Moores
Cover design by Pepi Bluck, Perfect Picture
Front cover image © 2025 Antelope Canyon, Arizona by Chris Coe
Back cover Top left: Atlas Mountains, Morocco by Chris Coe; Bottom left: Venice, Italy by James Rushforth; Top right: Sri Lankan Elephant by Juliet Coombe; Bottom right: Pride in London by Rudolf Abraham
Part opener images Page 1: The Stari Most, or 'Old Bridge', Mostar, Bosnia by Petra Shepherd; Page 11: Peru Motorbike by Karolina Wiercigroch; Page 257: Sri Lanka Mask Making by Mark Julian Edwards

Layout and typesetting by Pepi Bluck, Perfect Picture

Production managed by Sue Cooper, Bradt & Page Bros

ISBN: 9781804693629

Digital conversion by www.dataworks.co.in
Printed in the UK by Page Bros

Paper used for this product comes from sustainably managed forests, and recycled and controlled sources.

**To find out more about our Journey Books imprint,
visit www.bradtguides.com/journeybooks**

THE BRITISH GUILD OF TRAVEL WRITERS CELEBRATES ITS 65TH ANNIVERSARY

John Carter is a long-standing member of the British Guild of Travel Writers, a TV writer/presenter, freelance writer, lecturer and scriptwriter.

'The past is a foreign country...' according to L P Hartley. As far as international tourism is concerned, the past – in this case the 1960s – was another planet.

Few Brits took holidays abroad. Not for reasons of cost (a couple of weeks in Benidorm was cheaper than a fortnight in Blackpool) but because holidays abroad were regarded as solely for the elite.

It sounds unbelievable today, when international travel is no big deal, that sixty-five years ago the original thirty members of the newly formed British Guild of Travel Writers had to put more effort into persuading their readers to go abroad than in describing the delights that awaited them if they did.

We were few but had tremendous authority, if for no other reason than nobody else had been to those mysterious foreign resorts. We knew what a paella was, and how to spell 'bougainvillea'. We and our readers had to pioneer without credit cards, mobile phones, internet search engines, or Google Maps, but we had a captive audience and little competition.

As the sixties passed, the boom in foreign holidays began. Printed persuasion was reinforced by radio travel programmes, then TV.

And we had a hand in that too. The appearance of *Holiday* on BBC television in 1969 was the result of an idea pitched to a BBC executive at our annual awards dinner.

And so it continues. Leap forward to 2025 and the creativity and skills of Guild members have already moved beyond the scope of this book. We are now photographing and storytelling travel experiences online in blogs, on social media, in long-form YouTube videography and podcasts, and short-form on Instagram, TikToks and live broadcasts.

As our younger members might say, 'The past is a foreign country.'

ROGER BRAY reports the historic Concorde flight

THE EARTH SHRINKER!

London
11.40
Bahrain
3.18
DISTANCE: 3500 MILES

Roger Bray takes the first Concorde flight from London.

ASIA & OCEANIA

CENTRAL AMERICA, CARIBBEAN & SOUTH AMERICA

NORTH AMERICA

PART THREE:
UNFORGETTABLE EXPERIENCES

BY RAIL & SEA

FOOD & FESTIVALS

HUMAN-POWERED ADVENTURES

INDIGENOUS CONNECTIONS

MEMORABLE STAYS

NATURE & WILDLIFE

WORKSHOPS & TOURS

INTRODUCTION

THE CHANGING WORLDS OF
TRAVEL AND TRAVEL WRITERS

*Hilary Bradt co-founded Bradt Guides in 1974.
In addition to writing and publishing she has
worked as a tour leader and lecturer.*

Sixty-five years ago a group of travel journalists got together to form the British Guild of Travel Writers to share information, ideas and a few drinks. The same year, 1960, I made my first independent trip abroad, to Greece. The government restricted the amount of money British citizens could take to travel at £50 – easily enough for my hitchhiking trip but hardly conducive to a luxury holiday. Travel articles in that decade reflected this reality.

Since then travel has undergone many changes, recorded here and elsewhere by older members of the Guild. But one thing has stayed constant: the thrill at the sheer otherness that travel provides, whether at home or abroad. An article in *The Times* recently reported that scientists believe that experiencing a feeling of awe on a regular basis is a contributing factor to long life. And surely that is the continuing essence of travel over the sixty-five years the Guild has been in existence? Travel can – and should – be literally awesome, and the ability to convey that awe through the written word is what good travel writing is all about.

Here are 101 articles and stories by professionals about places and experiences which stood out as being something special, something they wished to share. The vehicle for sharing has changed enormously through the years. In the 1960s there was no such thing as digital content; we had to write a letter to the travel editor of newspapers and magazines and wait for a reply. Something else that has changed is our awakening to the damage that tourism can do. A pivotal year was 1988 when the organisation Tourism Concern was founded to raise awareness of the effects of uncontrolled tourism on vulnerable communities in the developing world. One of their early examples was the regular watering of international hotel lawns in India, while the local people trekked miles to a standpipe. Articles started to reflect this and Responsible Tourism became a topic for debate.

The growing recognition of climate change has brought new challenges. 'No-Fly' holidays became popular as travellers struggled to match their conscience with their wish for adventure. Articles about wildlife tourism were welcomed, with a focus on endangered species and how tourism can help.

One thing is certain, members of the British Guild of Travel Writers will continue to reflect the times, and their sense of awe, for as long as there are readers to enjoy them.

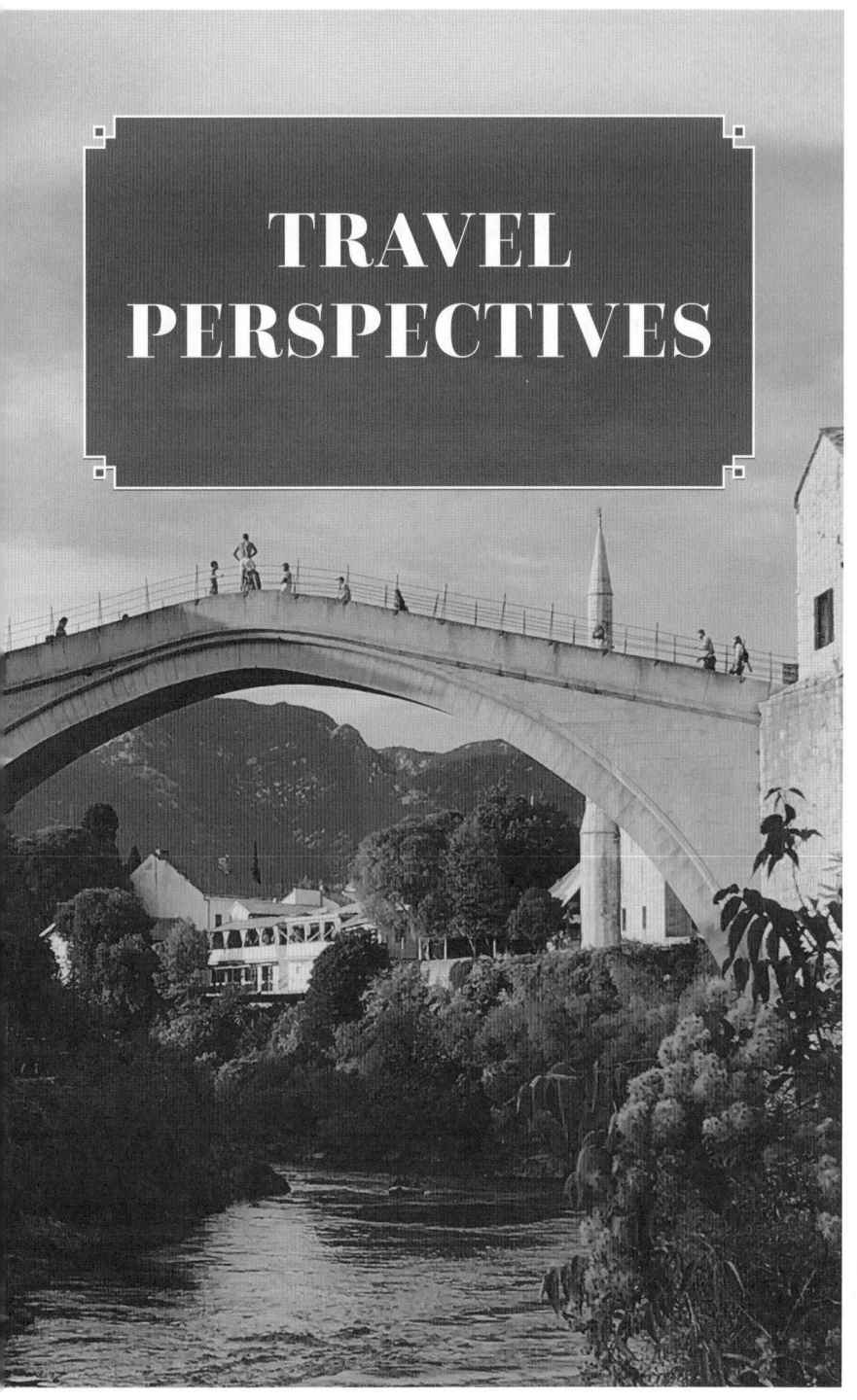

TRAVEL PERSPECTIVES

WHEN TRAVEL SHED ITS SHACKLES

Roger Bray looks back at the ever-changing seventies.

In the top-floor bar of a hotel, I asked for a glass of Californian white wine. The waiter, clearly perplexed, asked a colleague: 'Do we have any of that?' A shrug and a head shake. Sadly not. Disappointing, though, as I had read that it was pretty good – and hard, if not impossible, to find at home. But less gobsmacking than it would be today, for this was 1971, and most Americans were more familiar with Budweiser than the Napa Valley's finest. A cold beer would have to suffice but no matter, for as I looked down on the 'endless glittering lights' of Raymond Chandler's Los Angeles I felt privileged. I was there as a journalist. Back then few British holiday travellers carried home tales of massive steaks, burgers that put ours to shame, sandwiches you could barely stretch your mouth around and cocktails you could float a cruise ship in.

European package holidays by air had taken off in the early 1950s and expanded rapidly in the 1960s, amid horror stories of customers arriving to find their hotels unfinished. Brakes had been applied in 1966, when anxiety over the balance of payments persuaded Harold Wilson's government to impose a £50 limit on the amount travellers could spend abroad, and a year later when the pound was devalued. But mass tourism resumed its upward trajectory and the new decade would bring continual shifts in the ways we took holidays, where we went – and how much we paid for them.

At its outset the travel landscape was very different from today's. Few people possessed credit cards – and even if they did, shops, petrol stations, restaurants and hotels could not be relied upon to accept them. Most people took cash and traveller's cheques, or if you insisted at your bank, Eurocheques, issued in the currency of the country you were visiting. In America, cheques denominated in dollars were best.

Leisure travellers to the US needed visas. Catching a cut-price flight there at short notice was not an option. Competition between airlines was rigidly controlled. Bizarrely, many travellers got around the rules by joining clubs. Most famous was the Trowbridge and District Cage Bird Association. This raised hackles in London and Washington as officials tried to crack down on the perceived 'abuse'. But before long the ruse would become redundant. The advent of a new generation of aircraft carrying four hundred or more passengers, and growing consumer demand, created irresistible pressure for change. The first of them, Boeing's 747 jumbo, began commercial flights between London and New York in 1970.

In Europe competition was also on a leash. Minimum package holiday prices were set at the standard scheduled fare. The newly created Civil Aviation Authority (CAA) relaxed the restriction, prompting a wave of bargains like short breaks to Mallorca… at £10.

Tour firms also devised a ruse to undermine the straitjacket around European scheduled airfares. They began offering 'seat only' deals that masqueraded as packages but with accommodation customers were not intended to use – in one instance, caves. One operator told me how he tried to persuade the irate Spanish authorities, tongue firmly in cheek, that his firm's name, 'Just the Ticket', was nothing more Machiavellian than an English way of describing a perfect solution. Which, of course, it was. Resistance began to melt.

During the Cold War, countries beyond the Iron Curtain were largely off the radar. In 1972 my wife and I adventured to Hungary in our Riley Elf, a posh Mini with a wood veneer dashboard and a small boot into which we stuffed a tent. The country was less austere than expected and in Budapest you could dine well, by eastern European standards. No problem getting wine there. The tent was our accommodation on Lake Balaton, which provided a perfect vignette for the times. This was one of the few foreign places most East Germans could access. One of them arrived in a Trabant and pitched a hike tent opposite ours. Later a West German couple with a Mercedes and caravan rolled in. At huge risk, the former had ferried the latter to the west during the 1953 East Berlin uprising. What did he want his western friend to bring him, I asked. 'Just newspapers,' he replied.

Later I joined Thomson Holidays customers on one of the first package tours to the Soviet Union – four nights in Moscow for £29. The trip left abiding memories: of a wintry Red Square; a vodka-soaked night watching State Circus performers at the Intourist hotel; the amazement of Russian children queueing for the Kremlin Museum as Monty Modlyn, Lambeth-born market trader turned broadcaster, magicked instant Polaroid photos of them; and shopping in the vast GUM department store for watercolours that still hang on a wall at home.

In 1973 the Arab–Israel Yom Kippur War sent oil prices and the cost of aviation fuel soaring. The UK government introduced the three-day week. Candle sales rocketed; holiday bookings slumped. Tour firms were already fighting fierce price wars. In August the following year the Court Line travel group, owners of Clarksons, the country's biggest package operator, collapsed – slap in the middle of the summer peak with some forty thousand customers abroad. The crisis – the worst ever to have engulfed the travel industry – also dragged down Horizon Holidays. There was, however, a silver lining. The government backed a much beefed-up system of financial protection for future package customers, the broad basis of which exists today.

Changes in the air also made headlines: in 1973 British Caledonian made its inaugural commercial flight to New York. The CAA approved cut-price transatlantic 'advance booking charters'. You had to book and pay for seats weeks before the flight – and stay for a set period before returning. One entrepreneur launched a £49 return fare.

In summer 1977 the ebullient Freddie (later Sir Freddie) Laker finally won consent from President Jimmy Carter, who had campaigned on a platform of small government and low prices, to launch his much-trumpeted walk-on Skytrain service. The first flight left Gatwick that September, carrying 272 passengers, each paying £59. I queued all night to be one of them. By now you could tell someone had been to America when they ordered cheese and ham *on* instead of *in* brown bread.

At the other end of the price scale, Concorde, which had made its first commercial BA flight to Bahrain in 1976, finally cracked American opposition with the launch of supersonic services to Washington DC, adding the much-prized but long-frustrated New York route in 1977.

The British had already discovered the manifold joys of the Dordogne, but there were swathes of France they barely knew. Rural gîtes had been introduced in the 1950s to breathe life into villages becoming moribund as locals decamped for the cities. In the seventies they were marketed proactively in the UK. Mostly fairly basic – and absurdly cheap – they took us far beyond the Dordogne. With my young family, for example, I discovered the gentle green landscape of Limousin.

Rising numbers were taking ski holidays, once largely the preserve of the well heeled or those who had learned the skill in the forces. French purpose-built resorts with their vast piste networks – Val Thorens, the highest, opened in 1971 – were tempting skiers to desert the traditional alpine villages. In 1978 I had my first taste of the legendary Rocky Mountain snow when the long-established winter sports operator Inghams began selling packages to Colorado.

The following year, Harry Goodman, one of the last of a dwindling band of colourful holiday innovators, launched summer package holidays to Florida – the Americans' winter retreat. Summer there was hot, sticky and sometimes rainy. Hoteliers thought he was mad and refused to accept the room prices Harry demanded but, with some subterfuge, he broke their resistance. The weather didn't bother the Brits, though few then were adventurous enough to rent cars and explore the state beyond Miami Beach.

Countless thousands would discover the US in their wake. And whether because of demand from European tourists, a shift in American tastes or both, ordering a chilled glass of California Sauvignon Blanc would no longer perplex the waiter.

CHANGING WORLD

Telegraph Travel Supplement, 20 June 2020
*Ash Bhardwaj reasons that if we amplify voices from ethnically
diverse backgrounds, the planet will be richer for it.*

What's the worst travel experience you've ever had? Missing a flight? A hotel not living up to its billing? How about being spat at because of your skin colour? That's what happened to author Monisha Rajesh at a suburban railway station near Moscow.

'It was so unpleasant,' she says, 'and I could feel, under my skin, this sense of foreboding, that we shouldn't be there. I had never read about that experience of hostility in Russia. And that's because I had never read about any black or brown person travelling in Russia, in any newspaper or book.'

People of colour experience travel differently. Have you ever googled, 'How are white people treated in [insert country]?' Probably not, because you know that white people are treated well nearly everywhere in the world, and you regularly read about white people travelling there. But black and Asian people have to google their alternative.

Some experiences as a non-white traveller are awful. But others can be transcendent: on a group trip to Nepal, villagers chatted to me before any of the white guests, because they saw me as a 'brother'; a Māori guide in New Zealand shared his ancestral stories with me, knowing that I would treat them with respect, because I also knew what it was like for my heritage to be commodified.

Sometimes it's just helpful, like getting local prices at a market, and sometimes it's enlightening, like the Belarusian who had no idea that there were black or brown people in Britain.

These experiences are unknown to you because almost every travel writer is white – they can't tell these stories because they never experience them. It's important to recognise that this is a product of ignorance, rather than malice: there are black and brown travel writers out there, but I can name them on two hands, which leaves a sad gap in understanding.

Before my first visit to India, I read books by Paul Theroux and Eric Newby. But I couldn't connect with their experiences as middle-aged white men in India: observing the locals, rather than empathising with them. Remarkably, it wasn't until this year that I found a travel book about India written by a British Indian – Monisha Rajesh's *Around India in 80 Trains*. It was published seven years ago. That it took me so long to find it is a lesson in itself.

Even today, travel articles on India contain the tired old clichés of cows and slums, followed by spas and indulgence. There's a disparaging tone to these boring stereotypes, but read an article on India by a writer of colour, and you'll discover a completely different side to the country.

Terms like 'colonial charm' are particularly galling. They might evoke decadence and elegance to a white Brit, but to someone of African, Caribbean or Indian descent, imperial nostalgia represents tacit support of oppression and looting.

That's not to say we should wipe away the past. The nuance of identity and history is important: I say this as a half-Indian officer in the British Army Reserve, who proudly wears the Rifles' battle honours of the Indian Mutiny, even though my Indian ancestors fought on the other side. Those honours represent the sacrifice of my military forebears, and seeing them helps me to reflect on the complexity of the Empire.

It's scary to write about these matters, because they are sensitive, precious and make me feel vulnerable. It means admitting that I'm different to the white people who have commissioned me and the (probably) white people who will read my work. I fear that they will see it as evidence that I am not 'really British', or dismiss my experiences as irrelevant.

But in the past few weeks, I have spoken to friends of all ethnic backgrounds, who tell me that diverse voices make travel more interesting for everyone. Travel is supposed to be about broadening horizons and understanding different cultures, but all too often it comes down to repetitive clichés.

Now, more than ever, we must challenge dubious histories and narratives about the world. We've seen this with British Indians writing about India, but I want to hear more black voices in travel writing: what does a British Jamaican feel when visiting South Africa; would a British Nigerian have a different experience to me in Alabama?

You can't be what you can't see, and by seeing more travel writers that look like them, more people of colour will aspire to travel, and to write about it. Travel writers of all backgrounds should mentor and encourage them, give them opportunities and amplify their voices. Some of what they say might be uncomfortable. But their words will make travel richer, more complex and more inclusive for us all.

WE TRAVEL THE WORLD

65 STORIES FROM OUR TRAVELS

UNITED KINGDOM & IRELAND

DERRY AIRS

Sunday Independent, 29 April 2024
For decades plagued by Northern Ireland's sectarian struggles,
today an intriguing tourist destination where past and present
can co-exist, Isabel Conway delves into Derry.

Time frame: 1976. Location: William Street, Derry. Hearing a loud bang, an elderly woman rushes from her home in terror to hail a passer-by. 'Ah don't be worrying your head, Maggie,' Jimmy soothes. 'It's only another bomb going off up the town.' 'Oh Holy God, I thought it was thunder,' she sighs with relief.

True story, insists John McNulty of Derry City Tours, drawing laughter from his audience as he also recalls graffiti in the Bogside: 'Shop now while shops last'. 'We had this great ability to laugh at ourselves in the direst of circumstances and darkest of days,' McNulty tells assorted nationalities on his tour of Ireland's last remaining city walls, built four hundred years ago to protect English and Scottish settlers against Irish rebels.

Today Derry, with no hotel until the late 1990s, has changed hugely, and now enjoys the benefits of tourism.

Native Ciaran Quigley, who works in an integrated school, returned after twenty-six years to find 'a completely different place. The youth here are more concerned with jobs and social life than with flag-waving and tribalism.'

Nobody I meet, including customers in the famous traditional Irish music pub Peadar O'Donnell's, has yet seen *Kneecap*, the Oscar-tipped film about the West Belfast rap group who sing their pro-Republican songs in Gaelic.

Visitors from all over the world are drawn to Northern Ireland's second largest city to learn first-hand stories of how Derry emerged from decades of conflict. They visit landmarks like the pedestrian Peace Bridge over the majestic Foyle, linking the east and west banks, Nationalist and Unionist, Catholic and Protestant.

A hot September sun is splitting the stones of Derry's 8m-high, 9m-thick city walls as we reach Roaring Meg, the most famous of the twenty-two cannons used during the 1689 Siege of Derry, as part of a walking tour along the ramparts.

On my first ever visit to Derry, childhood memories of October 1968 come flooding back, the RTÉ evening news on our black-and-white television showing a peaceful civil rights march savagely set upon by the notorious B Specials and RUC. Ireland is watching the dawn of The Troubles. Protesters drop their banners and run for their lives through the streets of the Bogside in shocking scenes.

Below in the Bogside today the Tricolour flies over Free Derry Corner's monument, a big lump of painted stone, bathed in sunlight. Murals stand sentinel on gable ends of houses, commemorating key moments of The Troubles – Battle of the Bogside, Bloody Sunday, Operation Motorman, the 1981 Hunger Strike. A mural, Death of Innocence, is dedicated to Annette McGavigan who walked into a gun battle in 1971, the first child to die in the conflict.

The Museum of Free Derry is a prominent Bogside landmark established by the Bloody Sunday Trust to tell the story of the eponymous civil rights movement and is dedicated to the fourteen unarmed demonstrators who were murdered, and the many injured, by the British Army on 30 January 1972.

The Peacemakers Museum, a ten-minute walk away in the former gasworks on Lecky Road, continues the story, exploring the period from Bloody Sunday to the 1998 Good Friday Agreement. Using artefacts, oral history, archive footage and interactive features, exhibits explain how the Agreement was reached and the role played by three Bogsiders – John Hume, Martin McGuinness and Mitchel McLaughlin.

The family of the late John Hume, joint winner of the Nobel Peace Prize together with deceased Unionist leader David Trimble, distanced themselves from the project, on the grounds that it lacks 'inclusivity'.

Two of the three politicians at the centre of the project were members of Sinn Féin. The SDLP and John Hume's late widow Pat have said their objections were due to the narrow ethos and focus of the project.

Showing me around, Linda McKinney, director of the museum, says: 'We want the Hume family to visit and we think if they do so they will be pleasantly surprised. We're telling the story from the point of view of the local community. There's the Unionist story to be told, and those of the British and Irish governments that can be told elsewhere – we never said we were telling the full story here.'

After an exploration of historic old Derry, including the Victorian-era restored Guildhall, severely damaged by bomb explosions, our tour group stops to admire the striking bronze sculpture of two men reaching out to each other in the spirit of reconciliation on the western side of the Craigavon Bridge.

Another example of the sea changes that have taken place is seen in the previously no-go area of Ebrington, whose vast sprawling former British Army barracks, dating back to 1841 on the Protestant Waterside, was returned to the city as part of the peace agreement.

More transformational projects underway for Derry include further development of the Foyle Embankment and Queens Quay. A double-decker bus (decky) and converted ship-container street food cafés are already a big draw along the Foyle marina.

Kevin Pyke, one of the city's best-known chefs, returned to his native city in 2013 and set about creating an exciting food experience here in a disused car park. 'Make our city taste better' is his motto, opening a bricks-and-mortar restaurant Pyke 'n' Pommes on Strand Road last year.

The army barracks is now a stylish four-star hotel and spa, The Ebrington, while on the square live bands and restaurants, such as the popular Stitch & Weave, have panoramic views of the Foyle and the Peace Bridge.

The Walled City Brewery, where we munch tacos and quench our thirst with a site-brewed lager, is housed in the British Army's former Intelligence Centre. The brewpub's manager Amanda Hamilton reflects on how small Derry is. 'It's like a village really. Lisa McGee, who created *Derry Girls*, sat in my sister's class [at school]. The show was so true to life for us growing up here, with the bombings and barricades. All we cared about was where we'd be going on a Saturday night, what we'd be wearing and what boys were out. That was normality for us, but of course our parents definitely struggled. They went through a lot.'

And on that note, last but by no means least: the immersive Derry Girls Experience at the Tower Museum on Union Hall Place incorporates virtual reality experiences, props from the hit TV series that ended in 2022 and memorabilia that draws legions of fans who take photos under the Derry Girls mural on the side of Badger's Bar.

SPARKLING HERITAGE: A MOMENT IN TIME AT ENGLAND'S BRIDE VALLEY VINEYARD

Among the chalky slopes of Litton Cheney,
Fran Bridgewater uncorks the story behind
Steven Spurrier's enduring English wine legacy.

It was one of those wistful evenings when the Dorset hillsides appeared gilded by the setting sun, sheep, like fallen clouds, dotting ridge lines and a tangy sea breeze threaded softly through row upon row of Pinot Noir vines. I slowed the car and rolled down the window. That honeyed light, warm and almost celestial, held me for a moment. Far more than wine tourism, I thought, this was a much-needed pause. A quiet pilgrimage to the closing chapter in Steven Spurrier's remarkable life story.

This was the man who had famously sold copious quantities of wine to the French from his Parisian cellar in the seventies. 'Your wine merchant speaks English' ran his slightly tongue-in-cheek ad in the *International Herald Tribune*. He had taught the art and science of wine appreciation at his Académie du Vin, and by 1976, had shaken the foundations of the wine world when the Californian upstarts he championed – from Stag's Leap and Chateau Montelena – outshone Bordeaux's finest at the now-legendary Paris blind tasting that he organised to commemorate the United States Bicentennial.

Bride Valley was to become an estate where history, ambition and terroir would all collide to create something on home turf that the English never dared imagine: world-class sparkling wine.

Spurrier's wife Bella ran a two-hundred-acre sheep farm, tucked away in a natural amphitheatre just inland from the Jurassic

Coast. He discovered to his delight that it boasted precisely the same Kimmeridgian chalk base as the acclaimed Grand Cru vineyards of Champagne. The slopes were south facing, the climate was evolving and his vision was clear: if chalky soil and Chardonnay grapes could triumph in France, why not across the Channel in Dorset?

However, his plan was far from straightforward. The terrain was way too steep for tractors so many of the vines were planted by hand, southwesterly winds biting at their backs. Spurrier was a firm believer in the minutiae of detail, so he imported the finest Burgundy clones, sought advice from top French oenologists and meticulously tested soil samples across the estate to pinpoint the optimal vineyard sites.

So, when the first grapes were hand-harvested in 2011, they whispered a promise. After appropriate maturation, the inaugural wines released in 2014 reflected Spurrier's palate: clean and elegant with characterful 'racy acidity'. A Blanc de Blancs, a Brut Reserve and the delicate sparkling pink Rosé Bella, named in honour of his wife and lifelong companion. Hugh Johnson OBE described them as 'precise, intense, sophisticated, acute'.

I tasted the Crémant de Dorset at the converted stable block where weekly wine flights were hosted. The mousse was delicate and creamy, unveiling bright notes of sherbet lemon and ripe apple, layered over subtle brioche with just a whisper of sea breeze. I was reminded of Jancis Robinson's fond line: 'When his grandson asks him why he is famous, wine writer Steven Spurrier shows him George M Taber's book *Judgment of Paris* – a tangible reminder of the fateful blind tasting he organised'. However, this wine was tangible in a new way: Steven's legacy in a glass.

'Dorset Crémant is a wine born of necessity,' he would explain. The 2015 vintage had struggled to ripen so, ever the innovator, Spurrier leaned into the acidity. With a balance of Chardonnay,

Pinot Meunier and Pinot Noir grapes and half the effervescence of a classic fizz, the result was England's first and only Crémant and its character was unmistakable. 'A wine which sparkles, rather than a sparkling wine.'

It won silver at the Wines of Great Britain Awards in 2021. More importantly, it won hearts and palates the world over. Spurrier passed away that very spring, just shy of eighty, but not before completing his magnum opus. His friend and colleague Andrew Caillard MW called him 'one of England's great modern renaissance figures. A colossus in the world of fine wine.'

I walked through the landscaped gardens afterwards, past his gallery and tasting room, where a lifetime of awards and accolades were quietly displayed. The sun dipped behind the vines and I savoured this moment in time – a legacy rooted not merely in cherished nostalgia, but in what the English countryside was set to deliver.

Now, thousands of miles from Dorset in the heart of California's wine country, Spurrier's personal archive rests in the UC Davis Library. Letters, press clippings, tasting notes and mementos from the 1976 Judgment of Paris are preserved here, commemorating the moment when New World wines toppled French icons and he had, single-handedly, quietly changed the course of wine history.

Spurrier had always championed outsiders: California in the seventies and English fizz in the 2010s. With Bride Valley, he proved once again that great wine isn't born from tradition alone, but from firm belief, an appetite for risk and a healthy dose of rebellion.

ISLAND-HOPPING ON TWO WHEELS

The Independent/Independent Digital
News & Media Ltd, August 2011
A cycling trip covers the Outer Hebrides from end to end.
Following its 131-mile route, 'casual cyclist' Ben Lerwill falls
under the archipelago's spell.

They didn't give me a bike lock. I was about to embark on a five-day cycling tour from one end of the Outer Hebrides to the other: here was my map, here was my eight-speed hire bike, here were my snazzy panniers, here were my B&B bookings. But hang on – shouldn't there be a lock as well? The bike, after all, was a handsome machine. 'Out there?' Patrick smiled, nodding in the general direction of the hills south, and then down at his company's bike. 'No, I'd say you won't be needing one of those.'

So I set off, freewheeling into a world of cascading coastal scenery without so much as a key to my name. Scotland's Western Isles hang north to south in a 130-mile-long pendant of bays, highlands and lackadaisical bike thieves. A mere 26,500 people make their homes here, two thirds of them clustered in the north. In terms of long-distance cycle rides in the UK, it's as enticing a route as you'll find.

Patrick, it transpired, knew his islands. Earlier this year, he and his colleagues at tour operator Hebridean Hopscotch noted the archipelago's growing appeal to two-wheeled travellers and introduced an all-in cyclists' package with bike hire, ferry tickets and end-to-end accommodation. I'm what should be termed a casual cyclist (I wobble into town two or three times a week when at home, but wouldn't know a derailleur if I ran over one) so the simplicity of the adventure was attractive.

I'd arrived on to the northern island of Lewis, meaning I was setting off from Stornoway, the region's administrative centre. In the local tongue – a form of Gaelic that shares much with the Irish language – the name becomes Steòrnabhaigh, lending the place a touch more exoticism than its pebble-dashed cottages probably warrant. It seemed a proud, pubby little town, perched in the Atlantic at close to the same latitude as John O'Groats, but as a precursor to what the island chain was to hold, it gave barely a hint. Barra, my journey's end, was nine islands, six causeways and two ferry crossings away.

Seventeen miles was all it took. By the end of the first day's cycling, the shortest leg of the week in terms of distance, I was smitten. Lewis is a fiercely beautiful island, softened by sea lochs and rounded by hills that layer and rise into the distance. Traffic had dissipated to a trickle within a few miles of leaving Stornoway, so soon it was just me, the afternoon and the winding road. I learned that getting lost in the Outer Hebrides is nigh impossible and, by the evening, that fresh langoustines, cask ale and a view of Loch Erisort make for a worthy post-cycling combination.

'Time has its own pace here,' said Bernie, the owner of Loch Erisort Inn, the next morning, 'which is how we like it.' I'd been told that the 40 miles of water separating Scotland's Western Isles from the UK mainland were more than just a geographical divide, and so it appeared. Things operate differently out here. Daily papers arrive at no fixed o'clock. Nine out of ten passing drivers wave at cyclists. Even the sheep, in coats destined to become Harris tweed, chew through the day with a kind of ocean-sedated mellowness.

As the days went by and the sun, shockingly, made itself a familiar sight, the various islands came upon me quietly. It was bliss, really. Viking invaders settled here centuries ago, and they wouldn't have needed to look far to find landmasses to divvy up.

Within forty-eight hours of setting off I'd become acquainted with Lewis, Harris, Berneray and North Uist. Harris itself was astonishing, marking the highest point of the route (and the only truly lactic-legs uphill slog) with a tumbling panorama of moorland and mountains, then following it up with a genuinely breathtaking mile-wide beach scene, its colour scheme apparently pinched wholesale from some tropical atoll.

More of the same was to follow. The cycle route itself can be done either north to south or vice versa – I passed a total of some thirty people pedalling the other way – but to my mind it felt right to be beginning in the relative bustle of Stornoway and flowing gradually down into the croft land, valleys and low-roofed villages of the south. They say the prevailing wind usually favours those heading north, in which case the breeze was kind to me.

As well as being spectacularly attractive, the islands are also deeply religious. 'Presbyterian in the north; Catholic in the south,' one local explained, adding with a wink: 'You'll see people's propensity for fun increases the further down you go.' It meant that on Sunday the roads were ludicrously quiet (and the shops, it should be noted, very much closed for business). But no-one told the wildlife. On Berneray, not long after the flick of a tail signified an otter that had noticed me first, I watched a group of five seals hefting themselves onto rocks, then later stopped to gawp at a pair of hen harriers in the skies above North Uist. The same island's famed golden eagles, apparently greater respecters of the Sabbath, sadly remained hidden.

The cycling itself was split into manageable chunks – 41 miles being the longest stage, a distance easily fuelled by the mound of eggs, potato scones and black pudding that constitutes a Hebridean breakfast – and the further south I reached, the clearer it was that each island had its own defined character. Benbecula was a flat, peaty palette of greens and yellows. Grimsay was folded into coves and humpy headlands. South Uist, a real heart-tugger, was a vision of beaches and wildflowers, where the hills seemed to lean out of the landscape to get a better view of the butterwort and orchids. I cycled in a rare contentment.

The long decline of crofting and the predictable exodus to the mainland of university-age youngsters mean the Outer Hebrides are changing with the times, but the islands nonetheless remain very much their own place. 'I'd say we're less wary here, more trusting,' a South Uist bartender told me, and as the single-track road continued to spool south, I found myself agreeing, lulled into a hard-to-define freedom that comes from being somewhere both welcoming and remote. There were times when paying in sterling or spying a Royal Mail van momentarily took me aback: this was still the UK?

My legs were tired by day five. When Barra appeared, rumpled and olive on the horizon, I spent the ferry ride to its shore feeling a mixture of elation and relief. It seemed fitting, though, to have saved arguably the prettiest island for last, and my final two hours of cycling took a circuit of the clichés and superlatives that were its coastal contours. That evening, in golden light, I sat outside a hilltop pub looking on to a castle in the bay below. Two local drinkers – straight out of central casting, as they say – unpacked accordions and played into the sunset. It was, like much of the week, almost laughably magical. And the bike? Propped outside each night, and quite probably still where I left it.

I DIDN'T SEE ANOTHER SOUL: BRITAIN'S MOST MAGICAL WALKING ROUTE

The *Daily Telegraph*, August 2023

*Daniel Stables walks the breadth of Britain,
from the Lake District to the Yorkshire Moors,
on the 50th anniversary of the legendary Coast to Coast Path.*

Not all those who wander are lost, but I was. On the western ascent of Kidsty Pike, a windblown fell in the eastern reaches of the Lake District, a thick duvet of white cloud rolled in, smothering first the distant views over Ullswater to the west, and then the drystone wall in front of me, spilling over the steep ridge like dry ice over the lip of a beaker. I wandered lonely in the cloud until a cry of salvation came through the soup, directing me back to the path – from a pair of American tourists, up ahead of me on the trail for most of the day, who had turned around to notice I had vanished.

Getting lost on the Coast to Coast Path is a venerable tradition stretching back half a century, since the legendary fell walker Alfred Wainwright created the trail in his 1973 book *A Coast to Coast Walk*. Since then, thousands of ramblers have made the 190-mile schlep from St Bees in Cumbria to Robin Hood's Bay in Yorkshire, across the Lake District, Yorkshire Dales and North York Moors. Going off course is likely to become a thing of the past soon, however, once the path becomes a fully fledged (and signposted) UK National Trail – a process which was set in motion in August 2022 and slated for completion by October 2025.

In the meantime, I was walking the route in its entirety, to find out what had changed and what had stayed the same in the fifty years since Wainwright minted it. My journey had begun a week before my wayward wanderings on Kidsty Pike, at the western trailhead: the Cumbrian coastal village of St Bees.

The sky was a deep blue veined with white, like sodalite. Crackling gorse filled the air with the scent of coconut, and bluebells flowered right to the cliff edge, which plummeted sharply to a green sea and the pink rock of Fleswick Bay. I followed Wainwright's directions closely, noting sadly that the former miners' cottages of the down-at-heel village of Cleator still matched his grim description, 'cheerless monuments to a brief prosperity that withered and died', and following his advice for crossing a barbed-wire fence by placing my jacket over the spikes. 'Better a torn garment than impaled testicles or what have you,' he sagely observed, and it's hard to disagree.

I entered the western reaches of the Lake District on descending a hill into the pleasingly named Nannycatch Beck – still an 'Arcadia-in-miniature beneath the cliffs of Raven Crag' just as Wainwright described it. I sat to rest beneath a birch tree, watching peacock butterflies flutter their eyespots amid stands of moor grass, and tucked into the cheese and pickle sandwiches packed for me that morning at Stonehouse Farm, my B&B in St Bees. 'If it wasn't for Wainwright, we wouldn't be here,' proprietor Tony Beattie had told me as he'd prepared my lunch. 'My mother-in-law set up this hotel thirty years ago, and the Coast to Coast has become so popular since then. We owe everything to it.'

Wainwright is a legend around these parts; it's a rare pub between Rosthwaite and Richmond which doesn't serve his namesake ale, Wainwright Gold. An eccentric sort – he was famously antisocial towards other walkers and wrote that he took his walks wearing his 'third-best tweed suit'. By the time he published *A Coast to Coast Walk* in 1973 he had already achieved fame for his series of guidebooks to the Lake District, each painstakingly handwritten and accompanied by wry observations and hand-drawn maps.

His description of Ennerdale Water as 'remote from the usual haunts of Lakeland's visitors' still holds true. I didn't see another soul all the next morning as I scrambled along its southern shore; all was still but for a diamond sprinkling of sunlight dancing on the lake's surface, and everything in sight – clouds, rocks, trees, hills – was reflected as a strange, blurry mirror-world.

Beyond the water lay Ennerdale Forest, a dark mass of non-native spruce and larch planted from the 1920s to the 1950s by the Forestry Commission, much to Wainwright's disgust. A lover of the windswept hills, he appears to have harboured something of a prejudice against trees in general; in *A Coast to Coast Walk* he makes rather catty comments about a view being 'attractive in spite of its dark forests of conifers', and prefers at every turn 'fellsides open to the sky, singing birds and grazing sheep'.

What Wainwright failed to acknowledge is that those barren hills are the topographical equivalent of a plucked chicken – once covered in native woodland, his beloved grazing sheep have now nibbled them down to barren scrub, representing a disastrous decimation of habitat and biodiversity. In Ennerdale, the authorities are taking steps to repopulate the corridors of imported conifers with native trees, and the forest is becoming a haven for endangered wildlife. I spotted marsh fritillary butterflies flitting orange and white through the ferns, and managed to photograph a red squirrel scampering up a tree trunk. There are also plans to reintroduce pine martens. The forest has taken on the feeling of an abandoned human place, like an amusement park left to overgrow. Once arrow-straight, the conifers are becoming gnarled and crooked, bearded with mosses and lichens; sap spills from gashes in their trunks like oil from a breached hull.

Before long, civilisation began to reveal itself. I stopped for a coffee at the YHA Black Sail, still 'the loneliest and most romantic of youth hostels', in Wainwright's words, which has been sheltering weary wayfarers since 1933. Then came Grasmere, where I joined the throngs of tourists poking around Dove Cottage, erstwhile home of William Wordsworth and his housemate from hell, Samuel Taylor Coleridge, who would wake screaming from opiate nightmares and demand boiled eggs seasoned with cayenne pepper.

Wainwright's book does not devote much space to human culture, however – he tended to see humanity in general as an inconvenience – so soon I was back out into the hills, leaving the Lakes behind for the Yorkshire Dales. I was met in the village of Reeth by Craig Ralston, Senior National Nature Reserve Manager at Natural England, who walked with me for an hour to discuss conservation challenges along the trail.

'In Wainwright's day, this verge would've been covered in wildflowers,' he said, indicating a roadside strip of neatly shorn grass. 'Because of health and safety, and our modern fixation on tidiness, they are mown nowadays – it's all habitat loss. You hear a lot less cuckoos today than fifty years ago, and plants like Yorkshire sandwort are getting squeezed by climate change.

'On the other hand, we've worked with Kew Gardens to repopulate the lady's slipper orchid, which only grows here in the Yorkshire Dales. We're also seeing a lot more buzzards, red kites, little egrets, and butterfly moths than Wainwright would have seen.

'Ultimately, we are just another species. Yes, we have a much greater impact than most – but we are also the only ones able to recognise that, and to do something about it.'

Becoming a National Trail should make the Coast to Coast more accessible to greater numbers, even if it loses some of its choose-your-own-adventure appeal. I met many walkers along the way, some from as far afield as the USA and Australia, whose only complaint was that the walk was not well signposted enough. In places, in fact, it isn't waymarked at all, and in others, the path degenerates into a boggy morass which must be navigated, hopscotch-style, with a series of carefully landed leaps.

On my final day's walk, a trying 20-miler over the moors from Glaisdale to Robin Hood's Bay, I picked a route carefully across the boggy Graystone Hills until finally the skeletal ruin of Whitby Abbey revealed itself in the distance, and beyond that, the North Sea. I emerged from the moor and met a main road, and, soon afterwards, a junction with a road sign signalling 2.5 miles to Robin Hood's Bay – straight as a die, downhill on tarmac all the way. I withered somewhat as I consulted my map and realised that Wainwright, in typical style, had forgone this direct route to the finish line in favour of one final exhausting, undulating clifftop push around a craggy, hilly headland.

I was tempted, I will not lie, to follow that straight road, to the promise of scampi and chips, a cold pint and a warm bed. But I resisted, keeping to Wainwright's suggested route, propelled by the quote which adorns a tiled mural to the great man in his native Blackburn, and which could be said to be a hillwalkers' credo: 'You were made to rise and soar, to crash to earth, then to rise and soar again'.

AFTER IT BLOWS OVER

The *Sunday Telegraph*, May 2001
William Gray sets sail for the Isles of Scilly,
eager to discover whether the archipelago – renowned for
its sunny, mild climate and dazzling turquoise seas – does
indeed have a toehold in the tropics.

essy. That was the weather forecast and that, undeniably, is what we've got. No wonder there's a grim silence on board the *Scillonian III*. The ship's commentary, waxing lyrical about Mousehole and Wolf Rock, is obviously pre-recorded. We can barely see the Cornish coastline, let alone any landmarks. But it gets worse. 'As we head towards the Isles of Scilly,' the voice croons, 'you can sense the ship lift eagerly as she meets the great swells that have travelled across three thousand miles of open ocean…'

A woman next to me flinches as the ship shudders from another crashing broadside. There's a pale, stoic look about her as she clasps an empty cup and tries to ignore the fresh slick of coffee at her feet.

The Isles of Scilly are something of an enigma. Despite being just 28 miles southwest of Land's End, they seem to have a toehold in the tropics. Abbey Gardens on Tresco, one of the archipelago's five inhabited islands, runs rampant with exotic plants, while the surrounding seas are brilliant turquoise – teeming with corals, sponges and sea fans. All this is nurtured by the Gulf Stream and one of the UK's mildest and sunniest climates. But the flip side, of course, is that anything the Atlantic decides to hurl at Britain reaches the Isles of Scilly first.

After three stomach-churning, coffee-drenched hours we reach Hugh Town on St Mary's – home to most of the islands' two thousand inhabitants. People with ruddy faces and hunched shoulders are waiting for the *Scillonian III*'s return run to Penzance. Spray cascades over the jetty wall onto their heads, blending miserably with a grey squall racing across the harbour. It's the kind of weather that would make the toughest Doberman turn tail and hide its walking leash under the sofa.

In the town centre a sodden procession of holidaymakers browse the curio shops. Clad in waterproofs and with droplets of rain dangling from their noses, they scowl at the brazenly sunny postcard stands. A long weekend in the so-called 'Sun Isles' promised a short cut to spring – a few lazy days of warmth while the mainland struggled to shed a bitter and stubborn winter. I feel a big mope coming on as I trudge towards my B&B at the far end of the waterfront. But an unexpected glimmer of inspiration is hanging on my bedroom wall in the form of an old travel poster promoting the Isles of Scilly. 'Ocean air', it boasts, 'is the greatest of all curative agents'.

Thirty minutes later I am stalking Old Town Bay on the southern shore of St Mary's, snatching breaths from the full force of the gale. A small church provides momentary calm before I scale the ruthlessly gnawed headland of Peninnis. Thick gobs of sea spume quiver around granite cliffs that have been chiselled by rain and sea into a spectacular gallery of leering faces. Buffeted by the wind, I stagger around like a drunkard, my jacket flapping wildly like a loose sail on a doomed yacht.

The following morning, gusts are still reaching force 8. I wake from a deep ozone-drugged sleep – my face flushed with windburn, my eyes red and sore. It hasn't taken long to shed the wan pallor of a newcomer. After devouring an enormous cooked breakfast, I stride down to the pier where boatmen are chalking up the day's excursions. Only Bryher and Tresco are on offer – heavy seas have severed St Mary's from the other islands. So I take an exhilarating, gunwale-grabbing ride in an open launch called the *Guiding Star*.

On Bryher, surf is blooming on the headlands above Hell Bay – a relentless procession of sinewy waves hurling themselves onto the rocks and filling the air with the salty sweat of their exertions. The smell of angry sea is like a pheromone and, along with dozens of other day trippers, I watch transfixed as the sea flexes its muscles.

A scything blast of sleet finally sends us scuttling back to the jetty. Huddled in the bows of the *Guiding Star*, I am unaware of the brightening sky to the west. As quickly as it arrived, the wintry squall is whipped away and the wind ushers in paler wisps of cloud. By the time we reach nearby Tresco, I look up to find an insipid, but promising sun.

Emerging spontaneously, like mayflies from a Scottish loch, children descend on sandy beaches and ride bicycles along the traffic-free roads of New Grimsby – a cluster of timeshare cottages, a shop and a café. It's only a forty-minute stroll to Abbey Gardens, but the subtropical oasis (built around the ruins of a 12th-century priory) seems to sprout from another world. Not only do I find Mexican yuccas, South African proteas and Australian bottlebrush plants, but the fine, calm weather that goes with them.

Shedding waterproofs, hat and gloves, I stretch out on a stone bench snugly situated in a suntrap. If ocean air is indeed the greatest of all curative agents, the last twenty-four hours must have equalled a month in a health farm. Now it's time for some indulgent sunshine.

FLOATING FREE –
A CANAL BOAT TRIP TO WORCESTER

The *Daily Telegraph*, June 2025
*Adrian Phillips and his family return to Worcestershire to
repeat an infamous holiday of the past.*

It had been thirty years since we last went canal-boating. Now, as
I misjudged our speed into Astwood Top Lock, triggering howls
from the galley as cans cartwheeled from shelves and red wine
sloshed on the floor, it felt as though nothing had changed.

The narrowboat break of 1994 has gone down in Phillips family
folklore. 'Remember when the dog went overboard and Dad fell
in trying to pull him out?' we'll say to each other at Christmas. Or
the 'Titanic' incident, when my brother caught the rudder at the
back of an emptying lock, and the front of the boat dropped and
dropped with the water until finally, thank goodness, the rudder
ripped off and the stern came crashing down. We'd had to call out
the engineer, of course. He'd come again to unblock the loo when
Mum tried to flush cotton wool pads. He was a stoical sort.

All of which added up to one of the best family holidays ever,
one we often swore to repeat. And here we were at last, Mum
mopping wine from the floor as we headed out on the Birmingham
and Worcester Canal for a week-long return trip from Stoke Prior
to Worcester. Same canal, same mopping, same season: springtime,
the birds pairing up and buds starting to soften the bony trees –
although 1994 had been icily cold, which made Dad's dunking even
more enjoyable.

There were other differences. Three decades on, that grey-haired
man working the windlass to lift the paddles to drain the lock wasn't
my father. We'd faced some choppy water when my parents divorced,

but Colin had come along, and the way became smooth again. He's Grandpa Colin now; those nine-year-old twins were mine, lined up beside him to push open the gates, puff-cheeked with earnest endeavour. Yes, a big difference: this time I was father as well as son, with more life behind than ahead.

A tight parade of tatty industrial buildings gave way to banks of rushes and hawthorns frothing white with early blossom. Six locks came in quick succession, testing our processes, but we fell into roles without debate. Grandpa Colin and Monika, my wife, were the gatekeepers, jumping off and on with windlasses in hand to bookend our passage through each lock. Mum despatched a steady supply of coffee and muffins from the galley, while deckhands Matty and Kitty clambered about on the roof and offered a running commentary on the mistakes made by the helmsman at the back.

I was that helmsman, tight-browed with the burden of responsibility. Stretching ahead was a craft measuring 70ft – the length of two-and-a-half London buses, the kids informed me with a certain sadistic relish. There were three bedrooms, two toilets, a shower, a galley and dining area, four adults, the twins and two dogs, all to be threaded through narrow locks and nosed around blind bends. It was a pretty boat too, dark blue and glossy, with red handrails running along the top and its name painted with a dainty flourish on the side: *Eden*. Not a scuff mark to be seen. Sorry, *Eden*.

But a canal is balm for the nerves. Olive-green water slipped beneath the banks, pirouetted around protruding stumps, toyed lazily with a twig and a feather. It vented and thundered in the lock chambers, before swirling away on release and settling on its journey once more. I found pleasure in the simple geometry of the architecture: the arc of the little bridges, the interlocking teeth of the cogs in the lock mechanisms, the horizontal timbers that levered the gates. There was beauty in the robust functionality of this manmade waterway, iron and wood and brick working in harmony since the year Wellington won Waterloo. It seemed to slot into its landscape, like nature with neatened edges. And as we moored at dusk near a grand old oak tree, and a hundred chuckling jackdaws landed as one to roost in its branches, I felt more relaxed than I had in a long, long while.

We spent much of three days meandering the 11 miles down to Worcester. There would have been rather more urgency in the 19th century, when working men managed heavy horses to pull barges piled with salt from the works at Stoke Prior and chocolate from the Cadbury factory at Bournville. It must have taken some choreography, particularly when barges had to pass one another, horses rubbing shoulder to shoulder and towlines manoeuvred over or under the hulls in a three-way tango between man, boat and beast.

Today you'll see a purposeful jogger panting up the towpath, perhaps, or a kayaker racing the clock, but otherwise the canal is a place of gentle journeying and parallel existences. At Hanbury Junction, we chugged through a corridor of narrowboats moored bow to stern, some scruffy and others immaculately kept, but all obviously permanent homes. Smoke curled from the chimneys of boats called *Adventure Before Dementia, Seize the Day*, and *Bob Along*, the mission statements of people who had untethered from a hurrying world.

We kept left at the junction and carried on, through the dripping darkness of Dunhampstead Tunnel and out into air full of barnyard smells. On the right was a cameo of idyllic yesteryear, with a foreground of skittish lambs and behind it a medieval church bowing with age. At Tibberton, we moored for the night outside The Bridge pub and rewarded ourselves with a beef carvery dinner and pints of Butty Bach.

'Avast, me hearties – we're coming alongside!' cried Grandpa Colin next morning as we set off past a boat called *Polly*, and the trio of middle-aged women on board brandished imaginary cutlasses and pulled faces at the twins. Numbered bridges continued to tick down towards Worcester, but there was no sign yet of the city. We heard the soft pop of a farmer's gun in the distance. We watched a pair of herons lumber into the sky and a swan sleeping on an untidy nest in the reeds, neck folded over her back.

There were plenty of mishaps to reminisce about during Christmases to come. The propellor got snarled in someone's discarded pants; the dogs tripped Grandpa Colin over on the towpath. But we became a fairly well-oiled outfit as we navigated locks with names straight from a Dickens novel: into Blackpole Lock and barely a nudge or scrape; through Bilford Bottom, slick as a bar of soap. Then warehouses started to appear, and a string of canal-side back gardens containing beach huts, hammocks and self-built outdoor bars.

The bells of Worcester Cathedral were ringing as we tied up outside Sidbury Lock. We visited the Museum of Royal Worcester, tried and failed to crack the escape room at the Commandery, ate upmarket burgers for lunch (the kids' choice) and Japanese food for dinner (our choice). And then we began the slow chug back the way we'd come.

It was just a few weeks later that Grandpa Colin had his stroke. The choppiest of waters. But the way will become smooth again, and when his right arm is strong enough to wield a windlass, we'll book another narrowboat trip because thirty years is too long to wait to measure out some days in locks and bridges, cups of tea and games of cards. *Seize the Day*, *Bob Along* – the boat people have it right. It's good for the soul to float a little freer.

EUROPE

THE GREAT OUTDOORS

Trailblazing, **December 2022**
*Anna Richards tackles the Transcaucasian Trail in
Armenia where Asia and Europe meet.*

Knocking back vodka shots with a group of beekeepers as skewers of pheasant crackled on an open flame wasn't what I'd expected to be doing that evening, but then, nothing about my trekking across Armenia was what I'd expected. It's difficult to have preconceptions when you're part of the first cohort to tackle a trail.

The Transcaucasian Trail (TCT) spans 1,500km across Armenia and Georgia, and, political situation permitting, will one day double in length when linked with Azerbaijan. It had been a work in progress for seven years, and two years of lockdowns had hardly been conducive to building a transcontinental hike, but as I bushwhacked through foliage taller than me, it was clear that Covid-19 hadn't been the only problem when mapping a route here.

I caught the bus from the capital Yerevan to Meghri, on the southern border with Iran. For northbound hikers, it's the start of the trail. As the rickety old *marshrutka* rattled and lurched through the nine-hour journey, the landscape became increasingly arid. As I chatted to an Iranian man heading home, relishing what would be my last social interaction for some time, an almighty bang punctuated our conversation. The driver skidded to a halt at the side of the highway, pulling over long enough to retrieve part of the bus roof that had fallen off. We set off again, this time with a skylight.

Meghri can be hot, and never more so than early August when I began my odyssey in 37°C. Arevik National Park, the first stage of the trail, hardly looked hospitable. Blanched white sheep skulls littered the rubble, forest fires had reduced most of the trees to charcoal stumps (and obliterated most trail markings), and I climbed steeply until I could blot out Meghri, now a tiny green dot of civilisation, with my finger.

Six months earlier I hadn't heard of the TCT, but after seeing a post about the new trail on Twitter, my interest was instantly piqued. In under twenty-four hours I'd committed. I joined a training programme with hikers from across the globe, enrolled in Armenian conversation classes and tried desperately (and unsuccessfully) to obtain good-quality physical maps of the country. I'd never prepared so thoroughly for a hike, nor felt so clueless.

Mountains often look toothy, but Arevik National Park was more like the abrased, chipped enamel of an ill-cared-for mouth, creating a natural and impenetrable-looking border with Iran. I felt very alone that first night, and very small. The wind funnelled thick layers of stormy clouds across the sky and every so often a beam of sunlight would break through, spotlighting solitary mountain peaks. I imagined the mountains rolling on forever and ever, with my tent no bigger than a grain of sand amid them. It was three days before I saw a human face, a beekeeper in a village 54km from my starting point.

As I adjusted to the solitude I passed ruined villages, sometimes so overgrown that the first I knew of them was a large boulder under my boot. I scrambled up scree into dense cloud and followed barely visible tracks through sticky patches of forest peppered with giant hogweed. I adopted a family of four stray dogs (or rather, they adopted me) that accompanied me for several days. I gave them all names and spoke at length to them. If I hadn't been insane to embark on this adventure, I certainly would be by the end.

After largely climbing the first few days, the trail began to yo-yo, plunging into the belly of gorges, and I began to pass settlements. Rows of wooden beehives, Soviet-era LADAs taking day trippers to picnic sites, and wizened men, chain-smoking by village water fountains. I sought shade between the cool walls of millennia-old monasteries which, while almost derelict inside, were often perfectly preserved on the exterior.

With civilisation came legendary Armenian hospitality. Meal invitations came in their flurries, and I'd leave with my bag full of ripe apricots and thick, folded blankets of *lavash*, Armenian flatbread. As the land flattened, the people multiplied. Places where I slept now had names: Tandzaver, Tatev, Shamb.

Vayots Dzor, or the 'Valley of Woes', sounds like a Lemony Snicket creation, but looks like a setting in an Indiana Jones film. It was still impossibly dry, but the rocks were flame-hued and pockmarked like giant termite mounds. 'Rush hour' was meeting a herd of cows, their hoof prints interspersed with the fat paw prints and berry-filled droppings of bears. Postcard-worthy monasteries perched on clifftops and the sun reflected from every surface, evenly cooking me from each angle.

After scorching temperatures, Wild Western canyons and the threat of night-time visits from Paddington Bear's less amenable relatives who might have fancied more than a marmalade sandwich, the wide-open plains of Armenia's highest mountain range, the Geghams, were a welcome change. Rising to 3,597m, the route covers over 100km without passing a settlement and is described as the remotest part of the trail.

There is a complete silence which falls above a certain altitude. All of a sudden, the orchestra of crickets fell quiet. There were no bees, no flies, no trees to rustle in the breeze. With this muffled, cotton wool silence the landscape became more grandiose, a volcanic plateau laid out before me in epic proportions. I no longer struggled to identify overgrown livestock trails because my route was visible for several kilometres. The sheer space elated me, lifting my mood with the altitude. Resilient patches of hard-packed snow still clung resolutely to mountains that sparkled with loose rubble.

Silence was soon broken, however. Nomadic camps with herds of sheep and gruff-looking shepherd dogs began to appear around every corner. Usually the dogs would smell me before I saw them, breaking the stillness with a cacophony of barks, snapping at my heels. As I shouted '*nstel*!' ('sit!') the shepherd would appear, and as though teleported, I'd find myself inside a yurt, enjoying thick Armenian coffee and fresh watermelon.

The full Armenian TCT is 832km, and with just four weeks to complete as much as I could, I began to get selective. I hitchhiked a couple of road sections and beelined towards the lush forests and limestone cliffs of Lori Province, in the north of the country. It was September now and the trees were turning. The route still lurched up and down, often gaining more than 1,500m of altitude in a day, but water sources were plentiful and good camping spots easy to find.

When I arrived in Tumanyan, an old textile-making town in a gorge between limestone cliffs, I'd walked 580km. A little arts festival was in full swing. A former textile factory had been occupied by Russian refugee artists, and although it had attracted only a hundred or so people, I felt as though I'd arrived in a bustling metropolis.

Preparing myself for a final night in my tent on the football pitch, as the little town was bursting at the seams, I found myself instead sharing a crumbling Soviet-era townhouse with an Armenian silk printer. Coffee, cakes, salted sheep's milk cheese and fruit packed the little table. Once again, Armenian hospitality had turned up trumps.

AZERBAIJAN, THE LAND OF LEGENDS

The *Daily Telegraph*, 12 January 2021
*Can fire-worship and yetis survive as Europe's highest village
modernises? James Stewart journeys to Azerbaijan.*

Deep in the mountains of northeast Azerbaijan I was discussing Noah with an elderly villager. Wrapped in a headscarf and woolly hat, Malaksima, a formidable eighty-something (she wasn't sure) with a weathered face like a walnut, was collecting spring water in a silver teapot. I'd asked about a tale that the people of Khinaliq were direct descendants of Noah. Had the Bible's original sailor really dropped anchor on these flat summits?

'Noah?' Malaksima said. She laughed. 'Show me: where's the ocean? Noah's not even Muslim.'

Though Khinaliq lacks two-by-two wildlife, from aardvarks to zebras, it might pass as somewhere from the Old Testament. At the head of one of Azerbaijan's remotest valleys, the village coils over a mountain spur above the valley floor. In the silence you can hear the river below. Natural gas fires burn like divine portents in surrounding mountains. Before Islam – before the Hebrews wrote about Noah even – Azerbaijanis were Zoroastrians, fire-worshippers who discovered magic, according to Pliny the Elder. Old habits die hard. Azerbaijan's favourite name for itself remains 'The Land of Fire'.

'Anyway,' Malaksima continued, 'everyone knows an angel founded this village. He was called Nabi. He was sent by Allah to build a mosque in the valley. Maybe he came with Noah, I don't know. But it's true. I swear on bread.'

'On bread?' I asked.

'Of course. It's older than the Koran.'

In the jigsaw of nations that forms the Caucasus, the least accessible, most interesting country is Azerbaijan. While Georgia is on the cusp of travel superstardom and Ryanair launched direct flights from Italy to Armenia in January, Azerbaijan has a blank-slate appeal.

Capital Baku has tarted itself up with oil money, ringing a historic core with ego-architecture in an aspiration to become a Dubai of the Caspian Sea. But life in rural Azerbaijan carries on much as it has for centuries: venerating bread, ritualising tea-drinking, tending sheep. Figuring the way to experience all that was on foot, I wanted to walk.

Sheki is in the foothills of the Caucasus Mountains, a five-hour drive west of Baku. That sounds a drag after your flight until you see the price of fuel (40p a litre) and the scenery. Beyond the capital the desert ends abruptly and you're rolling past wooded hills and vineyards and blokes scything rhythmically in fields. It resembles a long-vanished Provence, if Provence had ever included samovars and Soviet trucks for sale at the roadside. They go for a song since Azerbaijan shrugged off Russia's bear hug in 1991.

Last July Sheki won World Heritage status for its tangible Silk Road heritage. In the cool water garden of an old caravanserai I sat beneath arcades where merchants once bartered for metalwork, ceramics and silks. In the palace of the khans I toured rooms with walls painted like Persian carpets, a decorative fusion of the Middle East, India and China, of geometric Islam and the pictorial West.

The culture clash continued in a café beside the market. The owner flashed me a mouthful of gold teeth then rattled through the day's dishes: Central Asian sheep kidneys, Russian borscht, oriental *dushbara* dumplings, all washed down with watery sheep's yoghurt served by the pint. The local delicacy is Ottoman, a sweet walnut baklava. Let's just say Sheki has a lot of dentists.

For a change of scene I walked 3 miles to Kish village. As Sheki fell behind, woods took over, dotted here and there with former dachas. For the Russian elite Azerbaijan was a Soviet shire, a place to breathe mountain air and enjoy a simple rustic life facilitated by servants.

Kish was the real deal, with cockerels strutting along rough-cobbled lanes. On the main square stood a bust of Thor Heyerdahl. The Norwegian adventurer has a cult following in Azerbaijan having funded the restoration of Kish's 1st-century church, the country's oldest. To understand why you need to know about his pet theory concerning Azerbaijan as the wellspring of Scandinavians. They went west when the Romans arrived, he thought, citing an Icelandic saga that describes Odin's homeland as 'Aser', east of the Black Sea, and petroglyphs like Viking ships at Gobustan, 40 miles from Baku.

Azerbaijanis seem happy to indulge the idea. At the church an attendant showed me two skeletons. 'You see?' he asked, pointing into the crypt. 'They're giants.' They were, although Bronze Age skeletons over 6ft 6in seemed on the large side even for proto-Scandinavians.

Throughout my time in Sheki people mentioned Quba Rayon. Near the Russian border in the northeast, the district was said to be a throwback even by Azerbaijani standards: a mountainous place that was almost isolated until a road was built in 2006, where traditional culture still thrived in sheep villages. It was beautiful, remote, fascinating, people said.

I returned to Baku and went north. Beyond Quba town, in the taxi of a rakish cove with a brigand's haul of gold teeth – my driver refused to risk his new car on the roads ahead – I ascended up a narrowing valley past slow cows and new guesthouses. The road swerved through a ravine, ducking under overhangs, to emerge on a broad plateau riven by canyons as if God had gone mad with a pickaxe.

An hour up the road we came to Khinaliq, the highest village in Europe (7,645ft), heaped above a shallow river like a braid of rope. As we arrived a boy cantered past on a horse, a blanket for a saddle, a toddler clinging to his waist.

The modern age has encroached with the new road but Khinaliq hovers uneasily beside the 21st century. Compacted manure and hay are burned for fuel. Most water comes from a spring – the hammam turned out to be the village shower (singular) in someone's basement – and loos are long-drops which smell several stages beyond ripe.

Khinaliq has a shop selling tea and wire, a school, two mosques and the air of permanence that can only be acquired through five thousand years' existence. The two thousand residents farm sheep, speak a unique language and live in boxy stone houses hunkered down against the weather. I was staying with Rauf and his wife Junata: four rough-walled rooms with space for the sheep downstairs – a cheap way to take the bite off chill mountain air if you don't mind the smell of ammonia.

In a place that seemed beyond time, outlandish stories swirled like the clouds over surrounding peaks. In 1988 a goat herder fell asleep in a cave. Babaali Babaaliev said he woke to see a huge hairy humanoid staring at him. Understandably, he has never quite been the same again.

I wanted to believe it. If Azerbaijan could accommodate Noah and angels and Vikings why not a lost yeti? Bilal, my hosts' sixteen-year-old son, was unconvinced. 'But there are bears in the mountains,' he said. 'Wolves too: you can hear them at night.' He'd taken me for a stroll around the village. Anything to avoid his parents – they were furious he'd dropped out of school. 'What would I do at college in Baku?' he asked. 'I'm a shepherd. I only know sheep and mountains.'

There seemed worse things to know. We stopped on a terrace. A few villagers in crumpled suits grinned shy grins and shuffled awkwardly. They directed my gaze across the valley to Shahdag, 'King Mountain', propped between peaks. Gilded by the setting sun, it shone like a crown.

The next day I went for a walk. Beyond women thwacking fresh wool in a trough, the old dirt road clung to slopes above the valley floor. I spent the day in this wild place, swishing through buttercups and harebells, watching jackdaws tumble across big skies and waving to shepherds following flocks of sheep which drifted across the slopes like clouds. When I dropped into Kalaykhudat village after a few hours a man invited me for mountain-thyme tea. He told me about a fortress of the Quba khans that had controlled this ancient trade route and of a fire temple recently rebuilt in the Shahdag National Park. Apparently the shepherds now used it to make tea.

Yet change may be coming. The Azerbaijani government is keen to promote Khinaliq. It has plans to transform my walking route into a tourist drive. Another project would create the world's longest cable car from Khinaliq to Qabala ski resort.

This is the point where you're expecting me to condemn both. I won't. Frankly, life is tough enough in these remote villages. If residents want a road and it sustains their futures, good luck to them.

That night, after a dinner of kid goat and shots of Tsar vodka, Rauf envisaged Saudi bus tours and new hotels. He made them sound as fantastical as abominable snowmen or Noah dropping anchor on a nearby summit. Great news isn't it, he said. No, I said, terrible. There was a brief silence then we both began to laugh.

I'm still not sure who's right. But I'd go sharpish if I was you.

PEAKS OF THE BALKANS

The Great Outdoors magazine, December 2017
Rudolf Abraham hikes through the Prokletije mountains,
in the spectacularly remote borderlands of Montenegro,
Albania and Kosovo.

It was a small black dog which finally pointed me in the right direction. I'd just crossed a nameless pass on the rocky, juniper-studded ridge which forms the southern boundary of the Rugova Gorge in Kosovo, and was looking – with increasing frustration by this point – for the correct trail down the other side. Any trail, in fact. Just not the beginning of that jeep track, which started here and swept off in completely the wrong direction – I'd already tried that one and had to come back.

I was on my final trip to research a guidebook to hiking the Peaks of the Balkans – a recently developed long-distance trail which winds its way for the best part of 200km through Prokletije (also known as the Accursed Mountains) in the rugged borderlands between Montenegro, Kosovo and Albania. It's a spectacularly beautiful and wonderfully hospitable place, a remote corner of Europe which few people know much about, let alone visit.

I walked back up to the grassy verge overlooking the shallow lake I'd just passed, before the path vanished, and scrutinised the way ahead again. Not left, since that led to the cliff-like buttresses of Guri i Kuq, one of the highest peaks hereabouts. Ahead and to the right, trail-less pastures led down to the edge of the forest, or dropped away steeply out of sight, with no guarantee that they wouldn't end in a cliff or a wall of dense mountain pine at some point on the thousand-or-so-metre descent to the floor of the gorge. I'd already tried finding a trail through head-high thickets of mountain pine earlier in the morning, and wasn't up for a repeat. Not for the first time, I cursed the map I was carrying.

It was at this point that a small dog suddenly appeared over the edge of the hillside – apparently out of nowhere – tongue lolling and looking immensely pleased with himself. Following the logic that a very domesticated-looking dog might have followed a trail up from a village, I walked off through the long grass to where he'd been standing (he'd bounded off again by this point, clearly with other business in mind) – and sure enough, down below me, beyond some rocks and bushes, was the beginning of a clear path. Two hours of steep descent later (during which the dog scampered past again, ears flying) I reached the floor of the Rugova Valley, and followed the road up the other side towards Rekë e Allagës.

The following day I hiked up from the Rugova Valley towards Liqeni i Kuçishtës – a beautiful, secluded lake wedged between steep slopes and a great swath of pine forest. After following the shoreline I dropped down steeply on a winding forest trail, then climbed past another, smaller lake, and across open slopes below the western flanks of Guri i Kuq, with the sound of a spring bubbling somewhere under a long finger of scree. From here a clear trail climbs more steeply to the Jelenkut Pass, above a prominent double rock outcrop, somewhere between the borders of Kosovo and Montenegro. I say 'somewhere' and 'between', because the actual border up here remains deliciously vague – further north, where the road from Rožaje crosses the border heading towards Peja, it descends through a stretch of exquisitely beautiful no man's land, several kilometres wide.

A couple of hours along the ridge I reached the Zavoj Pass, from where a path drops gently into Montenegro through masses of blueberry bushes – here as elsewhere along the route, hiking in berry season generally means progress is reduced to grazing pace.

Beyond the small settlement of Babino Polje, where I spent the night, the southern side of the valley is cloaked in thick pine forest. It's through this that the route led me the following morning, to Hridsko Jezero – a lake at just under 2,000m, below rocky peaks. Here a small group of German hikers were braving the icy temperatures for an impromptu dip, while I (rather less energetically) munched on a sandwich. Later that evening I descended through farmland to reach Plav – the only town of any size encountered on the entire route, though it's still very small – located beside the largest glacial lake in the Balkans. Then one more day took me over Vrh Bora, with jaw-dropping views of the wild jumble of rocky summits hereabouts, and down to the village of Vusanje, at the mouth of the Ropojana valley.

The stage between Vusanje in Montenegro and Theth in Albania is one of the most beautiful on the Peaks of the Balkans. From the long, broad green floor of the Ropojana valley the trail climbs to a seasonal lake, fed only by snowmelt, below the jagged line of the Karanfili peaks. I found the lake empty, and followed a well-worn trail through the long grass – across what, on a previous visit, would have been the bottom of a large lake – and crossed an invisible border into Albania.

Thanks to the Peaks of the Balkans, what was once a closed border crossing here at the end of the Ropojana valley is – along with some half a dozen other border crossings associated with the trail – now open to trekkers (though you do however still need to apply for a special cross-border permit to hike the Peaks of the Balkans).

From the lake the trail climbs through forest to open pastures, where I filled water flasks at a spring near a couple of simple, low-roofed shepherd huts, occupied during the summer months when local shepherds bring their livestock up to the high pastures.

Further on the trail climbs past the domes of two small concrete bunkers, enigmatic remnants of Enver Hoxha's isolationist regime – the former ruler had some half a million of them built all over Albania between the 1960s and the 1980s. A shepherd, sitting on the hillside above his flock – guarded over by a Šarplaninac, the breed of huge sheepdog kept in this region – waved me on towards a ridge.

The views from the Peja Pass are staggering. To the right, the southern face of Mount Arapit falls in a single sickening drop of some 800m; to the left, rocky summits stretch off towards Maja Jezercë, at a smidgen under 2,700m the highest mountain in Prokletije. Below lies the sprawling, rock-strewn floor of the Theth Valley. The trail ducks left beneath overhanging cliffs, and winds its way down to the valley floor. Here the path becomes a rocky jeep track, then a dusty farm track overhung with fruit trees in the late evening light before it winds its way into Theth, with its well-preserved 17th-century *kula* (tower house).

Over the next few days the Peaks of the Balkans crossed a succession of passes. From Theth, I set off for the Valbona Pass, on the watershed between the Theth and Valbona valleys, with the huge northwest wall of Maja e Boshit on the right, and unforgettable views of the Valbona Valley as I descended on the far side. The following day I crossed the Prosllopit Pass – a deviation from the 'official' route, which simply follows a road along the valley floor for most of the day – following a long, steep path up through old growth forest and open meadows with masses of wildflowers, my footsteps setting off clouds of tiny blue butterflies. Crossing the Prosllopit Pass took me back into Montenegro, below the sprawling summit of Maja Kolata (the highest mountain in Montenegro), then a trail led over a second pass and back down into Albania. Two days later there was a wonderful saddle overlooking Dobërdol, a remote summer settlement below the point where the borders of Montenegro, Albania and Kosovo meet – and of course there's that nameless pass above the Rugova Gorge, with its elusive trails.

One offshoot of the Peaks of the Balkans, over the decade or so since it opened, has been the establishment of small, simple but wonderfully hospitable guesthouses – serving delicious home-cooked food, and offering a genuine slice of rural hospitality which is frankly a million miles away from anything you'll find in resorts on the coast.

It was at one such guesthouse in Drelaj – around halfway through dinner as I sat at a long table on the terrace with the German hikers that I'd later bump into at Hridsko Jezero – that the dog popped into conversation. 'He followed us for two days, over the border from Albania,' said one. 'A small black dog, about this high,' he added. 'Oh, that sounds like the same one I saw too,' threw in another guest, who worked for the German NGO which helped set up the Peaks of the Balkans. One of the party pulled out a phone and tapped on a photo – and sure enough, it really did look like the same dog. Apparently he'd been wandering around in the mountains for days, or weeks, happily enjoying his own cross-border ramblings. Perhaps he's still there.

JUST STRAP ON
THE FOOTWEAR AND WALK

***The Guardian*, 7 December 2023**
Mike Unwin snowshoes with the ramblers in Bulgaria.

'You lift one foot and you put it down,' says Alf, my guide. 'Then you lift the other foot and you put it down.' For the newbies in our group – me included – these simple instructions are reassuring. At least snowshoeing has no complex manoeuvres to master; no vertical take-off, double-twist snowplough, or whatever it is that skiers get up to. You just strap on your strange footwear and walk. Phew.

The strapping-on part has its challenges, though. As I crouch in a squall of windblown snow, my gloved fingers struggle to adjust the ratchet clasps. And when I finally get to my feet, I tread with one snowshoe on the rim of another and immediately hit the deck again. Alf hands me my poles. 'Better not use the loops,' he says. 'You might break your wrist.'

Thankfully, I have seven days in which to improve. It's late March, and I'm here in Bulgaria's Pirin National Park at the start of a ramblers' snowshoeing week. There are ten of us, together with tour leader Alf Robertson – a lean, mountain-honed Aberdonian – and local guide Simeon Dimitrov. A quick glance suggests my companions are largely older than I am. They also look fitter.

We arrived yesterday afternoon in the historic town of Bansko, two hours south from Sofia and now a popular ski resort below the Pirin Mountains. A quick stroll around the historic centre revealed the famous Sveta Troitsa Orthodox church, complete with stork nest on top, but also an ominous bank of cloud cloaking the promised panorama. Over dinner, Alf confirmed what any true rambler knows: that mountains are unpredictable, and itineraries must remain flexible. 'It depends on the snowpack,' he explained. 'Too much snow can be dangerous.'

As it turns out, blue skies have blessed our first day and, instructions over, we are soon tramping up the trail. The first kilometre is forest, where lighter snow cover allows a gentle baptism of our new footwear. As the trees thin out we hit the virgin snow of the open slopes. Now, the snowshoes earn their keep, carrying us lightly over deep drifts that might otherwise swallow us whole.

Snowshoeing is knackering; let nobody tell you otherwise. Slogging uphill through snow at 2,000m altitude tests thighs and lungs. But we soon find our rhythm and, with confidence growing, I can at last look up, admire the soaring peaks and even pick out a handful of distant chamois. The only sounds are the creak and crunch of snow underfoot, and our own heavy breathing. When we stop, the stillness is impressive: bird calls carry up from the treeline with pin-sharp clarity.

Our destination is a frozen lake. But clouds sweep in, vindicating Alf's caution, and after hurriedly downing packed lunches, we're soon trudging back downhill through a white-out, barely able to see each other let alone the Pirin panorama. Nonetheless, it's been a good first day. And as we near the resort, hearing the thudding beat of après-ski music and clamour of excited skiers, I feel a certain tortoise-beats-hare smugness; there's another way to enjoy the mountains, without simply hurling yourself down them.

By the end of day two, we've got snowshoes sussed. But on day three, we leave them behind and catch a train to Avramovo, the highest railway station in the Balkans, for a hike through the Rhodope Mountains. This range extends east to Turkey, and its rural communities constitute the country's Muslim heartland – the legacy of three centuries under Ottoman rule. From the sleepy village, with its gleaming minaret, we trek east along the Veliysko-Videnishko ridge, enjoying stirring views of the Pirin peaks to the south. Our trail remains below the snowline but forest shadows hold the odd treacherous frozen patch. 'Should have brought our snowshoes,' mutters one companion. Clearly, our new footwear has already become second nature.

Dinner that night is outside Bansko at the Deshka Guesthouse – a member of the Slow Food Association, which feels apt for snowshoers. At a large round table, we tuck into wholesome fare –

the *banitsa*, a layered dish of pastry, eggs and cheese, is especially delicious – and imbibe copious local wine. After dessert, our hosts fire up some Bulgarian folk music, and persuade us to don traditional garments (for me, a *nosia elek* waistcoat and *kalbak* fur hat) and hit the floor. 'What are your traditional English dances?' asks Simeon, coaxing us into action. 'The hokey-cokey?' I venture. The *rakia* helps, though, and soon we're all jigging around as though we hadn't tramped 15km earlier today.

Day four sees us transfer north to the small village of Govedartsi, below the Rila Mountains – our third Bulgarian range – for part two of our week. *En route* we visit the Rila Monastery, Bulgaria's most famous cultural attraction and the country's spiritual heart. It was reputedly founded in the 10th century by the hermit St Ivan of Rila, who lived in a nearby cave. Inside, I admire the gold-plated *iconostatis*, behind which the hermit's hand is said to be preserved. Outside, the afternoon sun gilds the gleaming domes and columns – until the advancing mountain shadows swallow their lustre.

The snowshoeing continues in the Rila Mountains, our exertions fuelled by home-cooked fare at the delightful Djambazki Hotel, where we scoff local trout, baklava and breakfast pancakes (though not all at the same time) and are soothed with a visit to hot springs in the spa town of Sapareva Banya. And our final day promises the famous 'Seven Rila Lakes' circuit.

The day dawns with dazzling clarity: minted blues, greens and whites. We board a chairlift and ascend silently over slopes embroidered with the zigzags of mountain hare and roe deer. On go the snowshoes and soon we're falling into now-familiar step, beetling steadily up inclines and along ridges. It takes two hours to reach the first of the lakes. Linked in summer by tumbling streams, these water bodies are now frozen solid: pancakes of white beneath the frosted cliffs of a grand cirque. We squint beyond the snowfields to the distant greens of the lowlands, as though looking from winter into spring. Faces are glowing. 'This is as good as it gets,' says Alf. 'It's all downhill from here.'

Thankfully, I know exactly how to get downhill. You just lift one foot and you put it down, then you lift the other foot and you put it down.

FABULOUS FINLAND

Adventure Travel Magazine, January 2014
Anne Gorringe snowmobiles to an ice hotel, drives a husky dog team and swims in an icy lake in the Arctic Circle.

'The setting on the heated hand grips goes from "off" to "barbecue",' says our snowmobile guide as he takes us through the last-minute safety checks on our machines.

I couldn't be happier. With the temperature at -12°C and falling, I whack the setting to maximum and, with toasty fingers, set off across a frozen lake in northern Finland.

It's my first time on a snowmobile but initial nerves disappear as I carefully increase my speed to keep up with the leader. In theory we are off in search of the Northern Lights but, with thick cloud cover overhead, we are out of luck tonight. Still, at one point when we all stop and turn off our engines, the glistening snow in the dark around us is magical. And it's the perfect way to arrive at the Lainio Snow Hotel, our base for the night.

The huge building of snow and ice has colourful LED lights frozen into ice sculptures and furniture. There's a bar and a stunning dining room with ice tables surrounded by benches… felt seats stop you sticking to them. Owner Rami Kurtakko tells us that each year the hotel has a new redesigned layout and theme.

Inside the sleeping quarters it's cold. The temperature is -5°C and we've been instructed to take off our thermal suit, lie it on the bed's mattress, then carefully step over the ice frame to slip into the thermal sleeping bag. That's the theory – but I'm reluctant to turn in for the night. Thankfully so is the rest of my group, and we wander down the corridor to discover the ice slide (labelled 'strictly for children') and cheerfully break the rules to play until midnight. We do eventually get some sleep, but the cold doesn't help and I'm delighted to be greeted by the morning call from a staff member with a glass of hot berry juice.

It's an action-packed couple of days. The first activity of the week is to learn from guide Juho Vlipiessa, a past winner of the Amundsen husky race in Norway, how to drive a team of six enthusiastic dogs around an 18km trail. The dogs are so eager that the tricky part is keeping them still once they are fastened in. Standing on the back rail with all my weight digging in, the brake only just works. And then we are off – fur and, yes, dog poo flying. The team stop for nothing, eating mouthfuls of snow 'on the go' when they are thirsty as we race through the forest.

In the afternoon it's skiing in the resort of Ylläs, where the February winds bring white-out conditions and freeze my hair into icy plaits. I also get my first real taste of off-piste when I, quite literally, land up to my ears in snow. My pride – but not my sense of fun – is dented but I need the support of laughing colleagues to pull me out.

That evening features a 'taxi' ride in a snow tractor in swirling snow to the tiny mountain restaurant of Ylläskammi 718. Covered in a thick blanket of snow, it looks like a refuge for an Arctic hobbit which, with the temperature nudging -10°C, feels appropriate. Inside we are welcomed by a roaring fire and our 'taxi driver', who quickly strips off his jacket to don an apron and hand out wooden cups of warming vodka and berry juice and a meal of reindeer meat. Strictly speaking, at an altitude of just 718m, the mountain restaurant isn't really on a mountain, but a fell. Still, it's the highest thing there is in Ylläs.

Next day, at a Sámi reindeer farm at Venejärvi on the Swedish– Finnish border, I fall in love. Rocky the reindeer's mesmerising face is creased into a smile that captivates me on my snowy 6km safari. This is easy – the reindeer knows the route. I simply have to shout encouragement and jiggle the reins.

A fish lunch warms me up for the early evening trip to try floating in the icy waters of Lake Ylläsjärvi where I exchange my thermal suit for a red rubber survival suit designed for Arctic expeditions. It comes complete with integrated shoes, gloves and zip-up hat and I look like a Teletubby.

Floating in icy waters and looking up at the sky in a warm survival suit proves surprisingly relaxing. Fun too, particularly when followed by a hot sauna where we dare each other to dash in and out of the snow to cool down.

Most package holidays to Lapland go to just one location but I have the opportunity to try the slopes in the nearby resort of Levi, where the runs are more suitable for intermediate skiers.

Here our instructor explains that often temperatures at the top of the hill are noticeably warmer than at the bottom. They are. Skiing in the glow of the orange afternoon light in -8°C is perfect. But arriving at the bottom of a floodlit slope in -23°C conditions is something of a shock. I am glad he has warned us we should try to keep our noses covered on the way down, and to beware of any white patches of skin – a possible warning sign of frostbite.

As I look up at the glittering snowflakes I still can't see the stars, let alone the Northern Lights. But I am almost glad. It's the perfect excuse to come back…

MY FIRST HOLIDAY MEMORIES

Mary Anne's France, 23 May 2019
Mary Anne Evans' trip to north France brings back memories;
what will her son remember?

Memory plays odd tricks. My first memories of France go back many decades, but I vividly remember lying in a bunk with my mother on a ferry from Newhaven to Dieppe. I was four years old and very sick; my two elder brothers were prancing around being terribly brave on the horribly bucking and rearing old ship. Those were the days before stabilisers.

It was not a good start to our summer family holiday to Mers-les-Bains on the north coast of France. Why they chose this resort with its gracious villas that harked back to the Victorians we never discovered.

My parents had booked a small hotel overlooking the beach. It was very old-fashioned with iron shutters at the bedroom windows, big heavy furniture, lumpy beds and wallpaper that followed the French decorative trend of the time: big red roses went up the walls, over the ceiling and down the other side. We loved it.

I can remember hot days with a shrimping net. Going back to this part of France I realised that it must have been quite difficult to catch anything with a shrimping net. There are no rock pools, though the odd puddle might have yielded a lucky catch. Perhaps I was just proud of having a shrimping net.

I remember the hotel owners who went by the outlandish name of Monsieur and Madame Pompilliou (at least that's what I remember; my brothers can't remember at all). I don't know if they had children of their own, but two days into our stay they offered to look after all three of us so my parents could go to Paris for the weekend. I was four and my brothers were eight and twelve. Absolutely unheard of today, but then? Absolutely OK and the Pompillious were just being kind.

I remember my parents coming back from Paris with toys, particularly a small model of a Paris bus. It had an open back, a bell that rang and was green. I would describe it as British racing green, but that would not be tactful, and perhaps not true either.

I remember the breakfasts at the hotel: hot chocolate served in mismatched and slightly cracked French bowls – so much better than porridge, freshly baked baguettes which were crisp outside and warm inside, and joy of joys… unsalted butter and sweet, sticky apricot jam.

Childhood memories are fragmentary things that return when you least expect it.

I had forgotten all about Mers-les-Bains until one year when my husband, our small son and I were returning from a holiday in our house in the Auvergne. We had a whole day to fill before the ferry and needed somewhere to stop within easy distance of Dieppe. My finger ran down the map of the north French coast and out it leapt… Mers-les-Bains!

It was October and fiercely stormy; the waves crashed on the beach and the wind roared along, propelling dogs and dog walkers and impeding overkeen runners. It was all we could do to stand upright, and we took bets on which of the beach cabins would be blown away. None did; France is good at resisting the weather.

It was out of season so most of the small restaurants were closed. We walked along the front past Chez Josette and Café de la Plage until we found a restaurant that was open. Pulling open the door, we staggered inside, the door crashing shut behind us. The windows were steamed up; it was full of locals who smiled a welcome and it smelt of fish.

Mussels and chips were the obvious choice. Along came steaming bowls of the molluscs and double-cooked chips with sachets of mayonnaise.

My son looked rebellious; this was the first time he had encountered a mussel. He opened his mouth to refuse this disgusting-looking pot. 'Ah, monsieur,' the waiter smiled at him, 'zis is 'ow to eat it.' He picked up an empty shell, used it to extract the mussel from another shell, downed the flesh and put the shell into the upturned lid. '*Et voilà!*' the waiter exclaimed triumphantly. My son has been a fan of mussels and chips ever since.

I wonder what he will remember and treasure from his holidays in France.

LAPPING UP LAKE COMO

National Geographic Traveller, March 2015
*Lisa Gerard-Sharp glories in Lake Como, luxuriating
in its moody mountains, medieval ports and
Mediterranean vegetation.*

With its timeless setting and silky lifestyle, Lake Como is endlessly alluring. Henry James praised these backwaters as 'out of the rush and crush of the modern world' – and Lake Como still luxuriates in its moody mountains, medieval ports and Mediterranean vegetation.

Lake Como suits incurable romantics but you don't need to be in love to wallow in romance. I'm here alone in Blevio, on Como, and relishing its operatic grandeur already. The musical links on the lakes resemble that 'five degrees of separation' game.

On Lake Como, Bellini composed *Norma*, Rossini *Tancredi*, and Verdi conjured up Act II of *La Traviata*. If wishing to hear their lyrics sung, the composers simply summoned neighbours such as Giuditta Pasta, the Maria Callas of her day. And now I'm enjoying the lyrical setting of her former villa, Casta Diva, reborn as a luxury resort in 2010.

From Blevio, it's an operatic ferry ride north to Bellagio and Villa Melzi's waterside gardens, passing scenery as lush as a score by Liszt. The lake's beauty lies in the sweet melancholy of snow-capped peaks, the deep conifer forests, the thin silhouettes of cypresses and the seductive curve of the shore. My spirits soar in spring when a southern warmth takes the chill off the Alps. April's magnolias, azaleas and camellias will make way for wisteria, silvery olive trees, palms and pomegranates.

The Neoclassical Villa Melzi captivated singers and composers, including Liszt. What first inspired him was the Moorish coffee house standing over the lake, a bold folly with lofty vistas edged by banks of camellias. Liszt wrote his *Dante Sonata* on these shores, supposedly inspired by a statue of Dante and Beatrice in the aforementioned villa. An intimate mood is created by the ornamental pool, framed by cedars, maples, camphor and myrrh. On the formal terraces above, Classical statuary gives way to gently rolling lawns bordered by a pine grove. As always here, the glory of the gardens lies in the interplay between villa and lake, and the shifts in mood between the manicured terraces and untrammelled alpine scenery beyond.

Como has been a retreat for weary romantics since Roman times, when Pliny's villas saved the orator from the stresses of ancient Rome. The Milanese smart set moved in long ago but since George Clooney bought Villa Oleandra in Laglio, Lake Como has been bathed in Hollywood glamour. The lake represents a realm of enchantment and repose, where even celebrities can potter in privacy. The desire to escape from what the Edwardian writer

Holbrook Jackson once called 'the chatter and clatter and hustle and guzzle' of high society is motivation enough.

Today's movie stars seek simplicity and so Clooney, like Pliny, wants to feel he can fish from his bedroom window or enjoy what Liszt called 'the melancholy murmuring of the waves lapping against the boat'.

Yet Como is also the most punctilious lake, a place where Victorian-style promenading is still in vogue. Not that doing Como in style means stuffed-shirt gentility and hushed hotels. The lake lifestyle is sedate not sedated, with blockbuster art exhibitions in Como, summer music festivals in Bellagio, and low-key beach parties on the lidos. Even so, Lake Como is for sophisticates, not cheapskates or hipsters. Splash out on a linen suit and a room with a view; dress for a stylish dinner; swagger over retro cocktails on a time-warp terrace. Stay in a grown-up hideaway and drop into 'grand-dame' hotels for fine dining. It might start as play-acting but before long you'll be yearning to hang out with the Grand Tourists of yore. Whether rakish or rich, the Romantics came for the scenery and a sense of surrender. So far, so contemporary – so Clooney. The lake's poster boy loves the smooth lifestyle of his Lake Como home, from his sleek speedboat to the simple dinners of grilled fish and fine Barbera wine, saying that 'the Italians have taught me how to celebrate life'.

There's nowhere better to celebrate life than in Bellagio, Lake Como's calling card. The resort commands the promontory of Punta Spartivento, 'the point which divides the winds' and splits the lake into two. My eyes lap up the genteel promenade, pastel-tinged façades, steep cobbled alleys and bijou craft shops – Bellagio is a litany of lakeside clichés. In summer, I'd daydream over sunset cocktails at the Lido di Bellagio beach club before lake fish at Silvio, but today it's Cava Turacciolo for dawdling over wine and cheese in a cosy cellar bar. I drift into a delightful reverie about *fin de siècle* glamour and cypress-spoked slopes during the ferry cruise back to Blevio.

Next morning's cruise explores the western shore, with the most magnificent waterside villas and gardens. The ferry criss-crosses the loveliest arm of Lake Como, moving from the shady eastern shore to the sunny western side. The cliffs on the dramatic eastern shore evoke the Amalfi Coast while the tamer west shelters the best resorts, villas and gardens. At Lenno, the final short stretch to Villa Balbianello is by fishing boat. Set on a rocky spur, this beguiling property was James Bond's retreat in *Casino Royale*. As ever, 007 has impeccable taste. Mirrored in the lake, Balbianello boasts 18th-century gardens studded with cypresses, magnolias and plane trees. Neither a Classical Italian affair nor a romantic English retreat, this is a wayward garden framed by wisteria-clad views accentuated by artful arches.

Just one landing stage north of Lenno, Tremezzo is an appealingly mothballed spot, despite a recent revamp. A short stroll leads to Como's icing on the cake – Villa Carlotta's gorgeously opulent gardens. The Baroque villa, a wedding present from a Prussian princess to her daughter, plays second fiddle to the grounds, despite its excellent art gallery. In spring, the vivid azaleas and camellias offset the villa's cool Neoclassical interior.

The profusion of pink and white frames a theatrical staircase leading to the citrus terraces. An ornamental pool, rockery and rhododendron grove act as stepping stones to a moody glade and rushing stream. The planting plots an exotic map of the world, from cedars of Lebanon to Egyptian papyrus reeds, Japanese maple, Chinese bamboo and Indian tea – all by way of Mediterranean agaves, New Zealand ferns, Australian eucalyptus trees, and giant South American sequoias.

After a day of wistfulness in grand gardens, I want to experience the lake more intimately, in a kayak. Based in Pescallo harbour, Bellagio Watersports offers refreshing tours, including the paddle I take across the water to Varenna. This central stretch of the lake is the most seductive. Rivalled only by Bellagio, Varenna is perhaps the lake's quintessential village, shaded by pines and plane trees but less picture-postcard perfect than Bellagio. Completing the scene are un-touristy cafés, terraced gardens, a turreted castle and Italy's shortest river, which flows only from March until October. Nearby, the brooding woods and wild limestone peaks inspired Leonardo da Vinci to use the shadowy landscape as the setting for his *Virgin of the Rocks*.

Finally, my ferry sweeps south to grand moorings and gourmet delights on Cernobbio. Villa d'Este is where celebrities come for peace, quiet, and the exceptional grilled fish. With only Henry James' writings for company, I settle for a champagne cocktail on the terrace. Caroline of Brunswick, the estranged wife of the Prince Regent, later George IV, sought a fresh start in this frescoed palace, where she installed her Italian lover in 1814, and scandalised polite society. Not that naughtiness is anything new on Lake Como.

THE FORGOTTEN TREASURES OF ONE OF EUROPE'S OLDEST NATIONAL PARKS

The Way **(Adventure Travel Trade Association), 2016**
*In the chilly remoteness of North Macedonia,
Tracey Croke discovers the country's oldest
traditions and warmest of welcomes.*

It's May in North Macedonia, and our journey is off to a crawling start in the capital's traffic when guide Marko Bekric's phone pings with a message to remind us that summer hasn't quite arrived yet. 'That's my grandmother,' he says. 'It's been snowing and the mountain pass to Galichnik is blocked.'

I admit my expectations weren't high when I searched for a mountain bike guide to show me around Mavrovo National Park. North Macedonia's largest and one of Europe's oldest such parks – first proclaimed in 1949 for its exceptional natural beauty – is only seen each year by a smattering of intrepid visitors. With several days spare before I joined another bike trip in the region, I was keen to see this protected area near the Albanian border where wolves, wild boar, brown bears and the critically endangered Balkan lynx roam.

What were the chances? I needed a local with a mountain bike who knew their way around 500km of meagrely marked trails in an isolated wilderness that is completely cut off in the winter. It was a long shot, but a message I sent out through the adventure grapevine surprisingly bore fruit. In a pedal stroke of luck, my contact Jane Josifovski told me his cousin had recently started offering mountain bike trips through Mavrovo from his grandparents' guesthouse in the pretty village of Galichnik.

'Marko will pick you up in Skopje and you will go mountain biking with him and stay with his legendary grandparents. They will be glad to have you as their guest,' Jane wrote. More info would follow later, but who needs details when you have mountain biking and legendary grandparents in the same sentence? I immediately agreed.

Now as we crawl bumper to bumper through the choke of Skopje, I'm gutted for us both that seasonally stubborn snow has dumped on our plans. I start to mull over what I'll do instead, but Marko has other ideas. 'Don't worry,' he says resolutely, 'I will arrange for someone to get us through.'

And sure enough, several hours later, we are crossing the pass to Galichnik on a freshly snowploughed, slippery strip of tarmac. I breathe in while Marko skilfully squeezes his Opel Astra G between a cut glacier and an almighty drop-off into amen.

Galichnik was once a thriving village in a mountain region of several thousand people dependent on the wool industry. Many *chobans* (shepherds) made good money from their trade. However, in 1965, wool prices fell off the edge of a cliff and the village suffered a slow and inevitable decline. Marko's grandparents, Borka and Pavle, were the last sheep farmers to leave the village in 1970. After a twenty-year stint in the capital of Skopje, they returned to Galichnik to open a small restaurant. The couple, who have recently celebrated their 50th wedding anniversary, remain the only permanent residents, enduring the harsh winter months when the access road is gobbled up by glaciers.

In summer, Galichnik is known as a holiday destination for North Macedonians seeking respite from the heat and pollution of the cities. The homes of past *chobans* now serve as holiday boltholes for the well heeled. It holds a special place in history as one of the oldest Mijak villages in the region. Mijak people are famous for their craftsmanship and masonry skills. Their intricate wood carvings and fresco paintings are found in some of the finest architecture throughout Macedonia.

At the entrance to the village, we pull up alongside an elevated house atop a grassy mound. On the veranda, Borka and Pavle greet me. 'We like everything here, the nature, the water and the air,' says Pavle who still makes *kashkaval* – a sheep cheese similar to feta. 'There is a specific cheese in almost every region of Macedonia,' Marko tells me. Galichnik village cheese is notably famed for its remarkable journey into the kitchens of the ill-fated *Titanic* after one of the investors met a luxury robe trader originally from the village.

These days you'll find *kashkaval* in Galichnik pie, a cheese and spinach speciality cooked up in the guesthouse restaurant by Marko's grandmother, Borka. Regular punters are locals such as Vasko Velichkovski, who runs horse-trekking expeditions into the mountains.

It's clear Borka and Pavle's passion has rubbed off on their grandson. After exploring the park's gorges, karst fields and many of its vast peaks, the twenty-six-year-old was convinced intrepid travellers would love it as much as he and his family do. The young Macedonian has a formidable vision to revive the region. With a government support scheme and money he saved up from working in technology, Marko gave up his job, added several guest rooms to his grandparents' original two-room house and bought seven bikes to launch his tours.

In their restaurant, solid stone walls crafted with Mijak pride tell a story of the family. Sepia photos of Pavle and Borka in traditional Mijak costume hang among fox pelts, horsemanship trophies and pictures of the national park's revered resident – the brown bear. Wild boars are hunted for their meat, but bears are strictly off limits. Pavle assures me bears are shy. 'We would be lucky to see one.' And even luckier to see the elusive lynx, also known as the 'ghost of the forest'.

Marko makes the most of my short time in Mavrovo. Over three days, we ride tracks into pine forests through bubbling streams to the rumble of distant waterfalls. One day we reach the top of a ridge in bad weather just as the sun's rays punch through the clouds and pour on the village below. The howling wind insists on being heard between rainy, snowy and sunny appearances. I am bewitched by clouds, which seem like they are on fast forward, changing the landscape in a blink. Vasko and his troop are the only people we meet until we reach Mavrovo town, which serves the ski slopes of Bistra Mountain in the winter. A café overlooking the lake makes a welcome respite and heavenly cappuccino.

At the information centre I learn bears are world-class sprinters – up or down – with speeds up to 50 kilometres per hour according to the WWF. I've no Tour de France talent stashed in my bike pants to outride them; however, rangers confirm (contrary to questionable YouTube videos) that bears have no interest in me nor my bike and will retreat into the forest as soon as their super senses detect noise.

We don't linger too long as the weather is turning again, and we still have 16km to climb over a snowy pass. Despite piling the layers on, including face protection from the wind chill, I feel the thwack of hail on my cheeks all the way down into Galichnik, where a concerned Borka and Pavle are waiting on the doorstep.

Passers-by from neighbouring villages are inside tucking into the day's specials. Borka pulls off my soggy shoes and rests them by the fire. A bowl of steaming pork and potato stew arrives on the table in front of me. It feels good to be back among the familiarity of fox pelts and familiar faces chatting around the wood burner.

'So, what happens when you meet a bear?' I ask Pavle. 'We're friends with the bears, we live together,' he replies. 'But if we see one, Borka talks to it first!'

As laughter spills around me, a twinge of melancholy sets in. My trip to fill a few loose-end days is coming to a close and I'm in no hurry to leave the warmth of a family I've been made to feel a part of. I leave with the realisation that among the forgotten treasures of Mavrovo National Park, I've discovered rarity – an unadulterated experience as pure as the driven snow.

NORWEGIAN FJORDS ON TWO WHEELS

Amy McPherson gets on her bike to explore beyond the Norwegian fjords.

Something's up with Njord, the Norse god of the wind and the sea. He is making his presence strongly felt as we prep our bikes outside St Olav's Church at Aveldsnes on Karmøy Island. This hilltop location looking over the Karmsundet Sound was where Viking King Harald Fairhair made Norway's first royal seat, and it is said that 'Karmsundet' was also called 'Nordvegen', the old name of this first royal settlement, which gave Norway its modern name.

It is only fitting then that I start a cycling tour around Norway's southern fjords from the Viking royal seat that marked the beginning of Norway. I had come to Norway to ride the roads and to experience the beauty of the fjords by bike, and not even the gale force of Njord could stop me.

Karmøy is an island along the southern fjords of Norway, known for its beautiful beaches, lush pine forests and a rich copper mining heritage that supplied the copper for the Statue of Liberty in New York. It was appropriate that we pay a visit to the mining museum at Visnes to find the small replica of Liberty erected against the blue of the sea and the sky.

'And this is our own Lady Liberty!' said Malla Holden, general manager of Hotel Amanda in the nearby city of Haugesund and my guide for the next couple of days. 'She is concrete,' Malla observed. 'Maybe we ran out of copper!'

A quick pose with the Lady before we set off again. The road on Karmøy winds its way in and out of pockets of water of the surrounding fjords. Other than the fjords, Karmøy also has two of the thirteen Blue Flag beaches in Norway, the larger being Åkrasanden, with its 1km stretch of a string of pristine sand.

We rode to the smaller of the two, Sandvesand beach, to test the waters. The cove itself is wrapped by diverse species of grass and succulents on top of a mixture of sandstone and conglomerate; the surf roared and waves crashed their white foams on the soft white sand. Malla was right. It was beautiful.

We ended our day at the southern town of Skudeneshavn, a nautical town with a shipyard industry and full of traditional wooden houses that are listed as preserved Norwegian cultural heritage. After a day fighting Njord's fury I was in need of a feed. A coffee and a muffin later, I relived the roads again in my mind on our drive back to Haugesund and a chance to chat to Malla about cycling in Norway.

Although three of Europe's networks of EuroVelo routes pass through Norway, cycle tourism isn't big in Norway, yet. Malla, just back from a cycling trip in Mallorca, wants to change that. 'We ride bikes ourselves and go on cycling holidays elsewhere. So there is no reason why we can't create a good cycle tourism network.' She is right. So many see the fjords from a cruise ship; I feel I have experienced so much more than just balcony views.

Malla has ambitions. Her hotel is about to undergo major branding changes next year and she has big plans to convince the rest of the associated hotels that they could be the first cyclist-friendly hotel network in Norway.

'The concept is still new, so while my colleagues in other locations are supportive of my ideas, they don't really get what exactly they need to do!'

Situated in the middle of two larger tourist cities on the southern fjords, Haugesund is often overlooked. The city used to be a hub for the herring industry; it is now a base for offshore oil activities in the North Sea. So while there are hotels aplenty, tourists are few.

Haugesund is perfectly located for a centre-based cycling holiday, as you could go north towards Bergen and south towards Stavanger on the long-distance cycle route called The North Sea Cycle Path. Or you could go east, as we have chosen to do on my second day, along the Old Åkra Fjord Road.

'I must have driven on this road thousands of times in the seventies!' Alf Einar Apeland said, cycling beside me. A retired truck driver, he had made the same trip from Haugesund to Oslo in his truck when this was the only way in and out of the cities. Now there is a wider and better-maintained highway for the traffic, this old road to Oslo has become cyclists' heaven.

The attraction is the position of the road, which hugs the edge of Åkrafjorden, just one of the many fjords you can explore in this area. Fjords are created by glaciers that have created deep wrinkle lines into the earth as they melt over time through the natural flow of water towards the ocean. And that's what makes cycling around the fjords of Norway unique. These 'hills' that line the water's edge can get challenging, testing the legs as the road rises and falls with the steep cliffs that surround it, a surreal movie-like panorama of the fjord landscape, decorated by laces of waterfalls.

'So many waterfalls, there is a big one coming up!' Alf Einar shouted as he sped ahead of me. I had felt it before I saw it. The mist of Langfoss sprinkled my face as we approached. The cascading torrent runs 600m from the top of the mountain, under the road, into Åkrafjorden below. Its powerful roar could be heard even as we continued our ride away from it. At another curve in the road, I looked back for one last photo of Langfoss and the surrounding landscape. It was impossible not to stop for photographs every few kilometres or so.

You wouldn't have known this, but Norwegian cider is world class, and it's all thanks to the apples of Hardanger. The microclimate created by the fjord is perfect for cultivation as it never gets too cold in winter and too hot in summer, and there's plenty of water to do its rounds of the orchards, making this ideal for apples and pears. Did I want to go on a cider tasting on our bikes? Yes, please.

'You should have come in May,' said Artiom Neznanov, a Lithuanian who had moved to Norway for work. 'That's when apple blossoms are all around the hills, so much you can smell them in the air.'

We rolled up to Aga Farm for a quick tour of the brewery and a tasting of the cider made on-site. I can confirm, the cider is good. Cycling a bit further, we stopped again at Åkra Farm for more tasting. It wasn't just the cider we came for. Hardangerfjord has some of the oldest settlements of Norway, with museums and historic houses to visit along our tour.

For the night, we stayed in Utne Hotel. Norway's oldest hotel is preserved in its traditional wooden house; it has continuously operated as a hotel since 1722. Staying here is like living history and while the rooms are small (it is, after all, three hundred years old), the atmosphere was friendly and cosy, and the meals were delicious. We were, of course, served a cider pairing tasting menu.

On my last day, Malla decided I needed a challenge. So, together with local cycling guide Kjell Martin Dyrset, we drove further inland on the old road to Oslo, past the fingertip of the fjords, seeking some altitude.

Once again we were treated to a road that clung on to the edge of the mountain and the incline was steady. Although we were no longer in the fjords, the many lakes that make up the scenery deep down into the valleys were just as gorgeous to look at as I climbed. The further up we went, the air grew thinner and colder. Up, up and straight up, and I watched the transformation of lowland greenery turning into bald grey rocks until we got to the top where I was greeted by a small wall of snow still clinging on to the cliff. From here, we reached a dam and crossed its wall to begin our descent, back down into greenery and villages to finish at the town of Sauda for one final lunch together.

That sounds like a rather anticlimactic finale to my trip. The thing is, there isn't a lot to say, but there is a lot to feel. Cycling in Norway isn't about the best pubs to visit, the best café stops or any famous 'must dos'; rather, it's like riding into a postcard. As you ride, you feel the environment change around you, you feel the power of the water, the wind and the rocks. I want to say you feel the power of the trolls, as you'll notice references to these mythical creatures everywhere. You cycle here so you're not just stuck on a balcony of a cruise ship watching the fjords go by, but to be right in the fjords, and feel it in your legs, in your heart and in the friendliness of the people you meet.

Except for Njord the wind god. Perhaps have a word in Asgard before you go, ask him to ease off for a bit during your ride.

SET SAIL FOR A
LONG WEEKEND IN THE ARCTIC

The *Sunday Telegraph*, 24 February 2019
*Can a long weekend in the Arctic offer anything
more than images? James Stewart takes a slow cruise into
the Svalbard archipelago by traditional sailing ship.*

In Svalbard anyone can become a citizen. Get an address at Longyearbyen, prove you've the funds to support yourself and you're in. It's that easy. What you're not allowed to do is die. Something to do with tricky burials in permafrost and no cremations 650 miles from the North Pole.

I mention this because Rasmus Jacobsen, the softly spoken owner-captain of *Linden*, spent the first ten minutes of my cruise enumerating ways to come a cropper. You could go overboard (hypothermia within five minutes) or get brained by one of the ship's spars (someone releasing the wrong brown rope. Easy to do – they're all brown).

If you were lucky the last thing you might see would be one of Svalbard's three thousand polar bears – a constant hazard during trips ashore, expedition naturalist Mette Eliseussen warned. A bear cannot be outrun by a human. A serious confrontation usually ends in death for one party. Get on the wrong side of the world's largest land carnivore and Mette had a tricky rifle shot. We ten passengers giggled. Mette scowled. She wasn't joking.

Wasn't that why we were here, though? Not for the death part, obviously, but for the adventure? I wanted to do more than just look – there's something unfulfilling about just looking in the Arctic. I wanted to experience the Arctic if not quite on equal terms, then not cocooned from it on a powerful cruise ship.

Previously that required a hefty time commitment. Now you can do it over a weekend. Last month Discover the World launched a three-day sailing cruise of Svalbard. You board at Longyearbyen on Friday mid-afternoon. You disembark late on Sunday. Catch the red-eye back and you can be at a desk in London by Monday morning. It sounded implausible and a bit intrepid and also intriguing. The ultimate adventure quick fix. Could it offer anything more than pretty pictures? The ship delivered those.

Having read about *Linden* as Europe's biggest wooden replica schooner, I expected something ersatz. Instead, with sails bagged on yards and bowsprit, and tarred ratlines up three masts, this 160ft recreation of a 1920 Finnish cargo trader was nicely salty. Within was a cottagey saloon (brass lamps, prints of ships under sail) and seven en suites with bunk beds. Being a Danish ship, there was also a sauna and a bottomless urn of coffee.

Discover the World's itinerary proposed a sail west. The wind suggested we go north. Fine by me – I also wanted, if only briefly, to be a windblown vagabond at nature's whim.

As we left Longyearbyen's fjord Rasmus told me about his past on tall ships in the Caribbean. He bought *Linden* 'to do something more interesting'. 'Instead of being a nuisance we come a bit more gently. We ask what we can do to help the environment and local people,' he said. I nodded. But I wasn't listening. There was too much scenery. No purple prose, no statistics prepare you for a first encounter with the polar wilderness on a small ship. It's vast. Imagine the scale of the Arizona desert. Submerge it and add ice. You're not even close.

We motored between snow-streaked mountains buttressed by scree and turreted by cliffs. Across one horizon a meringue whip of peaks glittered. Over three days I never got used to the punch of stepping from the saloon's embrace into such raw wilderness.

Amazing but not entirely what we came for. Wildlife was why we were here. It appeared within the hour – a polar bear that had sniffed out a whale carcass. It leaned a paw that could bludgeon a walrus senseless with one swipe on the whale's head, chewing only the blubber that could sustain it for four months, then waded into the sea, paddling in water that would freeze a man in minutes. Overheating is a bear's second biggest problem. The biggest is climate change.

Many of us were here to sail too. The sails went up in a blur of salty terminology – sheets, gaffs, peaks – that left my palms stinging. You don't have to climb the rigging afterwards but it seemed a shame not to. The idea was to maintain three points of contact, I was told. Good call: the ratlines wobble as you ascend. I'd recommend you don't look down. But what a view ahead: billowing canvas, blue-black sea, mountains to infinity.

At 11pm we docked in brilliant sunshine at Pyramiden. Russia abandoned the world's most northerly mining town in 1998. Now gulls nested on window ledges of derelict apartment blocks and Arctic foxes skittered past the cultural centre, where a pink granite bust of Lenin craned its gaze towards Moscow. It looked like the set of an apocalypse film.

Yet Pyramiden isn't entirely abandoned. Two men endure the single long night of winter to maintain Russia's territorial claim. That made summer party time – a brace of guides had arrived to lead passing tourist ships.

I joined some in the bar in Pyramiden's seasonal hotel. A hammer and sickle plaque was mounted above vodka bottles. For the barman this was a summer job after university. Kiril had no plans to stay. There was no internet, no phone signal. He missed his friends in Moscow. I asked how many weeks he'd been there. 'Two days.'

Such settlements are very Svalbard too, Mette said. 'There are very few of these really isolated places you can only access by boat left.' Probably. I still preferred the version at Adolfbukta the next day.

Linden nosed through brash ice into a bay of beaten silver. Whiskered like a Habsburg grandee and as rotund, a bearded seal slid past on a floe. After the anchor chain rattled down there was silence but for the dull boom of a glacier calving beyond the bowsprit.

From the RIB, Nordenskiöld glacier appeared chaotic, carved by wind, weather and time. For up to ten thousand years it had poured around inland mountains, the top slipping faster than the bottom to tear the ice into crevasses with cracks like gunshots. Now, at the sea, it came to a messy end, exposing an iridescent teal core, littering the surface with glassy chunks that released air captured before Christ was a boy. It sounded like popping bubble wrap.

We bobbed beneath wheeling fulmars and kittiwakes and a marauding skua. There was a sudden gasp and a white barrage balloon emerged. Then another. And, there, another – a pod of around twenty beluga whales.

They feed on fish and crustaceans at the glacier's edge. Their poo fertilises the zooplankton that feeds their prey. While the glacier tumbles into the sea, the ecosystem spins. But Svalbard glaciers are retreating ever faster. What happens when they don't reach the sea? Well, it's anyone's guess.

On our final morning we walked across a shoreline of flame-orange lichens and bleached whale vertebrae into a miniscule forest – 2in polar willow, the world's smallest, toughest tree. Four reindeer grazed the tundra ahead. Svalbard reindeer are yet to associate humans with danger. Anything smaller is generally lower in nature's pecking order. We sat. Two came within touching distance, assessing me with huge eyes. It was quite a moment.

I lingered afterwards; enjoying the silence, watching the fulmars soar and the icy mountains gleam and the sea shift from steel to pewter and back. If polar wilderness demands anything of us it's that we be quiet for a while. You do that on a sailing ship. You yield to your surroundings. Have to, really. Without even realising, you internalise Rasmus' unspoken message about polar sustainability – and fragility.

I've had less fulfilling fortnights away than my three-day trip. Just imagine what life's like for citizens.

POLAND – GRIM HISTORY, BRIGHT REVIVAL

Roger Bray took this trip only eleven years after the dissolution of the Warsaw Pact and Poland's first elections following the end of Soviet communism.

Anyone researching the famous German sense of humour should visit the Polish resort of Sopot. In the town's museum they will find saucy old postcards surprisingly similar to those sold on Britain's seaside promenades. While the British father with the huge beer gut, looking for his son on the sands, couldn't see his little Willy, his stout counterpart by the Baltic had an eye glued to a partition knothole as he spied on generously proportioned ladies in their changing room.

German postcards in Poland? In the 1920s and 1930s, heyday of such unsophisticated ribaldry, Sopot was part of the Free City of Danzig, the backdrop of Günter Grass' novel *The Tin Drum*. An overwhelming majority of its population was German. For a time in its bewilderingly complicated history it had been Prussian. German holidaymakers came from Berlin and elsewhere, to stroll on Europe's longest pier and gamble at the Grand Hotel, whose guests included Marlene Dietrich... and Adolf Hitler. It all changed in 1945, when Soviet forces arrived, prompting residents to grab such belongings as they could manage, and flee.

Today Sopot is part of the metropolitan district of Gdansk, where we start our journey from north to south of the country. The heart of this once fabulously rich mercantile centre was destroyed during World War II but the façades of buildings, often with elaborate Dutch Renaissance gables, have been painstakingly restored. At the former Lenin Shipyard, Lech Walenska's Solidarity, the workers' protest against the yoke of Soviet communism, began to gather its extraordinary momentum. In the Roads to Freedom centre are remnants from those hard times – among them a grey public phone kiosk where a recording warned callers their conversations would be monitored.

The city lays claim to being the world capital of amber, the solidified sap of petrified wood, which is sold at stalls along Ulica Dlugi Targ, or Long Market Street. We are told that the lighter its colour, the older it is – and that it was said to cure heart disease among other ailments. Soak it in pure alcohol or maybe vodka, says our guide. Leave it six weeks in a dark bottle and, if it doesn't work, 'You really do need to go to hospital.' One piece in the Amber Museum contains a tiny, perfectly preserved lizard, captured in the transparent resin for some forty million years.

In Gdansk we lunch on pork dripping with morsels of meat and lovely bread, goose or wild boar terrine with plum compote and horseradish, and herring with sour cream, onion and slices of apple.

At a popular tavern in Warsaw it is the seemingly ubiquitous *zurek* – soup made of fermented rye bread, with boiled egg, sliced sausage and marjoram, followed by mammoth pork schnitzels, apple pie and a light cheesecake with chocolate sauce and strawberry mousse. Traditional Polish cooking is *not* for weight-watchers.

That day brings a sharp reminder of those for whom such fare became desperate fantasy. At a small surviving section of the ghetto wall, part of two enclosures which sealed off the Jewish population until transports to the death camps began, an old man emerges with a large visitors' book. Though not Jewish he is its self-appointed custodian. He looks after it, he says, because he has also known suffering, having spent three years in a Soviet gulag. The book is the fifth since he began. It contains messages from visitors who lost relatives in the Holocaust and some from Germans anxious to distance themselves from the horror. The two ghetto enclosures were on either side of Chlodny Street. Jews had to cross it by bridge. The tramlines on which other Poles rode through the divide are still there.

At the Warsaw Uprising Museum we watch astonishing footage from the 1944 uprising, filmed by the Home Army resistance movement. Fighters, hoping to speed up liberation from the Nazis, take cover behind barricades; teenage couriers scurry; women stir a cooking pot in the rubble; a couple wed amid the mayhem, the groom with one arm in a sling. The Germans levelled much of the capital in reprisal for this defiance (the old city centre was rebuilt in meticulous detail after the war). Whether or not the uprising was foolhardy, it was surely betrayed. From the viewing terrace of the Palace of Culture, that hulking Soviet power statement described wryly as 'Stalin's gift', you can look out across the Vistula River and imagine restless Red Army soldiers, ordered not to go to the insurgents' aid, waiting to enter the city until the uprising had ended in surrender and its defences razed.

In Lazienki Park, with its red squirrels, we stroll to the Chopin Statue, surrounded by benches amid beds of red roses where you can listen to free concerts on summer Sundays while a bust of his rival Liszt looks on. Once forbidden by the Russians (Chopin was a great figurehead for nationalists), the statue was erected in 1926 during Poland's interwar period of independence, blown up by the Nazis but copied and replaced in 1958. In Warsaw, Chopin's legacy is everywhere. Press a button on benches at places associated with him and you hear a fragment of a nocturne, étude or polonaise.

I love this city. Somehow its history seems to have created a vibrant reaction, a feeling encapsulated one balmy evening on Novy Świat, a boulevard, lined with restaurants, cafés and bars, as a cavalcade of rollerbladers sets off on a carefree circuit.

The train south rolls through rolling, undistinguished scenery. From Zakopane, a modest ski resort and major ski jumping centre in winter, we take the cable car to a switchback trail at almost 2,000m. You must book ahead or face a wait of maybe four hours for a ride. We follow a ridge ducking in and out of neighbouring Slovakia, the frontier marked by white posts. On fine days like this there are hundreds of other walkers on this and other paths. We see nuns hiking in full garb, with rosaries, crucifixes and boots barely topped by their habits. Their convent below may be unique in having walls topped with electrified tape to keep out brown bears. Before you set off you're warned to back off calmly if you encounter one.

On Zakopane's heaving, pedestrianised Krupówki Street we drink cold Tyskie beer. Characters from *Star Wars* parade for the kids. In the evenings there's a big queue for *placki* – potato pancakes with sour cream. Stalls sell the local smoked ewe's cheese, *oscypek*, which is slightly chewy and often served grilled with cranberry sauce. There's a crowded market at the street's lower end, selling everything from wood carvings to leather jackets.

Away from the throngs, attractive wooden villas catch the eye, some with elaborately carved balconies and wood-shingled roofs.

There are intricately constructed wooden churches. The oldest has a cemetery whose inmates include heroes of the wartime resistance.

Lastly, to Krakow, once Poland's royal capital, whose architectural gems survived the war mostly undamaged. Its huge main square, with the traders' Cloth Hall at its centre, may be compared with St Mark's in Venice (though prices at its cafés are much less jaw-dropping). From a tower of St Mary's Basilica a trumpeter plays on the hour. His refrain stops with apparent lack of logic, reflecting a nice legend: a 13th-century trumpeter was blowing a warning that the Tatars were coming, when he was silenced by an arrow to his throat. The basilica's great altar, decorated richly in gold, is one of Europe's finest works of Gothic art. A master craftsman from Nuremberg based its main figures on local people, carving their likenesses from the wood of a single lime tree.

Krakow has much to savour. In its cathedral is the throne on which all of Poland's kings and queens but the last were crowned. The Royal Apartments contain over a hundred 16th-century Flemish tapestries that were evacuated to Canada – via Romania and France – as the invading Wehrmacht approached. One of them includes the depiction of a dodo.

Just out of town we descend into the mind-boggling Wieliczca salt mine, a UNESCO World Heritage Site. Workers produced salt there from the 13th century until 1990, carrying it, before technology advanced, to lifts powered by horses. It has been open to tourists for over two hundred years. Goethe came to visit, and Chopin, presumably hoping the mine's air would relieve his chronic respiratory problems. Miners turned caverns into chapels. Three of them made St Kinga's, the star attraction, in the 19th century. The floor 'tiles', the chandelier crystals, and the biblical scenes on the wall reliefs are all carved from salt blocks. It is evidence of humankind's most inspiring creativity.

But not far from Krakow is evidence of the brutal opposite: Auschwitz. But after experiencing a country so palpably still enjoying resurgence following years of inhumanity and repression, we cannot face it.

THE FRUITS OF LAND AND SEA

Sainsbury's Magazine, March 2022
Renate Ruge delves into the gourmet delights of the Algarve in Portugal.

Cloud parts through the plane window revealing a bird's-eye glimpse of the Algarve below: emerald hills blanketed with vines stretch to a coast peppered with salt pans. A swirl of turquoise and white marks the point the Ria Formosa lagoon meets the azure Atlantic. It looks like it's been stirred by a giant spoon. Fishing boats head home followed by clouds of seagulls chasing their fresh catches of mackerel or sardines.

On landing there's only one thing on our minds… *pastel de nata*, Portugal's famous custard tarts. Local guide Catia leads us around Faro's historic streets, shaded by white sails, to *pasteleria* Gardy, where warm tarts sprinkled with cinnamon remind us of Portugal's historic explorers bringing spice back from the East Indies.

Reluctantly leaving the cake counter's fruit-shaped marzipan, our foodie group gets on the pans at nearby Tertúlia Algarvia, taking a cooking class learning how to make traditional seafood stew *cataplana*, named after the copper clam-shaped pot it's cooked in. Fish stock is ladled over hunks of cod, fired up with fresh paprika with just-caught razor clams scattered on top. As the stew simmers, we nibble *tiborna* – carob bread topped with paper-thin slices of smoked tuna, known as 'ham of the sea'.

After lunch, we check into cube-like villas at Quinta dos Vales winery's The Vines, where owner and modern artist Karl Heinz Stock displays his flamboyant sculptures around the estate. It's harvest time and son Michael traces the vintner's process from fruit to bottle and we pluck plump, ripened grapes from the vines to blend our own wine.

As the sun appears over the vines the next day we hike the Seven Hanging Valleys trail at Armação de Pêra, a coastal path winding around sheer cliffs. People paddleboard and kayak in the sea below as a man cooks fish over coals on the beach, its scent signalling lunchtime. Eating with water views is joyous at O Patio in Carvoeiro Beach, where tureens of colourful *arroz con mariscos* (seafood rice) studded with giant prawns are comfortingly soupy. The Moors brought citrus fruit and almonds to Portugal, so almond tart with orange-flavoured sponge is a fitting finish.

Later, larger-than-life tour guide Nuno takes us 'off the beaten track' on a foodie safari, pit-stopping first at Vila Sodré Silves. Owner André welcomes us into his candlelit cellar. Oak barrels are covered with platters of antipasti, and we taste a blushing local rosé, Al-Mudd, made from native Negra Mole grapes.

Back aboard the jeep, Nuno drives past Monchique village's whitewashed houses and accelerates through rivers into the mountains. Stopping at beekeeper Antonio's place, we sample sweet golden honey and shots of Aguardente de Medronho firewater – a schnapps-style liqueur made of medronho fruit. Reaching the summit of Fóia, 902m up, the air's fresh and scenic views of the Serra de Monchique mountains are breathtaking, the ocean on the horizon splashed by the last rays of sunlight.

Monchique Resort & Spa tapas offer tempura organic beans or 'fish from a garden', roasted octopus in silky red pepper coulis and creamy rice pudding with medronho-marinated figs.

Tonight, we're staying at São Rafael Atlântico with palm-fringed pools perched above Albufeira's golden beaches and come morning we're gliding across electric-blue waves aboard a speedboat with AlgarExperience. Jetting along the craggy coast is exhilarating, dipping in and out of inlets and spectacular caverns.

Back on dry land, we make a pilgrimage to Guia, famous for its barbecue and Restaurant Ramires' piri-piri chicken, legendary since farmer José Ramires set up his stall in the sixties. Fiery and flame-grilled, the chicken is delicious, with crispy fries dusted with extra chilli for the brave. Queues form outside as we leave.

Tasting local wine under the shade of a two-thousand-year-old olive tree at Morgado do Quintão is a lovely way to spend an afternoon. This gem of a boutique winery produces wine made only from Portuguese varieties. Salmon-hued rosé flows, perfect with tuna, beans and feather-light goat's cheese; citrusy orange *torta de laranja* pudding jives with a chilled red Tinto '18.

Later at Vila Vita Parc's Adega restaurant, we dig into delightful '*pica-pica*' (share and play) dishes. Roasted chorizo sausages are flambéed with medronho liqueur at the table and huge grilled tiger prawns swim in saffron-and-garlic Mozambique sauce.

As we're now officially hooked on clams, a visit to lively fishing village Olhão is the order of the next day. Following guide Christine, our walking tour weaves through blue- and green-tiled streets with street art mapping the lives of fishermen and we marvel at huge tuna and epic piles of prawns at the fish market.

Culatra Island is reached by ferry from Olhão. A walkway snakes through old houses and sand dunes to a quiet beach where people dig for clams as the tide goes out. Tasting clams and plump oysters straight from the seabed is wonderful, shucked for us by community leader Silvia Padinha, who's passionate about preserving the local clam-digging heritage. At Café Janoca, a blue-

and-white shack on the jetty, we savour juicy sardines, blackened by the chargrill and the smell is pure Portugal.

Further east at Vila Real de Santo António, where the Guadiana River meets the sea and dolphins play, we check into the Grand House hotel where pretty canaries in golden cages sing us a welcome. Lunch here, overlooking the infinity pool, is a feast of dorado sprinkled with *flor de sal* from nearby salt pans as we watch boats sail down the Ria Formosa. Bartender Filipe's bespoke cocktails are made to 'suit your mood'. Mine's a Green Witch.

Our last night is spent at 3HB Faro, a hotel handily fifteen minutes from the airport, where chef Adérito de Almeida's Hábito serves oyster ceviche, seared tuna and carob churros with rosemary ice cream – the perfect end to the day at the rooftop bar toasting our foodie odyssey with a zesty caipirinha. As they say in these parts… *Saúde*!

A FIRST BRUSH WITH THE RUSSIAN MILITARY

TNT Magazine, July 1997
Robin McKelvie rattles off for a rollicking rail ride across Siberia with a carriage full of Russian soldiers, who are intent on putting an end to glasnost and perestroika.

We were hoping to meet 'real' Russians, but had not bargained on Dimitry. I guess no-one really bargains on guys like Dimitry, but there he was, all 6ft 2in of him, lurching around in his army fatigues, a half-empty bottle of vodka swishing like a cutlass in one hand and a pistol threatening us from the other.

Setting out from our native Edinburgh in search of adventure, we craved realising many a traveller's dream of riding the legendary Trans-Siberian Express from Moscow deep into the wilds of Siberia.

The reality quickly proved more nightmare than dream in a vast, fractious nation still reeling from the collapse of the Berlin Wall only half a decade earlier.

Tossing his gun onto my partner's pillow, Dimitry clamped my sweaty hand in introduction. 'Hallo, my name's Dimitry. We are friends,' he bellowed. Did we have a choice?

Dimitry was not alone. Also sharing our small four-berth compartment was his comrade, Yuran. He filled the doorway behind; his massive hulk squeezed into the frame. Some people are blighted their whole life looking like a film star. Yuran did not have this problem. I had no doubt he was Sly Stallone's colossal adversary Drago from *Rocky IV*, played by the pumped-up and muscle-bound Dolph Lundgren. I laid out a limp hand in welcome, which he refused. 'I like sprinting,' he said in a voice that made Arnold Schwarzenegger sound emotional. Somebody had forgotten to tell Yuran that the Cold War was over.

For the whole journey the only English Yuran spoke was the repeated, android-like refrain 'I like sprinting'. Dimitry did not like sprinting. He liked drinking, pausing only occasionally to spout invective against anyone he could think of. As we hurtled on into the night, he set about single-handedly draining Russia's vodka lake and polluting the air with his unique world view. The choice was to stay sober in wide-eyed terror for the rest of the evening, or to join in.

Vodka it was. We meandered through his views on American movies and briefly found common ground: '*Rambo* nyet good,' sneered Dimitry. I raised slurred toasts to glasnost, but they fell on deaf ears. Then Dimitry decided that sharing my vodka was not enough, and, following a very rough interpretation of Communist principles, he decided to try to collectivise my partner. Capitalism took on communism in the battle of the top bunk while I snored straight vodka through my nostrils below.

Fortunately, capitalism stoutly fended off communism's advances. The next morning a formal warning over the serious breach of international etiquette by the Russian delegation was in order. Being honest was not an option – a line like 'Well, Dimitry, I know you are really drunk, not to mention armed, and of course you are backed up with another twenty armed Russian soldiers, but…' seemed likely to ignite a conflagration of hostilities beyond our compartment. An accusing point towards my partner in the top bunk, and a mumbled, 'Dimitry, nyet good, nyet perestroika,' was the extent of my bravery.

It seemed to work. Dimitry looked sheepish, or as sheepish as a malevolent Russian wolf ever can. But the ceasefire only lasted for a couple of hours before the drinking began. In earnest. A coiled Dimitry wound himself into a frenzy as we rattled on across Siberia. And ever further from a home that had never felt so distant.

By mid-afternoon spurned Dimitry was firing through his second bottle of vodka and had given up on conversation. Swinging his loaded pistol around the confines of the carriage he guzzled from his bottle, pausing only to offer rants like, 'Chechnya, Scotland bang bang!' I've long petitioned for Scotland to get more recognition, just not this kind. My partner cowered on the top bunk. I lay impotently beside her, forming a human barrier as Dimitry cranked up the radio and grooved to his favourite seduction serenade – 'Shut up, shut up and sleep with me, we're young, we're free. Shut up and sleep with me!'

It was surreal, verging on hilarious. But Dimitry was deadly serious. As he flailed his gun and our lives around to the frantic sounds of Russian techno we fed a constant stream of sweets over to the opposite bunk to Yuran in the hope of bribing him into keeping Dimitry under control. It seemed to be working. At least for now, but Dimitry remained a human hand grenade with the pin pulled out.

Then we ran out of chocolate. And Starbursts. Yuran caught us taking a powder-dry vitamin tablet. With no way for us to communicate what it was he insisted on having one and his face showed emotion for the first time, sheer disbelief that these strange Scots ate such disgusting sweets. For a moment as his face contorted and he scowled over we feared our lives might be lost due to the powdery taste and texture of British supermarket vitamins.

Just when it looked like we would never see home again, our nightmare came to an abrupt halt at Novosibirsk. Some 2,000km after they had bundled into our lives, Dimitry and Yuran were gone. We had lost a bottle of vodka and my male pride had taken a major dent, but we were still alive. Dimitry had even been kind enough to leave us a present. How thoughtful. Underneath our bunk lay a sprawling mess of vomit, an apposite souvenir from our first brush with the Russian military.

BACK IN THE CCCP

Doug Goodman, former PR Manager for Thomson Holidays, remembers exciting times in the Soviet Union.

They said it couldn't be done, impossible to organise, too much red tape and no-one would want to go there in winter anyway. It was 1973 when the marketing department of Thomson Holidays was planning new places for the following season and someone suggested winter weekend breaks to Moscow for 73/74.

From a PR perspective, holidays to Russia at the height of the Cold War would be an immense headline grabber. After two months of feverish activity all was ready: it worked and the rest became history. Three nights to Moscow for £29 on Britannia Airways' 737s sold out rapidly and a further 2,500 packages were added, taking the total number of visitors in that first winter to nearly seven thousand. After the Soviet capital came Leningrad. I was asked to visit Russia's second city to prepare a report on the tourist infrastructure. Thomson worked closely with Intourist, the State Travel organisation, who made us very welcome – they clearly needed foreign currency.

Leningrad was very popular and soon weekends there and twin-centre holidays were launched. Then came Kiev, Murmansk, Georgia, central Asia, Siberia and Mongolia. Back in the seventies and eighties it was easy to visit most of the fifteen Soviet Socialist Autonomous Republics as Intourist made all the arrangements for visitors.

I made nineteen trips to the USSR with Thomson before setting up my own PR agency in 1988. I had studied Russian language and literature as a student in Leningrad in 1964. The opportunity to see so much of the previously 'forbidden' land from 1973 onwards offered a wonderful chance to learn more and to meet friends from student days. With frequent visits to Russia I was suspected of handling PR for the KGB but I never stepped out of line or became involved in illegal activities (unless you count taking gifts to friends and offering bribes to obtain entry to the top restaurants).

Visitors were controlled, mainly because few understood the language and the lack of time meant many of the excursions were rushed. Dinner was served promptly at 6pm before leaving for the ballet or circus; if you were late a cold meal or nothing at all awaited you. Questions on political problems, shortages of food, alcoholism, lack of good healthcare, censorship and other topics were seldom answered by Intourist guides. Local people were forbidden any dealings with foreigners and were obliged to report on those they met. Lenin was revered; political posters were everywhere, and images of party bosses abounded.

The Hotel Intourist, home for Western visitors and now long replaced, had 'special' rooms; my press guests were usually put in room 14 on each floor. In the hotel's basement staff were apparently monitoring conversations. I always used a public phone to contact friends rather than the room phone – just in case. The joke was that if you required room service you spoke into the lampshade or two-way mirror.

I spent many happy evenings with Russian friends in their homes drinking *samogen* (homemade spirits), listening to music or discussing the latest banned books. If I missed the last metro back to central Moscow, I followed the example of the locals who flagged down any passing vehicle hoping it was going in the right direction. Offer a few roubles and the car was invariably going in your direction. I once even got a lift in a snowplough.

Arriving at or leaving an apartment block my friends insisted that I spoke Russian for the benefit of the concierge, who had to report on foreign visitors. In my friends' flats the telephone was always moved out of the room as conversations could be monitored. I doubted that but on an occasion in a hotel room, where a friend was staying, the radio was turned to full volume so we could hardly hear each other: neither could 'they', it seemed. He was a party member and Soviet Army officer. At the flat of a UK journalist I was shown the bumps under the bedroom wallpaper where microphones had been installed.

The rail journey from Moscow to Leningrad on the Red Arrow; drinks with the captain of a fish-processing ship in Murmansk; bargaining for melons in Samarkand; touring the world's largest hydro-electric power station in Bratsk on the Angara River; and being interviewed by BBC TV on frozen Lake Baikal in Siberia were the highlights of my visits. Memorable was a banquet in Tbilisi hosted by the tourist board chief. Etiquette had to be strictly followed, our guide advised: only drink when a toast is proposed and finish all the drinks placed before you. Suitably forewarned it was still a shock to see a full bottle of wine and a half-litre of vodka at each setting. All this was preceded by Georgian 'champagne' with a final toast to peace and friendship in Armenian cognac.

Despite seeing so many fascinating destinations in the USSR I felt most at home in Moscow. Revolution Day parade was held on 7 November so our press visits were often timed to see the spectacular show of military power. Although we couldn't get a place in Red Square, the corner of Gorky Street outside the hotel provided the perfect public viewing spot. At dawn we were woken by the sound of engines revving and soldiers marching. Blue smoke drifted up from the tanks as positions were taken for the drive into Red Square. Hot coffee was sold in cardboard cups to spectators for a few kopeks. Plastic cups were unknown so the scalding-hot, very welcome coffee had to be drunk before the cup dissolved.

My favourite restaurant was the Aragvi in Gorky Street, a place loved by Stalin for its Georgian food and frequented by top party bosses. A *shevitsar* (doorman) decided who would be allowed in but a packet of Marlboro's always worked. Dishes on the menu might be *deficitney* (off), but a small gift ensured that the dish you really wanted was suddenly 'on', along with more than the usual 100g of vodka and the much-sought-after sweet Shampanskoye.

A friend lived in a block opposite the Aragvi. Visiting one day I passed a well-dressed man who looked vaguely familiar. I was told he was English and always had a 'minder' accompanying him. In 1988 I received a letter from Moscow with a postage stamp depicting Kim Philby, the MI5 operator who spied for Russia and defected. I realised whom I had encountered. Once I was refused a visa and on another occasion locked up in an isolation hospital. But those stories are for another time.

Thomson really did open up the Soviet Union between 1973 and 1989 and provided a new experience for visitors, ranging from the curious holidaymaker to members of UK trade unions. Most visitors saw only what the authorities wanted them to see but it still gave them the opportunity to witness communism at work and to make up their own minds. In 1977, after only four years of operating holidays to Russia, over 100,000 people had made bookings and at its peak Thomson had five weekly Moscow flights and two to Leningrad on Britannia and Aeroflot.

In 2001 I toured the 'Golden Circle' cities. In 2005 I returned to Moscow to catch up with friends and in 2019 took a Volga cruise. But where was all the mystery, intrigue and excitement I had known before the 1991 revolution?

It's still there, though you have to dig a little deeper into the soul of Russia to find it. But assuming anyone wishes to go there, it may be some time before the country welcomes you again.

FACING FEAR ON AN ANCIENT SWISS PASS

Olly Beckett faces and overcomes his nightmares in Switzerland.

In my nightmares I'm teetering along narrow icy paths with deathly drops. Conversely, I daydream of being in the mountains where such paths abound. Usually I avoid them, but then I heard about a mountain hut high in the Swiss Alps, on a remote and precipitous pass that's been used since the early Bronze Age. Time to live the dream and face that nightmare.

I'm spending the night before in the tucked-away town of Kiental. While the Postbus struggles up Switzerland's steepest road, I opt for a pretty path from Reichenbach train station.

Kiental is timbered buildings with sun-blackened window shutters huddling beneath soaring mountains. Across the road from my 112-year-old hotel (with what seem like original carpets), a bakery sells sweet cakes and gives away friendly smiles. Despite it being shoulder season, the chairlift is still operating and costs just CHF10. Tomorrow's hike has been on my mind for many months, but I'm now distracted by enormous snow-capped peaks and pristine pine forests. Over there, on the other side of those mountains, is the Lauterbrunnen Valley and its crowds of tourists. Up above Kiental I enjoy a bonus warm-up walk all by myself.

Nerves prevent me from eating breakfast the next morning. Instead I board an early bus, then train, to Kandersteg and await the minibus I've booked to Selden. I'm encouraged to see other hikers join me. From Kandersteg the tarmac road becomes a gravel track which rises sharply and passes through unlit tunnels. To the side and far below the Kander River roars.

In the tiny hamlet of Selden every passenger but me heads for Berghotel Gasterntal, a large wooden building that has been accommodating and feeding visitors for a century. I walk alone towards the Lötschenpass, across a long suspension bridge and up a switchback path that for the next hour rises 1m for every 4m walked.

I'm now on the edge of a plain dotted with boulders and swaying with tall grass, a hidden alpine wonderland with slopes raking sharply upwards either side and, at the far end, an ominously looming cliff. At 2,000m altitude those hardy pines begin to thin out. I realise I'm at a point of no return; if I turn back I can still catch one of the trains that rush through a tunnel hundreds of metres beneath my feet. Opting to continue all the way to the hut I think I see a path chiselled into that distant cliff, a terrifying prospect. But there are also the tiny shapes of people on top of it. They must have taken another route.

Deploying some optimism I conclude that there must be a different way to conquer the cliff. Sure enough, I realise that the path veers right and takes what some would consider a more sedate route. I, however, consider it unsettling. It's narrow and roller-coasters steeply up and down along scree and beside a horribly long drop.

At the top of that cliff I look down on to that grassy plain. Next: a glacier covered in rocks. The only indications that I'm now walking over a giant lump of ice are the occasional flash of white and channels carved by water through the freezing base layer.

Posts mark the route across the glacier; on the other side I face my greatest fear: the path now clings to another cliff, has narrowed again and has patches of snow. There's a sturdy steel rail I can cling to but there are large gaps. Stopping only to take photos I climb and climb. It's only when I look back at those photos that I realise how big a drop there was.

Despite the trepidation I am, strangely, enjoying myself. In my ears is nothing but the whistle of high-altitude breezes, in my lungs nothing but cool alpine air. On the periphery of my vision mountains rise over 3,600m. This is my happy place and I'm glad my fear of heights hasn't kept me away.

That place gets considerably happier when the path levels out and I stroll on to rocky ground which, minutes later, dips slightly to reveal a wind turbine. I've made it.

Lötschenpass Hut is entirely powered by green energy, has three storeys and bunks for dozens of visitors. I've arrived on a sunny day and people have hiked here from the easier southern approach. They rest and refresh before returning the way they came. It's just me and two Dutch ladies staying the night, along with the welcoming staff. Adrenaline fuelled me up here faster than I expected and so I've plenty of time to gaze at hundreds of peaks.

'Hut' doesn't adequately describe this building. It's large, warm and comfortable, despite the harsh environs at 2,690m. Because there are a few bunk rooms I have one all to myself. That evening, while I refuel on Rösti, ibex stroll past outside, their magnificently curved horns outlined against snowy, dusk-lit mountains.

People have rested on this pass for millennia. In 2017 archaeologists found an early Bronze Age wooden food box close to the hut, just one of many pieces of evidence that show this was once a trading and migration route.

Expecting the next day's hike to be easier I depart in eager anticipation that is tempered by scrambling over icy rocks close to another precipitous edge. A damp mist descends once I'm on a safer path and, shortly after frightening a marmot into its flower-rimmed burrow, I plod wearily into Lauchernalp Village.

A grotesque face greets me through the murk, its deformed visage staring from the side of a chalet. Then another appears and another. These are the masks of *tschäggättä*: fearsome – and fictional – creatures that roam the Lötschen Valley from February until midnight on Shrove Tuesday.

I opt for an easy, wide track down to Kippel and the valley floor. I've overcome my fear of heights and met terrible *tschäggättä*, seen ibex and remote waterfalls, walked across glaciers and hidden plains, and spent a night on an ancient pass among the peaks of snow-covered Alps. What a dream.

YUGOSLAVIA '76 MADE ME
WHO I AM TODAY

The *Daily Telegraph*, 31 May 2019
Mary Novakovich recalls how her love affair with her parents'
hinterland region of Croatia began after being shipped off
there as a child for the summer.

Summer 1976: Europe was melting in a heatwave. Elton John and Kiki Dee were topping the charts and Canada was preparing for its first Olympic Games.

I was oblivious to most of this – not because I was too young to remember, but because I spent that summer in the mountainous wilderness of what was then Yugoslavia. No phone, no TV and certainly no internet.

My parents had decided to ship me off to the Old Country, back to their home region of Lika in what's now Croatia, so I could brush up on my Serbian and get to know my heritage first-hand rather than through the immigrant bubble.

I was put in the care of an aunt and uncle I had met precisely once, briefly. I was eleven, a somewhat indulged child (ie: a spoilt brat) and had never been away without having a close member of my family with me. What could possibly go wrong?

Flying while wearing my 'Unaccompanied young passenger' lanyard was exciting, the doting cabin staff taking my mind off my temporary separation from my parents. But within minutes of arriving at my aunt and uncle's flat in Belgrade, my language difficulties manifested themselves.

I thought I spoke Serbian reasonably well – it was my cradle tongue, after all. But I hadn't reckoned on how much English had crept in even at that age. I could not make myself understood, and

I could see my aunt wondering what she'd let herself in for. It was going to be a long summer, I thought, as we got ready for the big drive to Lika through Serbia and Bosnia.

What awaited me was a small house with primitive plumbing surrounded by orchards, mountains, rivers, waterfalls, meadows – simply the most gorgeous landscape I'd ever seen. (It still makes me sigh every time I go back.) But for this homesick city child, it took a while to appreciate the wild beauty now all around me.

First, I had to get used to the plumbing – or lack of it. Fortunately, my aunt and uncle's house had the only indoor toilet within 10 miles, but visiting others was tricky. 'Where's the loo?' Points to earth closet at the bottom of the garden. 'Over there.' Oh.

Unknown cousins burst out of nowhere and wondered what to do with this sulky kid with the funny accent. They did what all kids do – take the mickey, then get to know you and take you into their world. They were a mischievous bunch, though. I still remember my cousin Ilija insisting that I carry a stick with me as protection against snakes on our walks. That was when I still had a childhood horror of reptiles. 'See those holes?' he said, pointing to little mounds in the fields we trekked through. 'That's where snakes live. Bash them on the head if you see any poking out.' Just as well I didn't take him at his word, as the cheeky beggar was pointing at rabbit holes.

My language skills eventually got better: the day I told a joke in Serbian (and got a laugh) still fills me with pride. My cousins taught me how to write in Cyrillic, which I used in my postcards home – but using English words. My parents laughed their heads off when they read the cards.

Did I miss my parents? Not more than I missed everything else that I was familiar with. I really can't recall speaking to them on the phone more than twice, probably because the only phone was in the next village, also about 10 miles away. As with so many things in life in the seventies, I was just left to get on with it. And my aunt and uncle were kindness personified, even if my stubbornness and truculence tested their patience.

Every few days, they would send me to the farm up the lane to retrieve two large pails filled with warm, steamy milk, fresh from the cow. My aunt would boil it, skim it, and then grimace with annoyance when I refused to drink it. So my uncle would have to drive to the next village to pick up supplies of UHT milk that came in those odd little triangular cartons. I really was a horrid child.

Slowly, though, my homesickness melted. The farm with the cows had a huge hayloft, which made a fantastic launching point for screaming jumps into piles of hay. We would play hide-and-seek in the maize fields, and generally be left alone by the adults to run wild.

I inadvertently contributed to the family annals of amusing tales by making a fuss of trying to wade through the ice-cold river Una, stumbling on the slippery rocks. My friend Sanja (who was my age, and tiny) volunteered to carry me. My cousins still won't let me forget that, and chortle about it mercilessly even forty-three years later. I've since been back in the Una, which was icy as ever, but much more enjoyable with swimming shoes.

Tough as I found it at the beginning, I grew up treasuring that summer. I had the one and only chance to meet my father's stepmother, as well as one of his sisters (who I didn't realise was ill and died soon after). At the time, my step-grandmother was the sole remaining resident in my father's old hamlet – less of a hamlet, really, and more a run-down collection of farm buildings and cottages.

I couldn't imagine how hard her life must have been living alone in an old stone cottage with only a wood-burning stove for heating, and a well – her only source of water – that was at least a few hundred yards away. She was in her late seventies at the time, indomitable and kind. I've been back to the hamlet a couple of times, each time forgetting to bring the machete needed to hack through the vegetation that long ago smothered everything.

Over that summer, my enormous extended family became a little closer and more real to me, and we still see each other on my annual visits to Belgrade. And I discovered that, like most children, I was resilient and could adapt, albeit with some first-class whingeing.

I was grateful for the supply of books I had brought with me, and I was able to steal away occasionally into my own world – particularly in the early days when I seemed to be in a more or less permanent sulk and needed something familiar to grasp. At the time I was obsessed with the *Anne of Green Gables* books and read them again and again. But slowly I was realising that L M Montgomery's evocative rural life wasn't that dissimilar from what was around me – or so my overactive imagination thought at the time.

By the end of that summer I was thinking and dreaming in Serbian. In all that time, we'd had only one visitor who spoke English. Although my cousins were learning a second language at school, it was Russian, which was as much use to me as my school French was to them. When I came home, I was speaking English with a Serbian accent. I called my father 'Tata' – he was always 'Daddy' – and nearly made him cry. I wish my Serbian were as good now. Perhaps I need another summer of total immersion.

Nowadays, of course, I'd be staring at my phone, scrolling through Facebook, WhatsApp and Twitter, keeping in touch with family and friends, half the time oblivious to the world around me. I might not have spent quite so many hours jumping in haylofts, perhaps preferring to play games on a tablet. I might have used

Google Translate to get me out of a conversational jam, rather than sign language and charades that made everyone fall about.

If I'd had a child, would I do the same and ship them off into the unknown at such a young age? I probably would, if I knew they were in safe, loving hands. The chance to immerse myself in our culture and language was one I wouldn't have wanted to miss. When parents say 'You'll thank me for this later', sometimes they're right.

Peaks of the Balkans by Rudolf Abraham

AFRICA

WHAT SAFARI GUIDES REALLY FEAR IN BOTSWANA'S OKAVANGO DELTA

Inside the Travel Lab, 14 September 2022
Abigail King drifts along the world's largest delta.
But is it more dangerous than it looks?

Despite the stillness of the water, there's no sound of silence. Insects skim across the reeds with a soft buzz and woodpeckers tap against acacia trees. Birds chatter in all directions – yet the loudest by far are the doves.

'Chu charra, chu charra.'

'Work harder, work harder,' chants Rodger, slipping a pole into the delta and easing us forward. 'Drink lager, drink lager,' says another guide, Amos, illustrating a different point of view. From where I'm sitting, level with the water in a slender mokoro – Botswana's flat-bottomed canoe – I hear something else. Botswana, Botswana, Botswana.

Eight hundred miles from the Atlantic and a thousand from the Indian Ocean, the Okavango Delta looks like a miniature version of the earth from the air, an expanded jigsaw of land swirls amid deep and spreading blue. Its water seeps up through the soil, having landed as monsoon rain a thousand miles north in Angola. It's long been protected, both by government intervention and because its soggy, swampy nature makes building roads here impossible.

To get this deep into the delta, we've flown from Maun in a four-seater Cessna, a tiny contraption that trembled during the descent as though in awe of the expanse below. An elephant greeted us on the runway and warthogs scuttled past us in the camp.

Botswana takes its wildlife pretty seriously. Even on foot, guides can't carry firearms for self-defence, only a gunpowder-laced contraption resembling a syringe that produces loud blasts. When an elephant veers too close to the camp, guides let off a single empty shot that rips through the vast sky.

Should an elephant charge, or a hippo rear up from the water, our survival depends on our behaviour, we are told. Stand still, stay quiet – and if told to run, try not to fall into an aardvark hole. Not everyone is reassured. 'Why not take a gun with you?' asks one member of our camp. 'If you killed something by accident, what's the worst that could happen?' 'A lifetime in prison,' comes the reply. There's a rare moment of silence before we climb aboard.

Despite the danger, it's hard to imagine a more peaceful mode of transport. A cross between a punt and a canoe, mokoros used to be the only way to travel around here. Previous generations hand-carved them from ebony and kigelia trees but had to wait for more than a hundred years for the trunk to reach the right size. Since a wooden mokoro only has a five-year lifespan, the arrival of a fibreglass version was greeted with about the same enthusiasm as the discovery of sliced bread.

Today, boats use small motors to churn along the main waterway to Maun, carrying people, food and beer. The mokoros, however, fashion their own way through the reed fields, the long grass spreading apart before them in a deferential rustle. This off-piste navigation isn't just for entertainment, though.

'The only animal I fear,' says Rodger when I ask him, 'is the hippopotamus. That is why we stay away from the main channel.' 'But,' I state the obvious, 'we do need to cross it… eventually.' Rodger sinks the pole into the delta again and water sloshes gently against the thin-walled mokoro. 'I look for bubbles,' he says slowly. He grins. 'And I drive fast!'

Chu-charra, chu-charra. The doves reach a crescendo as we glide past giraffe, baboons and impala, while Rodger keeps watch. My mind drifts to his interpretation of what the doves are saying.

Like the rhythm of the mokoro itself, his version soothes me.

A PRIMATE LOCATION IN THE CONGO JUNGLE

The Independent/Independent Digital
News & Media Ltd, 11 January 2014

Congo's forests are teeming with wildlife, but not tourists. Sue Watt checks into two camps that put her within reach of birds, butterflies and wild gorillas.

Tiptoeing in the rainforest is never easy. Squelching underfoot and communicating only through hand signals, we tried to get closer to the shadows in the trees. Lango Forest is a popular haunt for monkeys, but these were something bigger, something special. Initially our guide, Karl, thought they were chimpanzees, rarely seen in the wild. But closer inspection proved him wrong.

'They're gorillas, wild gorillas,' he whispered, wide-eyed and elated, 'they've never been habituated, maybe never seen humans – unbelievable!' On seeing us, two giant apes rushed down the tree and disappeared into shrub. 'That's what I love about Congo,' he mused. 'The forests are full of surprises, full of secrets…'

The rainforests of Odzala-Kokoua National Park, spreading 13,600sq km across northwest Congo, certainly have an air of the unknown about them. Established in 1935, Odzala is one of Africa's oldest national parks yet is rarely visited, the country being adversely affected by people's confusion with its volatile neighbour, Democratic Republic of the Congo. With a unique biodiversity and Africa's densest population of western lowland gorillas (some 20,000 of the world's 100,000 population live here), the area is ripe for discovery, which explains the opening of two camps by Wilderness, an upmarket tourism/conservation organisation.

The timing is fortuitous. African Parks, a South African non-profit organisation that regenerates depleted parks, assumed management of Odzala in 2010 on a twenty-five-year mandate. With wildlife populations decimated through poaching, its first priority is to stabilise the core of the park, and for this it needs local people onside. Leon Lamprecht, AP's manager, explained: 'The only way this park can have a long-term life is if communities benefit from it. Short-term benefits are the prevention of elephant poaching for ivory… tourism dollars will help communities: they'll see the long-term benefits outweigh the short-term.'

Our two-hour flight from Congo's laid-back capital, Brazzaville, took us over seemingly endless expanses of rainforest. Beneath its canopy live some 430 bird species and 100 species of mammal, including 11 types of diurnal primates, more than any central African forest region.

Arriving at Lango Camp on a humid afternoon, it wasn't the beautifully rustic décor of the bar and lounge or the captivating view out over the river that struck me most: it was frogs, croaking and calling like a choir of thousands. The camp, inspired by the settlements of the B'Aka forest people, who lived here for forty thousand years, has stylishly simple tree houses built of raffia palms and wood, all perched on decking overlooking the river. After dinner, as we sat stargazing on our terrace, a tiny tree frog jumped onto my knee and we listened together to elephants trumpeting in the darkness.

The emphasis at Lango is on rainforest safari drives, walks and boat trips, and I soon realised that after years of travelling in southern and eastern Africa everything here is different. Elephants are shorter, with longer, straighter tusks. Forest buffalo look more like cows, red not black, and the impressive, bouffant-style horns have been replaced by short, stubby ones. Crocodiles are slender-snouted or dwarf, not Nile; monkeys putty-nosed or moustached, not Vervet; savannahs moist, not parched. There are new animals to see including the stripy, deer-like sitatunga and the beautifully named bongo, a huge, mainly nocturnal antelope.

After wading knee-deep through swamps and marshes we took a boat along the Lekoli River. Nearby, a lone bull elephant had also been wading through swamps, with watermarks almost to the top of his haunches. Drifting along the now calm waters, we received a running commentary of monkey mania from Karl and Fraser, steering our aluminium vessel. 'There goes a De Brazza's monkey,' said Fraser, then Karl urged: 'Check out those guereza colobus moving like ninjas.'

My favourites were the playful putty-nosed monkeys chasing each other in circles, so-called because their white noses look like squashed blobs of putty stuck on black faces. Bird lovers were in raptures: within five minutes a goliath heron emerged to our right and a giant kingfisher to our left, but both were outshone by the famously elusive Pel's fishing owl that suddenly darted across the river. 'That's a birder's equivalent to seeing an aardvark!' Karl said, explaining the excitement. 'Unbelievable!'

Still scarred from decades of poaching, wildlife here is skittish. But it will relax once it learns that the park's new guests are no threat. Gorillas, however, are more used to humans with three groups having been habituated by the renowned primatologist Dr Magda Bermejo and her husband German Illera.

A bumpy two-hour drive away, Ngaga Camp, similar in design to Lango, is Wilderness' gorilla-tracking base in the heart of the Ndzehi Forest. 'Welcome to the Gabon highway,' Karl announced *en route* as our Land Cruiser squeezed between the overgrown reeds and grasses that concealed what was little more than a severely pot-holed dirt track.

Even the gorillas are different here. Smaller than their mountain cousins and classed as critically endangered, the population is decreasing through disease, the bushmeat trade and loss of habitat. Visitors follow a strict viewing protocol to alleviate stress and the risk of contamination with human diseases. This includes restricting visitor numbers to four per group, keeping a minimum 7m distance from the gorillas, wearing masks when watching them and spending just one hour in their company.

We set off in mid-morning humidity to meet the Neptuno group, named after their mighty silverback. Our expert tracker, Zepherin, followed a grid of pathways cut through dense Marantaceae shrub, akin to gigantic aspidistras about 2m high. This is staple ape food, explaining why around 105 gorillas have made this particular area their home. Disturbed vegetation, half-eaten wild ginger stems and an upside-down ants' nest that gorillas had snacked on all proved that we were on the right track. Eventually, we turned off the main path down one of the 'tunnels' in the Marantaceae created by the gorillas. Then, we suddenly saw Neptuno sitting in a tree munching leaves. Around him were the rest of his family, eighteen in all, warming themselves in the sun.

Pan, a cocky two-year-old, lay on his back, sometimes scratching his tummy or brow, keeping an eye on us while Caco, aged six, climbed halfway up the trunk and just stayed there seemingly posing for photos. Ceres sat right at the top of the tree grooming her little baby, its spiky hair silhouetted against the sun.

Mesmerised by this happy family scene, our hour flew by. But just before we left, as if he was timing us, Neptuno performed his star turn, descending the liana vine like a brawny ballerina, elegantly sliding his 200kg of muscle down to the ground.

'Neptuno is special,' Magda confided that evening. 'The guides, the trackers, they all feel the same...' The next day, we tracked Jupiter's group of twenty-five gorillas for four hours, following footprints and discarded fruits, broken Marantaceae and fresh-smelling faeces on the trail. But it seemed they were constantly and rapidly moving on. Eventually Karl briefly spotted one gorilla in a tree about 100m away but the group was hidden in such dense vegetation it was impossible to penetrate.

Returning disappointed, we learned that a solitary wild male had been threatening Jupiter, forcing him to rush on without even stopping to eat. With the gorillas' well-being always paramount, Magda decided that Jupiter had suffered enough stress for one day and that we shouldn't return for another attempt to see him. And with the itinerary only allowing for two tracking experiences in two days at Ngaga, with no contingency for non-sightings, Jupiter would, for us at least, remain unseen.

It was a different story for the group who tracked Neptuno that morning. One guest showed me her photos, her face still glowing with amazement. There was Neptuno, big and burly on all fours in a clearing, feeding contentedly. Nearby, youngsters were happily fooling around and mothers were nurturing their babies. 'No-one spoke when they got back, not even the guide. They were just stunned,' Charlotte the camp manager told me. 'It's the best sighting we've ever had.' As Karl had said after our first, unexpected gorilla encounter in Lango Forest: unbelievable...

WHAT'S NEW IN ANCIENT EGYPT?
A JOURNEY BACK AFTER TWENTY YEARS

Inside the Travel Lab, 30 January 2025
Abigail King realises that nothing stays the same,
even in the ancient world.

More than four thousand years may have passed since the pyramids were built. But don't say there's nothing new in ancient Egypt. In fact, the country has a surprise up her sleeve. And it is well worth the wait.

Twenty-four hours is a long time in politics, and indeed with gastroenteritis, where a night spent doubled over beneath the stars gives a new perspective to the desire for immortal longings.

That took place on an island in the Nile on my very first trip to Egypt, nearly twenty-four years ago. It was an unfortunate part of a sun-scorched pilgrimage to see the wonders of the ancient world, from the pyramids of Giza to the arresting Abu Simbel. It also revealed the twists and turns of fate since the chivalry shown on the night in question by my then boyfriend played a large part in him becoming my husband.

But whether measured in years or hours, such time seems a speck when travelling in this part of the world. Tombs in the Valley of the Kings, where Howard Carter found Tutankhamun, were built around 1,500BC. The sphinx in 2,500BC. And the pyramid at Saqqara clocks in at around 4,600 years old.

They are phenomenal works of architecture and art, revealing powerful stories of the ambition, frailties and desires of the human race. They also demonstrate some of the world's best engineering.

For the pyramids are not just mounds of stone. They contain intricate passageways that travel right to the heart of the structure, without, somehow, causing the threat of collapse. Over 2.3 million stone slabs were assembled, each weighing between two and fifteen tons, before the invention of the wheel and before horses arrived in Egypt. The corners align perfectly with the cardinal points of the compass.

In Abu Simbel, Ramses II decreed that a temple be hewn into the face of the rock to instil fear in those approaching from the south from modern-day Sudan. Four towering statues loom overhead, a grown man barely reaching their ankles. These guard the entrance to a temple of Russian-doll segments, each lined with hieroglyphics and shadows, growing smaller and smaller until deep in the heart of the rock, you find four life-size statues in stone. This includes Ramses II, pharaoh of the time. Sunlight reaches his face only twice a year: on his birthday and on the day of his coronation. These dates are not six months apart.

In the 1960s, UNESCO teams relocated this stonework to protect it from the floods. In doing so, with all the technology at their disposal, they introduced an astrological error. We still cannot, it would seem, match the engineering brilliance of ancient Egypt.

So, what is the point in going back? With the whole world to explore, what more is there to see or say about a pile of old stones? I'm teasing, of course. Such study of 'old stones' could take a lifetime: intricate, sweet sketches on honeyed stone revealing bloodthirsty gods. Decoding cartouches for names like Alexander the Great, Caesar, Cleopatra, and Tutankhamun.

My journey this time, with a guide by my side and a brand-new adult's worth of life experience, gives me a completely different perspective. Since my first visit, friends and family have died. The concepts behind preparing for the afterlife and honouring your father ring differently this time. So too, since the birth of my daughter, do the gods of fertility and the biography of Cleopatra. I've even changed my last name, itself an intriguing emotion in the Valley of the Kings. But it's not just me who has changed. Egypt has as well.

And not only in the little things, like the paved walkways and electric buggies at Hatshepsut's temple; a move that morphs back-breaking pilgrimages into comfortable afternoons and opens access beyond the young, fit and able.

It's not just in the development of tourism, for want of a better word. When I visited before, the focus was simply the temples. Now, there are light shows at the sphinx and hot-air balloons fill the skies at dawn in Luxor. The bartering to get around is replaced by Uber; there are apps for everything; and I'm regularly approached by Egyptians asking for a selfie. We find such changes the world over. But in Egypt, it's the ancient world itself that's new. The empty plinths at Luxor temple are empty no more: the statues have been found, buried in shallow graves, Vegas style, in the desert. Ramses II restored.

But in Cairo, or to be more precise, Giza, is the greatest of them all. The brand new, shiny, colossal and unashamedly named Grand Egyptian Museum. Or as locals call it, the GEM. By the time I find myself walking along the long stretch of concrete that leads to the entrance, I am in danger of being underwhelmed. From cosy London corners to the steps of Cairo's citadel, I'd heard whispers about the greatness of the 'Jewel in Cairo's Crown'. The hype was immense.

The previous museum on Tahir Square, the Egyptian Museum Cairo, had the air of an eccentric Victorian collector. Incredible treasures tucked into wood-framed glass cases with hand-scrawled notes. You half expected Paddington Bear and Hugh Bonneville to leap out from a sarcophagus.

The GEM, meanwhile, carries the promise, no hype, of modernity. And to begin with, hype does seem to be all that it is.

There are no swirls of the Guggenheim, no sudden glass pyramid of the Louvre. Just a clean-enough, nice-enough paved walkway with multiple parking spaces for coaches, plus orderly ticket queues and security checks.

As I walk through the triangular door, my impressions starts shifting. The triangles are pleasing. The lighting soothes the eye. Multimedia exhibits bring hieroglyphics to life and the gift shop is secretly glorious. But there are two key places where the brilliance of this project really sinks in.

One, our friend from earlier, Ramses II. His statue stands in pride of place within the atrium, overlooking an inky-black infinity pool. In the ceiling, it appears as though a panel has fallen out, as though something is already missing. But this is no mistake. Just twice a year, sunlight reaches the face of the statue through this panel. On the day of his birthday and then his coronation. Exactly.

Beyond that, a series of escalators escort visitors through four granite stages, each with softly lit details. The stages symbolise four things: pharaohs, religion, the afterlife. And then nothing. The final level is empty.

I stand for a moment, blinking. For a civilisation devoted to the idea of life after death, why the anticlimax? My eyes adjust to the light. A crowd is forming in this layer of nothing, a blur of silhouettes. My eyes adjust again. And then I see. It's not nothing. It's a window. To the pyramids in the sand. And with that, the architects have pulled off a magic trick.

It is ancient Egypt, made new.

JOURNEY TO THE
CENTRE OF THE EARTH

Through successive trips to Ghana, Ian Packham has witnessed incredible sights, but also the real meaning of travel.

I t's hot and sticky, just as I love to hate it, and my shoes kick up a small cloud of orange-red dust with every step. But the sky is a bright baby blue, unknown birds are twittering in a nearby bush and there's been absolutely no tunnelling required – just several slightly sweaty hours on Ghana's main form of public transport, the goes-only-when-full trotro minibus.

Ghana's location on the Greenwich Meridian, which cleaves through the fittingly renamed Centre of the World Golf Club roughly 20 miles east of Ghana's coastal capital, Accra, plus the fact it's the closest point in mainland Africa to the Equator, has led to the country being dubbed 'the centre of the world'.

Before that, it was much more common to see the West African nation with the moniker of 'Africa in microcosm' or 'Africa for beginners', which is exactly what had me arrive on my original visit in 2006 as a nervy twenty-three-year-old on my first solo trip to Africa. At that time only one European airline was brave enough to fly there.

These three short weeks began an on-again-off-again love affair now heading towards its third decade, triggered by the continued authenticity of the welcomes I receive, a plethora of important historic sites, a fair share of wildlife and the chance to get beyond my comfort zone and have an adventure (just hit some of the roads in the far north during the rainy season), knowing it's unlikely to end with any of the mishaps that befell Otto Lidenbrock, the protagonist in Jules Verne's rather more literal *Journey to the Centre of the Earth*.

Add to that an ever-improving range of locally produced chocolates from the second largest cacao producer in the world – a surprisingly new addition to Ghana's long list of attractions – and it's frankly a surprise this sweet-toothed travel writer ever leaves.

While many of Africa's nations are so big it's difficult to know where to start, bite-sized Ghana – the approximate area of the UK – couldn't be easier to enjoy. Start on its Atlantic coast, where nesting leatherback turtles can outnumber sunbathers on the remotest of beaches and Africa's largest chain of forts age quietly beneath the sound of the lapping waves.

Celebrate amid the drummers of Kumasi's Akwasidae festivities with the King of the Ashanti and his chiefs, give back with a tour of Mognori eco-village on the boundary of Mole National Park, where walking safaris regularly encounter elephants, and be welcomed into mud-and-stick-built mosques that date back to the time of Christopher Colombus in the dusty north.

But whether you stick to the eastern or western hemisphere, head north, or linger in the subtropical south, Ghana won't fail to have you re-evaluating your place in the world. Every time I visit, and I'm now on the fourth tour of the country totalling months pounding those dusty roads, I return richer.

Even though I appreciate a home climate that doesn't have me sweating by daring to breathe, I come back home with more patience and willingness to help others, as complete strangers in Ghana have helped me, buying me roadside lunches entirely unbidden just to welcome me, going out of their way to lead me to the correct bus station, or stepping in to translate on one of the rare occasions when English doesn't quite cut it.

THE LONG NIGHT OF THE LION

The *Sunday Times*, October 1979,
and *Savannah Diaries*, Bradt 2014
Brian Jackman takes to a camel on safari in Kenya.

Northern Kenya is a harsh and unforgiving land, yet its beauty is undeniable, its wildness unsurpassed. Here, as soon as you leave the beaten track, disappearing into the fathomless Commiphora thickets and heat-hazy mountains, you can feel the years falling away and imagine yourself in the Africa of a century ago when there were no 4WD vehicles to ease your passage through the bush.

This is the age that Julian McKeand has managed to recapture, if only for a week or so at a time, by organising camel safaris into Samburu country from his home in the shadow of Mount Kenya. McKeand is a former game warden who later became a professional hunter before hitting on the idea of running camel safaris for Kenya's growing numbers of tourists.

Everything is as authentic as McKeand can make it. From the camels themselves to their clanking wooden bells and the ex-British Army saddles made by Makhanbal & Sons of Bikaner, India, in the last days of the Raj.

Camel trekking, I discover, has one big advantage over horseback riding: no previous experience is required. You simply hoist yourself aboard and then cling on tight as the animal lurches to its feet with an alarming fore-and-aft heave. Each camel is led by a man with a rope and simply ambles along in a tireless soft-shoe shuffle.

Every day on our safari down the Seya Sand River begins the same: the cold dawn coming alive to a chorus of doves and the sun's red glow igniting the still-sleeping hills – a reverie broken by the bellowing complaints of our camels being harnessed, like someone gargling with a bucket of gravel.

Under those huge African skies, in that wild, awesome country, I felt absurdly happy. Our Laikipiak Maasai crew were happy too. Their step was light, and they sang as they led the camels down the criss-cross game trails between the thorny thickets. They sang about the blue hills above us, where greater kudu roamed the stony paths. They sang about the beauty of their cows, which they valued above everything else in the world. In high, clear voices, they made up the songs as they marched along in their blood-red robes, and each impromptu solo cadenza was answered by a stirring, one-two chant of hunhh-hunhh that made the hair stand up on the back of my neck.

As for the camels, they varied in colour from a dusky brown to a pale creamy suede. At first, I had thought them ugly, ill-tempered brutes. But in time I learned to love their lugubrious faces, their curious dignity and tireless plodding gait. How well they were named ships of the desert. As for us, seated aloft and swaying through the amber light of early morning, we were strangers no longer, but lords of the bush.

Now it is night. Supper by a huge campfire of dead trees is over, and I have been guided through the darkness to the trestle bed on which I am to sleep, protected by nothing more than a flimsy mosquito net propped up on four poles. This is my first taste of fly camping, and as I lie there looking up at the stars, I feel for the first time the fear of the preyed-upon.

Suddenly a lion begins to roar, causing the camels hobbled on the dry riverbed to shift and grumble and rattle their bells. In the silence that follows, it sounds as if the whole world is listening. I feel my heartbeat rising and think to myself, this is how it must be for the zebras whose shrill squeals of alarm now ring out in the black and silver night.

Then the lion roars again, much closer this time, its deep voice dying away in a throaty series of rasping grunts. I stare into the shadows, trying to catch the slightest movement, ears straining to pick up the stealthy pad of velvet paws. But the lion does not roar again and, in the end, after what seems like an eternity, I pull the blanket over my head and sleep soundly until dawn.

WHAT HAVE WE DONE?

Hilary Bradt ponders the dilemmas facing
tourists seeking an authentic tribal experience.

It is hardwired into us travellers that in the developing world the traditional life, following the ways of the ancestors, is the best life, and that any influence we may have on tribal communities, however well meaning, must be harmful.

I can pinpoint the moment when I first questioned this. In the late 1960s I had visited one of the car-free villages dotted around Lake Atitlán in Guatemala and filmed, with my old cine camera, the village women collecting water from their communal well. I watched them scoop up the water in hollow bamboos and trickle it into their earthenware vessels, chatting and laughing together before heading back to their houses with the heavy pots supported on their heads. With their exquisitely embroidered blouses and the terracotta pots it was a beautifully photogenic scene, one I was proud of.

Returning a few years later I headed to the same village with my camera. Oh no! The women were still collecting water, but the well was now a standpipe and the pots were all made of plastic.

Not worth taking photos this time; the curse of plastic had even reached this remote village. And then I stopped to think. This material was far more suitable than clay for the purpose of carrying water: lighter and unbreakable. It made these women's lives much easier.

Belief that traditional lifestyles should be protected is nothing new. One hundred years ago Mark Twain wrote pithily about the Native Americans: 'Soap and education may not be as sudden as a massacre, but they are more deadly in the long run.' Books and television programmes champion the explorer who treks for days to meet uncontacted tribes, takes part in their rituals, embraces their way of life – and then returns to his comfortable home, changed, he assures us, for the better after immersing himself in their culture. But are the people he stayed with also changed? Almost certainly. They will have had a glimpse of another world, and the youngsters will want to be part of it.

As a guidebook writer and tour leader in Madagascar for over thirty years I have largely managed to avoid cultural tourism. There are villages that I've omitted from the guide because I'd seen their community in action, loved what I saw, and wanted to keep it that way. Visitors, with their gifts, would change it in an instant. So a few years ago, when our hotel in the southwest of the country suggested they try to seek out the elusive Mikea people for us, I was wary. This clan of hunter-gatherers has lived, unmolested, deep in the spiny forest that has now become a national park. But brushing my concerns aside, the hotel manager provided us with an interpreter and guide who had made contact with one family. They had only seen two other white people before, Andry told us proudly.

'Some local people believe the Mikea can make themselves invisible,' the guide explained. 'They see a smoking fire in a clearing, and they feel the presence of the Mikea but they're nowhere to be seen.' The sandy paths were narrow, and the thorny scrub vicious:

grey-green with fearsome spines, broken by the waving tentacles of Madagascar's octopus trees.

We walked into a clearing and there was our first sign of the invisible people: a smouldering fire. Whoever made it must have left very recently. We stopped to listen to the sounds of the forest: birdsong and something else, a baby's cry. Andry asked us to wait while he investigated. 'They say you can come,' he said, and led us to another clearing, with another fire and a family – man, woman, and two little girls – sitting on the ground. They were clearly terrified. Both the woman and man wore short, fringed loincloths made from material which might once have been blue but was now a dull charcoal grey. The children were naked. The woman kept her eyes downcast, and her face contorted into an expression of misery. The children hid behind her. The man nervously scraped a hole in the sand with a stick.

Eventually he spoke. 'Have you come to kill us?' Andry reassured them, and explained that we wanted to learn about them. Answers to our first questions were unrewarding. 'How old are the children?'… 'They don't know.'

'What do they eat?'… 'What they can find.' After some persuasion, the man elaborated, saying they dug for roots and sometimes trapped a tenrec (about the size of a rabbit). Occasionally they managed to kill a wild boar. He demonstrated the two sorts of trap. For a tenrec he would dig a hole and implant spikes in the bottom, covering the top with a fragile lattice of dry twigs. A different tactic was used for the immensely strong wild boar. An obstacle was created out of sticks and sand across their favourite pathway. On the landing side, when they jumped over, was a row of slanting pointed stakes.

Through Andry we encouraged them to question us.

'Are you human?'

'Is your blood also white?'

'Is it poisonous like the sap of the euphorbia tree?'

'Why is your hair like that?'

A quiet conversation between our two guides followed. They had difficulty finding enough drinking water, we were told. They used the large shells of land snails as receptacles, but they don't hold much and it was the dry season.

Our guide held out a plastic bottle of water. 'This is our gift,' he said. A ripple of concern went through the group. Oh my God, the demon plastic! My more nuanced response was that this family would never be the same again. What a wonderful present! Once the man had learned how to work a screw top (it was the first time he had seen one) he would use and re-use the bottle until it fell apart or was stolen. There was no danger of it joining the plastic waste that litters the island. But – and what a big but – will this family ever again collect water in a snail shell? And when they show their treasure to others in their community will a fight ensue? Will other families now seek out tourists with the hope of receiving similar gifts?

We walked back to the vehicles in silence. Yes, it had been an extraordinary experience. Unique in all my years of travel, but what had we done? And, actually, does it matter? Were we right to believe that the Mikea should remain untouched, that they should continue to scratch a living from their hostile forest, should go hungry and thirsty because we hold dear the concept of a simple life lived close to nature?

I don't know.

REHOMING MALAWI'S ELEPHANT HERDS

The Independent/Independent Digital
News & Media Ltd, 2016
*Sue Watt joins the first day of African Parks'
historic 500 Elephants translocations.*

A helicopter whirred overhead as I stood in shock on the golden floodplain. All around, elephants were falling, their legs collapsing under the weight of their extraordinary bulk. I'd been briefed it would be like this, but no briefing could have prepared me for the sheer visceral impact of seeing such powerful yet vulnerable animals, one by one, flopping suddenly to the ground.

Over the past century, Africa's elephant population has declined from around 10 million to just 450,000, resulting from a combination of human wildlife conflict, habitat loss and poaching. But these elephants weren't victims of callous criminals after their ivory: rather, they were being immobilised by a wildlife vet shooting darts from the helicopter above.

It was July, and I'd been invited to Malawi's Liwonde National Park to see the first day of the world's biggest elephant translocation operation. African Parks (AP), a non-profit organisation transforming the continent's reserves by battling poaching and restocking parks, was starting the complex process of moving five hundred elephants from Liwonde and Majete Wildlife Reserve, both in the south of the country, to Nkhotakota Wildlife Reserve in central Malawi. Peter Fearnhead, AP's chief executive, told me these parks are 'islands in a sea of humanity', explaining Malawi is so densely populated, there are no corridors between wildlife areas – hence the need for this huge operation.

But AP is accustomed by now to answering big asks. In 2003 the organisation took on the management of Majete, which had been ravaged through poverty and poaching. The park's transformation into a thriving wildlife destination is phenomenal. It's a beautiful reserve of verdant woodlands and gentle hills. AP acquired Liwonde and Nkhotakota in 2015, aiming to make them similar success stories, transforming Malawi into a major safari destination and rendering the parks both ecologically and socially sustainable.

Liwonde is a park dominated by the Shire River, which teems with crocs and hippos as it twists across vast floodplains. Elephants, too, are prolific in Liwonde. On a morning walk, our group spotted an eighty-strong herd dashing through dappled mopani woodland. Later, we took to the river, where we were mesmerised by a family of ten with a frisky calf drinking just 2m from our boat. Even from the relaxing wood-and-thatch lounge of Mvuu Lodge, which overlooks the river, we could see elephants wading in the water.

Both this lodge and nearby Mvuu Camp support nearby communities; most staff are local and I could tell they had a true sense of pride in their work. The wildlife seems happy here too. From the decking of our luxury tented room, we watched kudus, hippos, elephants, impalas and baboons wandering the lagoon and the river hosts fabulous birdlife, including rare African skimmers – elegant black and white birds with striking bright orange beaks, that seem to dance over the water.

'Liwonde's a special place', according to Andrew Parker, AP's operations director, whose energy and passion for the project is tangible. 'Once we've curbed poaching and brought lion, leopard and cheetah back, this will be one of Africa's greatest wildlife regions.'

Liwonde is special, but AP has its work cut out. Poaching is rife here: rangers have recovered thousands of snares since last August and in a single day found sixteen elephant carcasses. The human cost is staggering too: in four years, elephants have killed sixty people, usually in conflict situations when elephants raided much-needed crops. To help protect both communities and wildlife, AP is building a perimeter fence around the park. Moving 250 of their 800 elephants to Nkhotakota will also help.

On that first morning on the floodplains of Liwonde, a young elephant had run away, frightened and confused at seeing her mum collapse. As she rushed towards woodland, the vet feared he might lose her but darted her just in time. 'If the little one had escaped,' Peter told me, 'we would have woken up the whole family and let them go.' It's a mark of the compassion and professionalism of these conservationists, and the importance of family groups for elephants. Led by matriarchs, they bond together through generations, communicating in a language of rumbles, and even mourn their dead.

With all nine of Group A elephants darted, the team sprang into action, numbering and monitoring each one. 'Sue, check A3's breathing,' Peter instructed me. 'It should be around six breaths a minute. If it falls below four, she's in trouble.'

Sitting beside A3, with one hand at the end of her trunk, I counted her long, warm and fuggy breaths, staring intently at my watch. My role was miniscule in this giant operation, yet I felt intensely responsible for her. I saw the wiry hairs on her trunk, the mud encrusted on her huge ears, and stroked the smooth, slightly wonky tusks for which poachers would mercilessly kill her.

With webbing tied around her feet, I watched A3 lifted upside down by crane onto a low loader. 'It looks awful,' Peter had briefed us, 'but it doesn't harm them. The capture stress they feel is minimal and well managed with tranquilisers.' He was right: it did look awful. As the crane winched her up, A3 looked dead, a grey lump suspended in mid-air. Once I'd helped lift her heavy trunk onto the truck, the tears welled up and I had to walk away, even though I knew the bigger picture. I knew her family would have the space they needed at Nkhotakota and their chances of survival were now stronger than ever. Far better to be shot by a dart from a vet's gun than a bullet from a poacher's.

Nkhotakota, their new home, is a wild, hilly reserve with verdant miombo woodlands fringing the Bua River. I first came here in 2011, to the newly opened Tongole Wilderness Lodge. With a combination of community involvement and understated luxury, this laid-back lodge has remained one of my favourite places in Africa. You can hike, fish and canoe, sleep under the stars, or simply chill on the decks overlooking the river, a popular spot for the reserve's resident elephants. Tragically, only 80 survive from a population of 1,500, the park having been under siege by poachers. But Samuel Kamoto, AP's park manager, told me Nkhotakota will be 'unrecognisable' when AP's work is done.

It's here that I once again saw A3, easily identified by those precious wonky tusks, sauntering casually into the sanctuary. Under sedation, Group A had travelled 350km overnight in thirty-ton trucks, and this was their first morning in Nkhotakota. Calm and relaxed, and seemingly oblivious to the historic journey both she and AP had just made, I watched as she started to explore a new home abundant in food and space and hope for the future.

SONGS FOR ELEPHANTS (NIGHT MUSIC)

National Geographic Traveller, October 2018
*Enlisted to help Ugandan villagers protect their
vulnerable crops, Dom Tulett tests out the myth
that elephants are afraid of mice.*

Nelson plays the drums by firelight. Isaac sits on a tree-trunk bench and swings a bell with unending vigour. They carry no tune and I hear no rhythm, but still I join in, screaming my lyric: 'Mouse!'

A similar stuttered symphony had kept me awake the previous night at my camp on the fringes of Uganda's Queen Elizabeth National Park. At breakfast I asked the waiter, Barnabus, if there had been a party.

'No, sir. That night music was for the elephants, to scare them from the fields.' 'Could I see that?' 'If the elephants are there tonight, we will go.'

Our torches shine a trail through stony scrub, down to the village of Kikorongo. In the distance, Lake George glimmers under the moonlight, its shoreline marked with dots of golden light. The land around it is dark: safari plains that stretch to a star-lined horizon.

I'm introduced to Nelson. He's farmed this land for twenty-two years. His tired, bloodshot eyes flick from me to the fields, scanning for movement, as he tells me how months of drought have forced the elephants to extend their range, roaming out of the park in search of food. I want to help but have no instrument. 'You can shout,' says Nelson. 'What should I shout?' 'Anything to scare the elephants.'

'I'll think of something.'

We advance across patchwork fields of cassava, sweet potato and corn. The villagers blow whistles, beat sticks together. I see tracks through the dry earth, clumsy and wide, where the plants have been trampled and lost. The tough conditions affect every species – this harvest is more important than most. Nelson resumes his drumbeat and I shout the most intimidating cry that comes to mind: 'Mouse! Mouse!'

Urgent chatter tells us elephants are close. We increase our tempo, raise our volume. Animal numbers are recovering after rampant poaching in the Idi Amin years; the villagers know large wildlife populations attract tourists, boosting the local economy. They wish no harm on the elephants. Night music is the best deterrent.

Children pass around bunches of tiny bananas. A woman carries a flaming torch and by its light I can see our audience, their hulking bodies lumbering towards the fields. Nelson ups the intensity of his drumming. Isaac's bell-ringing reaches a frenzy. Whistles and sticks. The chorus swells – accelerando! Forte! 'Mouse!'

We stay until dawn drives a wedge under the eastern night and news comes that the elephants have retreated to the park. Nelson shakes my hand. His eyes are brighter now. He laughs as we part, 'Goodnight, Mouse.'

On my final night at Kikorongo, I hear the night music again. I think of Nelson, his challenges, his solutions, and silently wish him well before drifting off to sleep.

In the morning, I see Barnabus again. 'More elephants last night?' I ask. 'No, sir. Last night there were no elephants. They have moved to a different area.' He straightens my coffee cup, fills it to the brim and grins. 'We had a party to celebrate.'

GAME BOY VS THE ZAMBIAN BUSH?
NO COMPETITION

Independent on Sunday, 26 May 2002
Take your six-year-old on holiday to a rural mud hut in Africa,
writes Helen Truszkowski. He'll love it.

'*U*cokera kuti*?*' demanded the first. The next in line charged forward: '*Unazaka zingatti*?' An incoming toddler stared at us with dinner-plate eyes, opened her mouth and screamed. Not your average welcome.

George came to my aid. He smiled. The crowd of children smiled. Then, mouthing that miracle child lingo that transcends all other tongues, the herd circled away with George at its core. Saved by a six-year-old.

I don't know when it first occurred to me to take my son into the Zambian bush to stay in a village. It might have been after the Christmas holidays when he informed me that his friend Ben has 'a radio and a CD player and a TV and a telephone in his room. So when can I get my own telephone, Mum?' Maybe it was the cumulative effect of a year spent listening to George and his fellow classmates measure their worth in Harry Potter merchandise.

I stood alone eyeing the sunset's pink flush, listening to hippo vociferously reaffirm their claim to a stretch of river. Turtle doves warbled. Crickets rubbed shoulders. A football fashioned from newspaper and elastic bands reached my sandalled feet. I'm no David Seaman, so I let it pass. Cue the stampede and whoops of delight. 'Inde, inde, inde!' George was evidently making headway with the Nyanjan patois.

Just twenty minutes earlier we had abandoned our preconceptions and inhibitions on the tarmac as we drove on to a trail sliced through maize and cotton fields bound for Webby's Village, our home for two nights. With encouragement from Jo and Robin Pope (possibly the best-known safari operators this side of the Zambezi), the villagers first offered a few inquisitive visitors bed and breakfast 'Kunda style' some four years ago. The take-up has been surprisingly slow.

You might figure it takes a certain type of traveller to venture here. One that values personal discovery above prescribed experience, adventure over the passive predictability of habitual holidays. Highbrow it all you like. Truth is, I'm just a mum and George is just a schoolboy and the invitation to talk, to touch and to be touched by our tribal equals, normally a world apart, was both a rare and beguiling opportunity.

Sheathed in a chitenje (sarong) to protect my modesty, I joined the gaggle of women preparing supper on a reed mat. Plucking a still-warm chicken, they spontaneously broke into peals of joyful song. I responded with a tuneless round of *Under the bramble bushes, under the sea*. A fit of giggles later, I knew we'd bonded. Forty-eight hours later and I'd practically chained myself to the bamboo fence, willing the villagers to take me on as an apprentice.

Looking back now, my diary beggars belief. Tuesday I hauled water on my head (spilling more than I saved), learned to strip maize kernels and swapped candlelit tales over a meal of boiled groundnuts. At dusk I took a stick and scratched an unlikely map of the world, highlighting the extent of our journey to a chorus of sighs.

Trailed by his pack, George appeared and reappeared momentarily, increasingly unkempt, *Lord of the Flies*-style, his face smudged with sweat and dust. 'Dirt,' he enthused. 'I like dirt.'

Wednesday we got a peek inside the primary school at rows of enraptured students aching to ask: 'How old are you?' A daunting, girls-only ceremony saw me under the scrutiny of a traditional *singanga* (healer). Knocking on ninety, she was wiry, innocent and had a smile of irresistible charm. Her diagnosis was frighteningly accurate; her herbal cure unimaginably vile. The evening collapsed into revelry as George and I danced a dubious *chitelele* alongside bottom-jigging naturals way out of our league.

Our accommodation for those nights was a simple rondavel mud hut. A screened-off tin bath took the place of our regular en suite. No electricity, no cutlery, no flushing loo, no telly. Any doubters among you will be gagging to probe the shortfalls of a village stay like this, so insignificant may seem the tokens of modern-day comfort, even basic reassurances for visitors. Fair enough. Buzzing through a clouded *Simpsons* sky on board a mini-aircraft destined for a shaky landing on a duvet-size airstrip had seemed less than comical. Clicking our legs into reverse as the quick-witted villagers stoned a random spitting cobra was even less of a laughing matter.

On balance, though, the chance to exchange life experiences with these vanishing tribal people, to build a rapport with the incredibly hospitable villagers and participate in their day-to-day lives was far too good an offer to miss.

As late as the 18th century the people of Zambia had hardly any contact with non-Africans. It was the arrival of David Livingstone that broke Zambia's comparative isolation. At Webby's, on the day we arrived, the screaming toddler had thought we were ghosts. George played the 21st-century envoy, charming the ever-intrepid youngster with noughts and crosses scratched into the earth. Harry Potter's Game Boy Advance doesn't come close.

SENSES AND SENSIBILITY: WHAT'S A SENSORY SAFARI – AND WHY SHOULD I GO ON ONE?

The *Daily Telegraph*, 16 July 2018

Mike Unwin goes to Mana Pools in Zimbabwe to find out why.

'So, where else in nature do you find a spiral?' Rob Janisch, safari-guide-cum-ecology-tutor, holds aloft the shell of an African land snail. He contemplates his find, like Hamlet with poor Yorick, while we shuffle uncomfortably, cogs whirring. Behind us, a passing warthog snorts its derision.

'A kudu's horns?' I venture, recalling one of yesterday's sightings. Somebody else suggests a millipede, pointing to the one trundling over my trainers. Now the ideas flow. Rob, scrawling with a stick in the sand, explains how a spiral offers the most efficient transport in nature, from blood flowing through a heart to nutrients through a tree. The warthog trots away, reassured.

Two days in Rob's company and it's been a steep learning curve. But this is no air-conditioned lecture theatre. Our classroom is Mana Pools, Zimbabwe's wildest national park. In peak dry season, this spectacular reserve, sandwiched between the Zambezi River and its rugged escarpment, is big game central. But now, with the late rains having dispersed the herds, we can step back from the Big Five agenda and look a little deeper.

And that's the idea behind this new, six-night 'Super Sensory Safari'. Led by expert guides, we are engaging both senses and brains as we peek and prod our way through the bush. Rob wants us to see the natural world in a different way. 'How would nature make a chair?' he asks, as we search for somewhere to sit. Or, as we gather around a termite mound: 'How would nature build a city?'

Rob's passion is biomimicry: the concept of designing more sustainable products and systems for our human world by emulating those found in nature. 'We need to tap into the genius of nature,' he insists. 'It's our last resort for solving the problems of the planet.'

Inspiration lies all around. Take this towering termite mound. Not only is it a marvel of engineering, complete with air-conditioning systems and nursery chambers, its sustainable construction also enriches the soil and provides homes for everything from mongooses to mambas. Rob suggests that our own urban edifices could, likewise, enhance rather than deplete their environments. 'Cities could function like rainforests,' he explains. 'We could be turning all that CO_2 into oxygen.'

Kanga Camp, our base for the first three nights, is smuggled into thick bush around a permanent lagoon some 25km inland from the river. During downtime, Rob develops his theme. He explains how nature's ingenuity could be much better harnessed in technology, citing such recent examples as whale fins inspiring Danish wind turbines, and bacteria-resistant sharkskin helping advance hospital hygiene. 'Remember, nature has had three and a half billion years of R and D,' he tells us. As he talks, an elephant approaches the lagoon, trunk uncoiling to demonstrate just how nature came up with the siphon.

Mana Pools is renowned for its guided walking so tailor-made for this very hands-on safari, in which vehicles are largely eschewed in favour of tramping the terrain underfoot. Under Rob's guidance, every detail prompts discussion. He explains, for example, how the brilliant blue of a glossy starling feather is a 'structural' colour, its iridescence drawn from light refracted through tiny barbs. Could this offer an alternative to expensive, unsustainable oil pigments? An old weaverbird nest passed from hand to hand not only reveals impressive strength and elasticity but will also break down into the soil. Houses that biodegrade into gardens, anyone?

It's inspiring stuff. Armed with Rob's mantra, 'What would nature do?', we are soon planning a brave new world for our own beleaguered species. But while absorbed in minutiae, it is easy to forget that bigger beasts roam these parts. Thankfully our guides don't. Each walk starts with a safety briefing, and whenever Rob corrals us for a chat, I watch his colleague, Lewis Mangaba, scrutinising our surroundings. One trail reveals the dew-fresh prints of a large male lion. 'Just one hour old,' says Lewis, peering into the thickets.

Lewis offers more than just security. A walking textbook of medicinal and nutritional wild plants, he takes over one afternoon to lead an ethnobotanical walk. Now we engage more senses, sniffing the fragrance of wild basil and nibbling on sweet, nectar-bearing blooms. Lewis was raised in the Zambezi Valley and has a traditional take on biomimicry. He finds us wild jute, which in his village produces rope and soap; demonstrates how to set a bird trap from the runners of a spiny combretum; and crushes the leaves of a woolly caper bush to produce an infusion used to treat asthma.

Meanwhile, renowned sound recordist Derek Solomon, our third expert, has been working on our lugholes. 'We've learned to filter out sounds, important sounds,' he announced on day one, 'and we need to get our ears back.' On one drive, we turn off the engine and simply listen – not to anything in particular but just to the ambient soundscape. And the more we listen, the more we hear: from the pulsing rhythm of countless territorial doves to the throat rumble of a distant female elephant, trying to assemble her family.

Back in camp, Derek explains the science of sound: the difference between a bird's territorial song and its alarm call;

how a lion draws down its larynx into its chest cavity to produce that thunderous resonance. Out in the bush, he uses a microphone to reveal sounds that we never knew existed, including even the hissing of Matabele ants. After dinner, as hippo grunts and lion moans punctuate the insect chorus, he picks out other sounds: the mechanical chirrup of an African scops owl; the whistled chorus of painted reed frogs.

After three days, we leave Derek and Rob and move on with Lewis to Zambezi Expeditions, Kanga's sister camp on the Zambezi. The country opens out as we approach the river, revealing small parties of zebras, buffalo and elephants. The camp itself is gloriously appointed: in front, a grand sweep of Zambezi, its languid progress periodically broken by the hydraulic hiss of surfacing hippos; out back, a park-like floodplain, the smoky greys of the distant escarpment visible beneath a high browse-line of statuesque winter thorns.

Guide Richard Yohane now joins Lewis to lead us around. Lions are on the agenda, and each morning we head off in the direction of the roaring from the night before. At seasonal pools, we break for coffee, watching storks step around dozing crocodiles and bee-eaters flutter after dragonflies. Focused on tracking, there's now less chat, but still we haven't packed away our curiosity. Richard and Lewis gamely field questions about everything from dung beetles to meander loops – on one occasion, breaking off to shepherd us smartly into a dry riverbed as a family of elephants swings past.

Lions prove elusive. But other rewards materialise, including a crowned eagle in the branches of a fig tree and a hefty leopard tortoise crossing the trail. In one clearing, we meet a pack of eighteen wild dogs. Lewis shepherds us in a cautious approach, via fallen log and anthill, until we are within a stone's throw. For half an hour, we watch these endangered, tie-dyed canines sorting out

Royal Edinburgh Military Tattoo, Scotland (Daniel James Clarke)

Plymouth, England (Juliet Coombe)

Stonehenge, England (James Rushforth)

Dolomites, Italy (James Rushforth)

Jerez, Spain (Peter Ellegard)

Sahara, Algeria (Simon Urwin)

Rabat, Morocco (Kate Wickers)

Limpopo-Lipadi, Botswana (William Gray)

Seruwila, Sri Lanka (Juliet Coombe)

Tibet (Simon Urwin)

Saudi Arabia (Chris Coe)

Vivid Sydney, Australia (Daniel James Clarke)

Papua New Guinea (Jeremy Flint)

Cartagena, Colombia (Kate Wickers)

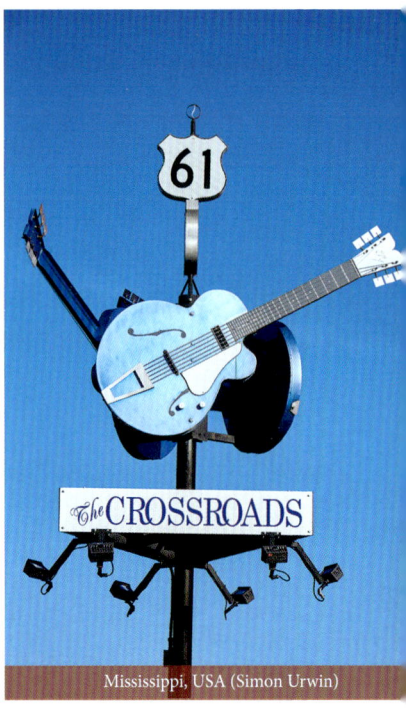

Mississippi, USA (Simon Urwin)

Mercado de Urubamba, Peru's Sacred Valley (Karolina Wiercigroch)

Tupungato Winelands, Argentina (Peter Ellegard)

Mayor Evelyn Hikoutini, Ua Pou, Marquesas Islands, French Polynesia (Nori Jemil)

Svalbard, Norway (Chris Coe)

South Shetland, Antarctica (David Lindo)

their pack politics, before – white tails raised – they trot away into the trees.

And then there's the river itself. One afternoon, we launch canoes upstream and drift back to camp, admiring stately goliath herons and hovering pied kingfishers. Buffalo look up from their grazing, and we hug the bank when snorting hippos surface in the deeper channels, goggle-eyed with outrage.

That night, a pathway of lanterns leads from the riverbank to a dining table beneath the stars. After dinner, Lewis gets out his mbira – a traditional Zimbabwean thumb harp – and the kitchen staff perform a Shona dance in front of the leaping flames, cajoling some of us into joining them. Later, as the fire settles, I let my chair sink deeper into the sand and tilt my gaze towards the heavens, where Scorpio and the Southern Cross loom alarmingly close. A hyena whoops from behind the kitchen. This week has been a refreshing new take on the usual Big Five safari formula, I reflect. And yet, however you slice it, the magic of this place is timeless.

And those lions? The next morning, we round a bend to find impala exploding wild-eyed in all directions. A tawny shape pads across the road and down into a bushy gulley. Three more follow, fanning out and disappearing. 'Let's see what's happening,' says Richard. We dismount from our vehicle and, after a whispered briefing, creep forward in single file. Cue a deep growl from the gulley – chillingly close. Richard holds up a hand. No further. We hear the crunch of bone.

What would nature do? Another step forward might see us making a personal contribution to the nutrient cycle: the ultimate in sustainable tourism, perhaps. But Richard, thankfully, has other ideas. Rifle cocked, he whispers his instructions: stick together; keep behind him; back up slowly. Right now, that works for me.

ASIA & OCEANIA

THE NEW TRAIN TO CAMBODIA'S PAST

The *Daily Telegraph*, 26 February 2018
Along jungle-strewn track laid during French rule,
Tristan Rutherford railroads through Indochine to
rediscover the ghosts of Cambodia-sur-Mer.

Phnom Penh railway station radiates the ghosts of passengers past. It's a gigantic white wedding cake where signs point commuters to consignes and toilettes. The destinations listed above most of the guichets are optimistic. After Cambodian dictator Pol Pot last held court on the concourse in 1975 only a few lamentable carriages continued to totter around the French colonial network until 2002. Now a bugling peep from the platform edge suggests there's a gentler revolution in progress.

Two trains painted with a thick shell of blue gloss twinkle in the afternoon sun. Like the SNCF Autotrain service that carries vehicles from Paris to Nice, here cars and scooters toot on to wagons to be pulled gently towards the sea. They recently carried a Rolls-Royce. The passenger carriages were built in Germany before the fall of the Berlin Wall. Like renovated hotel rooms, each one contains fitted carpets, air-conditioning units, ceiling spotlights and, plugged into a socket, the sort of Wi-Fi router that sits atop your address book at home. Incongruous but true.

Our departure time is strictly adhered to. There are simply no other trains on the network so we don't have to wait for the late running of the 8.10 from Eastbourne. With a clickety-click we're off.

Our destination is the Cambodian Riviera. Although the French left Indochina in 1954, the country's Francophone elite continued to sip Sancerre on the Gulf of Thailand shore. (The French also built the line to the Thai border, due to reopen one day soon, which will allow trains to run all the way to Singapore.) As this route hasn't run for fourteen years it scythes through a cross section of urban life like a clinking voyeur. It sees backyard barbecues. People doing dishes. Make-ups, break-ups and dusty games of football. Then the wagons sway out of the city limits like an angry boxer and pummel through jungle scrub.

Dusk brings a timeless portrait of southeast Asia. Silhouetted palms and rice paddies that glow ochre in the winnowing twilight. Calves run alongside our irregular service, while their mothers chew on with world-wearing indifference. Rural life travels by bicycle, not car. Goods by tuk-tuk, not truck. When the train stops, all is silent. You can even open the carriage doors for added birdsong and the occasional monkey shriek. Then stay perched there as the train picks up pace, and the 21st century is airbrushed away like the warm wind on your face.

A plunging sunset offers a violent ball of red. Moments later the tropical darkness heralds dinner. We putter into Takeo station for fast food. Here that means chicken legs and boiled eggs with salt from a communal shaker. Plus river fish spatchcocked over an open fire. There are tubes of crisps too, but not ready salted. Only squid and berry flavours, with 50p cans of Angkor lager to accompany. I wash my hands in the spotless toilet ('*serviettes utilisées*') as the little train wanders into the humid night.

Old elites alighted at the colonial outpost of Kampot. Now the riverine town is a place where backpackers come to die. Silver-haired travellers who once ate apple pie in Afghanistan can take an apartment, attend evening yoga or sip sunset G&Ts while reading

Albert Camus, albeit on their Kindles. The Rococo riverside strip is charming. Under droning fans one can savour *steak-frites*, play vingt-et-un or indulge in a £7 massage. It's as if a French *colon* would bluster in at any moment and sink a pastis.

My destination the next morning is even more chic. In a return to the swinging sixties the reinstated train will also call at Kep-sur-Mer soon, but until then it's a thirty-minute bus ride from Kampot. Before the Khmer Rouge, this beach town was Cambodia's Deauville. I hire a Parisian sit-up-and-beg bicycle for a tour.

The ostentatious villas of Kep-sur-Mer host more ghosts than Phnom Penh train station. Derelict Art Deco dreams gaze seaward like abandoned ocean liners. One has a rubber tree growing through the middle. Another Normandy chateau sits strafed but unbowed, with *fleur-de-lis* ceramic borders guarding the overgrown perimeter. During Cambodia's 'Golden Age', before King Sihanouk was exiled in 1970, a casino hosted games of *chemin de fer*. Then the lights dimmed on a once luminous era, as Pol Pot and his Khmer Rouge hordes turned the clock back to year zero.

Cambodia's modern elite prefer Kep-sur-Mer. They crowd the blissful beach with its imported white sand. Many hit the seafood restaurants – the town is famous for its sweet crabs – built on stilts over the emerald sea. Others recline inside a uniquely Kep invention. These are open-sided platforms, built seaside to catch the breeze, and rented by the day. Half the family can picnic on mats, while the rest doze in hammocks strung even higher above, a duplex if you will.

Scooter hire, dive schools and fried banana stalls usher in a new breed of tourists. The welcome memo was evidently not read by a family of macaque monkeys. From the branches of a carob tree they lob seeds at nouveaux riches applying sunblock in an attempt to stay pale in the tropical heat.

I ride the £4 return boat to Rabbit Island. That's a thirty-minute splash through limpid sea with a family of queasy Cambodian landlubbers. They are as pleased as I am to see the nodding palms and lines of hammocks along a half-mile of golden sand. Snorkels are a dollar a day. A bungalow with a ceiling fan and mosquito net doesn't cost much more. At 10pm the generator ceases, rendering the island as tranquil as a rural train stop.

The lights never went out at Île des Ambassadeurs, King Sihanouk's former private island, where feted nabobs were fed local crab and imported champagne. Nor does the partying stop at the Vietnamese island of Phu Quoc a few miles away. TUI started direct flights here from Gatwick, meaning I could trade a Robinson Crusoe lifestyle for rural Sussex in one swift move. A sobering thought.

My flight home is from Phnom Penh. The morning train from Kampot illuminates the picture I missed by night. Temple wats in jungle. The green sheen of paddy. Naked children swim in rivers, with water buffalo not far behind. The air con is set to freeze so I open a train door and watch Cambodia in 3D. With another clickety-click four hours pass in seconds, before we arrive to the tick-tock of a Tissot station clock made in Paris.

EXPLORE GUILIN'S CLASSIC LANDSCAPES – THE ECO-FRIENDLY WAY

Blue Wings (Finnair), June 2010
Tim Bird confirms that cycling is the most relaxed,
enjoyable and environmentally friendly way to explore
one of China's most beautiful regions.

Pedalling through the countryside in Guilin County is like drifting through a classical Chinese landscape painting – and provides a welcome rustic relief to the cauldrons of China's big cities.

If you set out in the morning on your bike in this magical corner of China, mist still clings to the sheer lush slopes and wide valleys of the karst limestone hills, the distinctive feature of the region. Bamboo rafts ferry fishermen with coolie hats across winding rivers and buffalo churn the soil in the rice paddies.

Another joy of the region is the quirky landmark names, from 'Camel Crossing the Hill', 'Three Colour Pond' and 'Tortoise Climbing up the Hill' to 'Lion Watching the Horse', and the even less snappy 'Elephant Out and a Horse into the Cave'. After an hour on your bike with a local map, you'll be thinking of your own names for the hills, streams and weirs as the fabulous crags and peaks march into the distance.

The tall karst hills soar in all directions, separated across the river plains by wide, flat valleys that lend themselves perfectly to cycling tours. If you are aiming for something more strenuous, park your bike at the end of one of the footpaths that spiral around the sheer outcrops and hike off into the hills. The rock faces are popular with climbers too. The area offers so many opportunities to leave behind the traffic and crowds of China's spreading urban giants and to savour some of the country's most exquisite natural landscapes.

The city of Guilin on the River Li is the main entry point to the area, but the smaller town of Yangshuo, downstream from Guilin and a two-hour drive, makes a more picturesque and leisurely base. In high season, a continuous armada of boats unload their tourist loads from Guilin a kilometre or so upstream at a dock reached via a shaded walkway. The town gets busy, but escapes in all directions are easy.

Wedged between gaps in the hills and spilling down to the riverbank, Yangshuo is compact but lively, full of affordable if often modest hotels, and bustling with craft shops, a riverside market and excellent restaurants. It's also the best place to rent a bicycle, with rental shops clustered around the streets leading off from the quay.

'No deposit needed, everybody knows me,' says Alice Cheng, my guide for the first day's cycling excursion as we choose our bikes from a stand just off Xi Jie, also known as West Street, a lively lane of shops, bars and restaurants. Yangshuo is like that: the taxi driver always seems to be the cousin of the bar owner, and the shopkeeper is best friends with your hotel receptionist. When we have paid our 2-euro fee for the day's rental and headed out of the town, Alice regularly waves at and stops to talk to villagers and farmers along the way.

Once we have cleared Yangshuo's outskirts the route snakes upstream along or close to the Yulong River, a tributary of the Li. We head off the small country roads and on to narrow paths skirting rice paddies and farming hamlets. Alice greets Li Zhao Du who is smoking a buffalo-bone pipe in the village of Jiu Xian and we watch a rice farmer guide his buffalo-driven plough through the heavy, saturated soil. 'The village is four hundred years old,' Alice tells me as I am ushered through low arches into tiny cobbled courtyards. 'These people have lived here all their lives and have never been further than Yangshuo.'

The morning mist clears and sunlight brings to life the lush green of the limestone fingers poking up from the plains. At about midday we reach our destination, the graceful stone Yulong bridge. A fisherman prods his boat into midstream, cormorants spreading their black wings at prow and stern. This ancient fishing method, whereby the birds' long throats are constricted to stop them swallowing the larger fish, is a dying practice, regarded as cruel and unethical. But Alice tells me that fishing is this man's livelihood, although she adds that the night-time displays for tourists offered in Yangshuo are rarely authentic fishing expeditions.

The quayside close to the bridge is cluttered with bamboo rafts – another fuel-free method of transport. Alice negotiates a fare of 200 yuan (25 euros) and we lift our bicycles onto our vessel. This seems like a generous fare considering all we have to do now is float downstream, but the scenery of looming hills justifies the outlay. Our boatman uses a pole to guide us down a series of weirs and we stop to buy beer and grilled fish-on-a-stick from a river-borne vendor. Alice serenades me with a river song. We drift about half of the way back to Yangshuo then cycle into town as the afternoon sun reaches full dazzle.

Thanks to Alice, the next day I feel confident enough to negotiate the vagaries of Chinese traffic on Yangshuo's streets alone, before leaving the tooting trucks behind on quieter country roads. As my destination I choose Moon Hill, a distinctive geological oddity some 10km out of town where the crown of a karst hill has been eroded into a huge half-moon aperture.

I set off early again to avoid the heat and crowds that often flock to picnic at the base of Moon Hill, crossing the picturesque bridge at Camel Crossing the River and passing the meandering

Assembly Dragon Cave. I reach the huge natural arch before the first coaches unload at the entrance to Moon Hill Park and I climb to its peak with two young students from Guilin. Spectacular limestone humps soar and dip to the horizon. 'Procession of Camels', I think, congratulating myself on getting the hang of this landscape-naming business.

My third and last cycling expedition the next day takes me west to the village of Fuli. Country villages hold markets on certain days of the month; it's the second day of May, a national holiday, but also Fuli's turn to attract the farmers and craftspeople of the area to set up their stalls. Fuli is a short ride that takes barely more than an hour from Yangshuo, so I take some detours through the patchwork paddies and down to the banks of the Li.

The market fills the centre of Fuli with vendors of every conceivable form of edible produce, from rice, maize, mushrooms, herbs and blood-red fiery chillis to slabs of unidentified meat. Steam wafts from boiling vats; chopsticks click and diners slurp. Elderly men gather to sip green tea, show off their caged birds and play board games.

Closer to the river, I find cheap and useful souvenirs in the form of knitted slippers at 30 yuan (4 euros) a pair. There are Chairman Mao hats and badges and landscape paintings of local landmarks in the classic style for sale here as well as elaborately painted fans drying in the sun. A stone causeway leads across a weir to idyllic pastures where cattle graze and the river continues downstream to Three Colour Pond and the town of Puyi.

I jump on another bamboo raft, this time with a motor to tackle the current, and head back to Yangshuo. I glimpse myself reflected in my camera's viewfinder and describe myself in the Chinese fashion as the raft chugs through a limestone gorge and the sun beats down: 'Lazy Fat Dragon with Sunset Red Head'.

KUMBH MELA

Globetrender, 12 May 2025
*It was the largest human migration the world has ever seen.
Noni Ware describes visiting the Kumbh Mela festival in
Uttar Pradesh.*

I arrived at Kumbh Mela on the back of a motorbike from Prayagraj. It was, as journeys can be in India, a thrilling if terrifying beginning to a trip exploring the state of Uttar Pradesh. The first part of the journey was at Kumbh Mela, one of the most important of the Hindu festivals, which is normally celebrated every six and every twelve years.

This year (2025) was an exceptional year to celebrate. An astrological super star line-up, the conjunction of Jupiter and the sun in Aquarius, a moment that many of us would have been unaware of, but in India is a signifier of enlightenment and purification. This celestial arrangement of planets had not occurred for the past 144 years and I, along with 660 million others, had come to celebrate the moment. Over a period of forty-four days, from 13 January to 26 February, more than double the entire population of the United States had come to Triveni Sangam near Prayagraj in Uttar Pradesh to take part.

There are four holy sites for Kumbh Mela (The Festival of the Sacred Pitcher). Prayagraj in Uttar Pradesh is considered the most sacred, where the Ganges, the Yamuna and the mythical Saraswati rivers converge. It is only here that the Maha Kumbh Mela (the Great Kumbh Festival) takes place, a once-in-several-generations celebration.

My arrival at the festival also coincided with one of the most important dates at Kumbh, 26 February, the Maha Shivratri Festival, which celebrates the divine union of Lord Shiva and Goddess Parvati. Over fifteen million people arrived to bathe from boats, the riverbanks or the bathing ghats (small areas set aside for people to bathe from the shore). A holy dip at Kumbh Mela signifies a cleansing of one's sins and leads to moksha (salvation).

It was incredibly joyous to watch. There was so much anticipation and delight at being here, for many it had taken weeks to make the pilgrimage on foot. In the water there was no difference between rich and poor, it did not matter where you came from, which caste you belonged to. The River Ganges made no judgement but silently flowed past us all absorbing the sins of 660 million people.

Trying to board one of the blue-painted boats required navigating through a crowd of almost unimaginable scale, an arterial flow of people surging towards the banks of the River Ganges. Tragically, there had been stampedes in the weeks before I arrived. Thirty people had died, the barricades breaking under the sheer volume of the crowd. Wading through fetid black mud, plastic bottles and discarded clothing, I managed to board my boat and we rowed upstream, while 'Ganga Bahna', offerings in the form of flowers and food placed carefully on wide green leaves, floated past us.

At the point where the three rivers met (the mythical Saraswati River is unseen but said to flow beneath the Ganges), the boats emptied as people jumped into the water, submerging themselves and offering up prayers. I watched as my boat, along with thousands of others, formed a floating wooden city in the middle of the river. From here as the River Ganges flowed beneath and around the boats that gathered in their thousands at this sacred meeting point, it was almost possible to make sense of the scale of humanity around me; to be just far enough away from the crowds rather than in them to comprehend what an extraordinary moment this was.

On land, stretching as far as the eye could see at this ten-thousand-acre site were tents. To put this in terms of a gathering we can conceptualise this is like twenty thousand Glastonbury Festivals. But the tents here at Kumbh Mela housed spiritual gurus and Akharas who greeted their followers – some with only twenty or thirty devotees, others with thousands. There are thirteen major Akharas which are very much at the heart of Kumbh Mela. Our guide informed me that nobody in India needs a therapist – the Akharas provide spiritual and personal guidance to each of their devotees. I sat with the Naga Sadhus, their much-photographed, ash-covered bodies and matted hair reflecting devotion to Lord Shiva, my forehead decorated in ash with the Tripundra mark. In one of the smaller tents I joined an orange-robed guru whose wise words I clearly did not understand, but the sense of peace was palpable, an escape perhaps from the madness outside as much as spiritual enlightenment.

Many families had spent the full month at Kumbh Mela, camping under roughly constructed tents made from saris and plastic tarpaulins, their pots and cooking utensils neatly delineating their tiny plots. Stalls selling long wooden beads, pyramids of orange carnations and mounds of bright spices lined the dusty roads. There were loudspeakers every five yards which for twenty-four hours a day echoed with either spiritual chants or the desperate messages from families who had lost a relative in the crowds and wanted to be reunited.

I was in one of the tented camps set up along the banks of the river. I did not sleep, but lay awake listening to the relentless beeping of motorbikes and cars making their way over one of the thirty bridges that had been built across the river.

Imagine India and the noise, the smell, the chaos, the colour, the rubbish all condensed into two stretches of riverbank.

Religious tourism is on the rise with an estimated 450 million trips made annually for religious purposes. For many countries religious tourism around its historical and religious heritage is a significant part of their tourism market. Saudi Arabia received 17.5 million religious tourists last year and by 2030 that number is expected to reach 30 million visitors. In Brazil, which hosts over two hundred religious events annually, including the Círio de Nazaré procession attended by 2.5 million people, religious tourism is valued at $15 billion. As more people seek deeper meaning and purpose in their lives and interest grows in visiting places of religious significance, it is predicted that pilgrimage tourism will become ever more popular.

I am not sure that anyone could have predicted the 660 million pilgrims who visited Maha Kumbh Mela and I could not have predicted that the stars aligned and I was lucky enough to be one of them.

AN OVERLAND JOURNEY TO INDIA

Mark Nicholls discovers some timely enlightenment as he makes his way to India.

Growling trucks with big engines and small brakes lined up in endless rows, ready to ship oil along the Anatolian Highway into Europe. Dripping sticky droplets into dark puddles, they waited in the chilled air for customs clearance on the land border between eastern Turkey and Iran.

On a frosty November morning in 1997, with the summit of Mount Ararat in the distance, it was this formidable gauntlet that independent travellers like myself had to negotiate to enter the land of the Ayatollahs. Eventually, I was ushered into a white-tiled oblong room having had my passport 'stamped' out of Turkey, but not yet admitted into Iran.

It was a curious, sheltered no man's land near the Turkish town of Doğubayazıt; on the Turkish wall, the paternal figure of Mustafa Kemal Atatürk looked down benignly on departing visitors.

As I lifted my eyes east, they locked with portraits of Ayatollahs and Iranian presidents staring sternly at those seeking entry into the Islamic Republic.

Momentarily transfixed, I subconsciously noticed a single red-tiled line passing across the ceiling, down each wall and along the floor. I was standing astride what I surmised was the border between the two nations. What I didn't fully appreciate until I arrived in Iran was at that very moment my right leg was thirty minutes ahead of my left leg.

It began a stage of a hugely memorable journey; from Tabriz to Tehran and the wondrous mosques and bazaars of Isfahan before heading further south to Yazd, Kerman, Shiraz and the hazy border town of Zahedan.

Once on board the 'smuggler's express' to Quetta, local tribesmen with AK-47s over their shoulders cooked and shared fried eggs on a gas burner as the train rocked on further into Pakistan.

What that crossing into Iran did acutely illustrate was the human ability to play with time, with nations 'adapting' time zones to suit sovereign interest, define individuality and national identity, seize economic advantage, or make optimum use of daylight.

While the position of the sun has decreed our daily routines for millennia, it was not until 1884 at the Meridian Conference in Washington that the world was formally sliced into a twenty-four-hour clock with longitude 0 degrees at Greenwich in London and longitude 180 degrees – the imaginary dateline which separates two consecutive calendar days – running through the Pacific Ocean.

But ever since, countries have continued to shift their time, leading overland travellers to factor that into their journeys.

Pakistan is a clear example; it moved its clocks back half an hour in the 1950s to emphasise its separation from India after the division of 15 August 1947. Even quirkier is Nepal where the time difference once you cross the border from northern India is a mere fifteen minutes.

Perhaps most dramatic is Samoa's leap across the international dateline. Set 30km east of the line, it skipped a whole day at midnight on 29 December 2011, missing out 30 December completely and going straight to 31 December to fall into line with Australia and New Zealand to strengthen trade links with the two countries. The move came 119 years after Samoa moved in the opposite direction when it wanted to improve links with the United States. In 1892, it actually had two 4 Julys.

On land, time in relation to distance travelled didn't matter much until the evolution of rail travel saw more precise timings required for timetabling and safety.

Now, as we fly long distances, we also need to be aware of our 'circadian rhythms' which influence our sense of time and place and can impact our physical, mental and emotional well-being. Time zones do bend somewhat haphazardly around the globe and some are not always easy to understand or live with.

Russia and China, two of the planet's largest landmasses, have approaches that could not be more different. From the extremities of west to east, Russia is 9,000km and covers eleven time zones, while China – which is 5,200km wide – is covered by one single time zone centred on Beijing. China's Communist regime moved from five zones to one in 1949 to 'unify' the vast country. And there are quirks within this; when returning to the UK by train from Beijing via Mongolia, time took on an unnatural sense once I crossed into Russia.

For the century or so prior to 2018, all trains and stations operated to Moscow time, whether running through Vladivostok, Irkutsk, Murmansk or Saint Petersburg. They now run to local time. But before 2018, you could stand on the street in central Siberia at 9am and the moment you crossed a station threshold you readjusted your watch to 6am.

But on my initial journey east, intrigue with time travel took on a new dimension once I finally arrived in India.

The country has a unique, and on occasions, frustrating concept of time. Any visitor to India knows that things happen when they happen. Now five and a half hours ahead of GMT, India was allocated two official and additional time zones at the 1884 conference. Bombay Time (using the 75th meridian east) was set at four hours and fifty-one minutes ahead of GMT, and Calcutta Time (using the 90th meridian) at five hours, fifty-three minutes and twenty seconds ahead of GMT. India has actually run on the single time zone for decades, though local times were retained in Calcutta and Bombay until 1948 and 1955 respectively.

India's history of defining time is long. One of the earliest known descriptions appeared in the 4th-century astronomical treatise Surya Siddhanta, using the span of one breath, called the prana. It is equivalent to four seconds, based on a breathing pattern of fifteen breaths a minute. (Just to be clear, holding your breath doesn't make time stand still.) The country also hosts a group of monuments which continue to capture my imagination through the way they reflect time with transparent honesty.

A chain of giant astronomical instruments was constructed in the 18th century by Maharajah Jai Singh to measure the positions of stars and the sun, with massive timepieces telling the time of day to the nearest two seconds. Four of the colossal pink structures, known as Jantar Mantars, survive with the best known in New

Delhi and Jaipur. As you stand in central Delhi with your watch set to standard Indian time, there is precise correlation between the Jantar Mantar and your personal timepiece.

But heading west to Jaipur, east to Varanasi or south to the sacred city of Ujjain (a fifth structure at Mathura has long since disappeared) the sundials will show slightly different times – all accurate to the sun, but not quite correlating with your wristwatch and the modern time zones the world is divided into.

What Jai Singh's Jantar Mantars vividly demonstrate is that the world does not naturally carve up into hourly slices of modern time zones but is a precise science and one inextricably linked to celestial bodies and the human body clock.

It also shows that however much we play with time, one thing is certain… nothing will stand in its way.

FIREFLIES AT BUAHAN, INDONESIA

Sydney Morning Herald/The Age **(Australia)**
Traveller section, March 2023
Penny Watson tries Bali's Banyan Tree Escape,
a 'no walls, no doors' jungle experience.

'I call the project "bring back the light", Wayan Wardika tells me as we nimbly navigate our way down steep muddy steps, over a rudimentary bamboo bridge and around the mossy edge of a waterlogged rice paddy. 'My dream is to bring them back,' he says, 'because I know they were here before, but… environmental issues have pushed them away.'

The 'light' he is referring to is that of fireflies or kunang-kunang, those enchanting lamplit winged beetles (yes, beetles) that were once a common sight in Bali as they zipped around the banana palms and sweet-smelling *cempaka* trees, danced across water *subaks*, and skimmed the rocks beneath burbling waterfalls.

Ask many a Balinese local, especially those from the cooler inland climes around Ubud, and they will, with childlike wonder, retell stories of how, as kids, they chased those luminescent blinks through moonlit gardens and the inky-green night-time jungle.

Such anecdotes often finish with 'but the fireflies have all left Bali now' and similarly melancholic refrains, which is why I'm trailing Wayan to A Banyon Tree Escape, a firefly conservatory in the jungle surrounds of Buahan, a resort north of Ubud.

Since opening in mid-2022, Buahan, with just sixteen luxury villas, has proved popular thanks mostly to the panoramic views stretching from its main dining area across the pool towards seven enigmatic mountain peaks that, most mornings, materialise majestically from the mist.

Its 'no walls, no doors' concept has also garnered attention. Guests reside in the cooler mountain air, with just a mosquito net separating the king-sized bed and a beautiful copper bathtub from the jungle. The concept has been lauded not only by guests, but also the hotel industry. Being open to the elements is considered a bold move in the luxury space, but it is one that fits the times, says resort manager Puspa Anggareni, who comes from the village of Selat in east Bali. 'People are looking for a real connection to deep nature, and this can't happen behind walls,' she says.

Puspa can take credit for luring the resort's inspirational chef Eka Sunarya away from a similarly luxurious five-star resort to head up the kitchen. Eka's approach is true zero-waste, farm-to-table style. And it's not just about micro garnishes; here 70% of the menu is plant-based, with herbs, fruits and flowers often plucked straight from the resort's organic farm and ungentrified landscape when not sourced from farms and producers in the region.

The firefly conservatory was Puspa's idea too. She met Wayan in his home village of Taro four years ago and they started talking about his firefly passion.

Since the resort opening, the project has been happily humming along in the background, but plans are afoot to release the fireflies during Bali's annual Nyepi celebration, an auspicious twenty-four hours of silence and the island's Caka New Year.

The conservatory is as enchanting as the fireflies themselves. The little bamboo hobbit house is tucked into the side of the hill and has a welcoming front door. Inside the fairy-tale terrarium, water spouts from a bamboo pipe into a lotus-covered pond; epiphytes clad the cross-hatch ceiling, and the garden is crowded with ferns, flowers and grasses. Small black gauze boxes are the 'honeymoon suites' where Wayan controls the fragile breeding cycle of the fireflies with the perfect combination of pristine soil, water and air. It is the pollution of these three elements that has seen their demise across the province, says Wayan, who works with biology experts from Bali's University of Udayana. Along with the fourth element, light pollution.

'Fireflies use light to communicate,' he says. 'Twenty to twenty-five years ago we could find fireflies almost everywhere because everywhere was dark. Now everywhere is bright.' He believes fireflies are an indicator of how nature is faring.

In the ecosystem around the conservatory, it is well and truly alive. Synchronised pairs of yellow butterflies twirl around each other, cicadas buzz and birds coo. The small hillside rice paddies, free of pesticides and agricultural chemicals, nod to Bali's burgeoning regenerative rice movement. On the edge of the property, water gushes from on high into the Agung River.

As I look from the conservatory I see that the resort is brilliantly camouflaged, the human-made elements hidden in a festival of tree trunks, palm fronds, vines and oversized leaves. On Nyepi, when the lights are out and not even a candle is allowed to flicker, the resort would be immersed in darkness. All the better to see fireflies that here, at least, still glow strong.

CELESTIAL MOUNTAINS

Independent on Sunday, 25 April 1999
Clive Tully treks in the Tien Shan mountains of Kazakhstan and Kyrgyzstan.

There's no doubting that the might and grandeur of big mountains can make you feel very humble. Doubly so when you look up at a summit in the certain knowledge that someone is up there fighting for their life. I'm at the South Inylchek Glacier base camp at 4,000m, gazing in awe at the towering bulk of Pobeda, 7,500m tall, and the second highest mountain in Kazakhstan. Somewhere just below the summit is a stricken Japanese climber, too exhausted to go down with his three team mates.

Making their way up in a desperate bid to rescue him is a party of Russian climbers, but the news on the radio isn't encouraging. It's halfway through the afternoon, and the Russians are so absolutely exhausted – it seems they may not be able to go on. It doesn't look good for the Japanese climber. He's already spent two storm-blasted nights up there on the edge of the death zone, and the chances of his surviving another are surely fading.

Suddenly the air is filled with the distinctive beat of helicopter rotor blades. It's the same machine that ferried me up on to the glacier yesterday. After a brief stop at base camp, the Mi-17 takes off again, climbing straight up the mountainside. Similar to those used by the Red Army as troop carriers and gunships during the

Afghan war, it's doing something I wouldn't have believed possible were I not witnessing it myself.

This flying Transit van has gone way, way beyond its operational ceiling of around 5,000m, and is now scuttling back and forth above the summit ridge of Pobeda, looking first for the Japanese climber, then his rescuers. We watch open-mouthed as a package is tossed out to the Russians – food, fuel and oxygen – then back it comes in a series of wide circles, touching down again at base camp. Although the helicopter evacuation of Beck Weathers from the top of the Khumbu Icefall (around 6,000m) below Everest is, I believe, the record for a helicopter plucking someone from a mountain, what I've just seen would almost certainly rank as the highest ever helicopter-assisted mountain rescue.

This is no mere Transit van, however. Doubtless ever so slightly tweaked, it's the Kazakhstan president's helicopter, leased out for the summer to Kan Tengri Mountain Services, the company which runs the South Inylchek base camp and the well-appointed fixed camp in the Karkara valley. Boss man Kazbek Valiev flies with the chopper as well, doing the daily forty-minute run from Karkara to the base camp – a stunning flight over mountains and glaciers, swooping close to spectacular knife-edge ridges. Perhaps it reminds him of former glories – he was a member of the first Soviet expedition to climb Everest in 1982.

For me, the trip on to the glacier – the largest by volume in the world – is like a journey to another planet. I'd spent most of the previous two weeks trekking in the lower Tien Shan (Celestial Mountains), soaking up a wonderful mix of birch forests, pretty valleys and mountain passes, with some beautiful flower-strewn alpine meadows thrown in for good measure.

There are plenty of opportunities to experience some of the local culture even before I get the chance to pull on my walking boots. Almaty, the former capital, has shops which vary between classy fashions with sophisticated window displays, and the more typically Soviet-style supermarket, barely identifiable as such from the outside. The market is a real education – this is the place to get your cold cuts of horse meat.

Almaty, I was warned on the flight out, is a hotbed of violent crime. Don't go out on to the streets at night on your own, I was told. But it seems as though there's an element of the Wild West here even in broad daylight. At a small open-air bar just outside my hotel, the barman casually toys with an automatic pistol, snapping the magazine in and out of the butt to impress a glamorous lady customer sitting opposite.

Outside Almaty, the tarmac quickly gives way to dirt roads, with people living much more rustic lifestyles. Before hitting our first night's camp, we visit a man training a magnificent eagle to hunt foxes, whose pelts are highly prized by Russians for coats and hats. The rapport between man and bird is tangible. Then he invites us in for tea and impresses me with his ability to crack walnuts with his bare hands.

Once you adjust to the routine, trekking is a brilliant way to experience a country. Your slumbers are broken bright and early with a cup of tea brought to your tent. Then after a quick wash (maybe), pack up and get ready for breakfast, served in the mess tent. The walking varies from easy strolling to hard work, particularly the steep climbs up over 3,500m passes, where the altitude has you gasping for breath.

Apart from making sure I was generally fit, I prepared my lungs for the experience beforehand using a gadget called Powerbreathe. Its spring-loaded valve enables you to improve the condition of the muscles surrounding your lungs, increasing their power and capacity. I know from previous treks that at least I would have suffered from some shortness of breath – this time I had no altitude-related problems at all.

Excitement too from the numerous river crossings. Some we cross by jumping from one rock to another; some simply by wading, with the really powerful ones forded with the assistance of our luggage-carrying horses – an experience in itself for an equine-phobic Tully.

The trek itself was split into two sections, with a rest day at Karkara in between. The end of the first section is especially memorable for two reasons. Firstly, it's the morning that I happen to severely sprain my ankle, landing badly on a tussock of grass as I trot downhill from my tent to the river below. The following four hours' walk to pick up our bus is excruciatingly painful – in fact the remaining two weeks of trekking and several months afterwards aren't too clever, either.

Secondly, we drive to Lake Issyk-Kul, Kyrgyzstan's jewel in the crown and number one tourist attraction, now, unfortunately, also number one environmental disaster. A couple of months previously, a truck on its way to the Kumtor gold mine overturned into one of the lake's tributary rivers, spilling nearly 1,800kg of sodium cyanide in the process. Large numbers of people were evacuated, and more than five hundred were hospitalised with cyanide-related illnesses. Incredibly, when I visit, there are people at a shoreside holiday camp – a jumbled collection of wood and corrugated iron chalets – bathing in the lake with no apparent regard for their safety.

I won't forget in a hurry the evening our camp is invaded by marauding cows. The advance guard sets about chewing the wrist straps of my trekking poles, which I'd parked outside the tent. When I shoo it away, it trips over a couple of the guy lines. Then the rest of the herd moves in on the camp – most entertaining without a doubt is the plight of the poor Russian crew member squatting over the latrine, suddenly finding himself hemmed in by cattle. Eventually the herdsman arrives on his horse, laughing his head off, and after a few cracks of his whip, the cows are away down the valley.

Wonderful memories, too, of the wood-fired sauna in a tiny cabin in the Ulken Kokpak valley – its low ceiling dripping hot water tinged with pine – and the short dash to cool off in a nearby icy mountain stream. Then there's a magical encounter with Tursun, a farmer who spends the summer grazing sheep and horses in this most idyllic of mountain settings, living in a yurt, the traditional cross between a circular shed and a large tent. The latticework frame not only holds the outer felt covering in place but provides numerous hanging points for all kinds of possessions inside – everything from a variety of belongings in plastic carrier bags to the large-bore shotgun used when the wolves get too close.

We ask him what he likes about the yurt lifestyle. 'The freedom,' he admits, 'and the beauty of the mountains.' He wonders why we want to come here for a holiday instead of going to a beach. Our answer, of course, is the same as his.

ADVENTURES IN THE MANGROVE

The Australian **newspaper, 25 May 2014**
Kate Wickers discovers a mesmerising
menagerie on Langkawi Island.

I've got a lot of respect for the female fiddler crab that resides happily in the mangrove forest on the Malay island of Langkawi. The sensible girl inspects the burrows of more than a hundred males before deciding whom she'll move in with and then expects him to keep up the good housekeeping once they've mated.

The ninety-nine islands of Langkawi are sandwiched between the Thai island of Phuket to the north and Malaysia's Penang to the south and when I first visited in 1994 the island's mangrove habitat, trapped between land and sea, wasn't accessible to tourists. Today, however, it's one of the island's most memorable experiences and you can navigate the waters to peer into a spider's web of black mangrove roots, in search of the gentle spectacled langurs, boisterous macaques and among the menagerie of weird and wonderful sea-dwelling creatures: fish that walk, crabs that box and snakes that swim.

In 2007 UNESCO made the wise move of giving Langkawi a Geopark status (the first in southeast Asia) to preserve the mangrove and 400-million-year-old limestone karst hills, which in age rival those of Halong Bay in Vietnam and China's Yangtze River. We visit the mangrove twice during our stay, exploring the first day by whisper boat, a traditional long-tail boat with an environmentally friendly and almost silent electric engine. You cover more ground this way, but it is while gliding in a canoe, during our second visit, that we discover the most: vipers curled around tree roots and mangrove leaves that 'cry salty tears' (a clever way of filtering out the salt from the seawater), and fish that saunter nonchalantly out of the water.

'Look, Mummy! There's a walking fish!' shouts my wide-eyed eight-year-old son Freddie, leaning over the side of our canoe and pointing to where the mudskippers shimmy over the glistening sludge, fanning out their top fins like sails on a ship. And although we don't set eyes on the Malayan pond frog, we certainly hear her screaming for a lover. But it is the male fiddler crabs who entertain us the most with one giant red claw, which they wave to attract the vivid blue females and to box rivals with. When things get a little too serious, they cleverly cut doors in the mud, which they retreat into and slam shut. It is like watching a cartoon.

Our interest peaks when we come across a diminutive white flower on the rock face and learn that it is the rare white slipper orchid. A sapling can reach up to £30,000 on the black market. 'Let's pick it!' suggests Ben, my rather unscrupulous eleven-year-old. Our guide, Aidi, gives him a gentle lesson on protecting endangered plants and the fact that there's a similarly large fine if you're caught trying to steal one, and he soon sees the light.

There are regular mangrove clean-ups and encouragingly, for an island that hosts three million tourists annually, we don't come across much litter. Visitors to the mangrove are encouraged to help keep the forest clean and *en route* we fish out a lost flip-flop, a length of rope from a fishing boat and a few fizzy drinks bottles. As we float along, Aidi is also on the lookout for fallen mangrove saplings, which he replants by spearing them back into the muddy banks. To protect the environment only licensed boats are permitted to enter the forest and numbers are restricted, so Aidi keeps an eye out for unlicensed boats, reaching for his camera to take zoom shots of the pirate skippers. My sons enjoy being eco-warriors and get in the swing of things by pointing to boats being driven too fast, churning out fumes or missing licence plates, until I feel like an extra in an episode of Langkawi Five-0.

Langkawi gets its name from the Malay word for eagle, so it was somewhat embarrassing when the population of white-bellied sea eagles, which glide on warm thermals above the mangrove, dwindled to just 10% in the 1990s. The government quickly introduced a feeding programme which continues today, and tourists are allowed under supervision to take part. With noses firmly pegged my gagging sons throw a gruesome jigsaw of chicken's body parts out onto the water. The raptors are soon ominously circling our boat, their wingspan of up to 2.2m on glorious show. We cheer as they plunge, yellow talons outstretched to retrieve their lunch, which with fearsome hooked beaks they tear into once perched back in the forest canopy.

We all learn a lot from our visits to Langkawi's mangrove forest. 'Just remember the fiddler crab,' I plan to remind my husband and sons, while making threatening pincer movements with my fingers. 'Pick up those towels, put your plates in the dishwasher and keep that toilet seat down because if you don't, I'm off to inspect a few more burrows.'

OFF THE RAILS

Wanderlust, Summer 2015
Anthony Lambert takes New Zealand's Otago Central Rail Trail through some of the wildest and most spectacular landscapes, a journey made by the hospitality of its remote communities.

I'd read about the wind, the way a gust can come out of nowhere and blow you off your bike. So it was no surprise that I soon found myself looking at the next curve on the trail and figuring out whether it would speed my progress or add to the sense of challenge, though that's not quite how I put it at the time. I knew Kiwis really get the wind; they know all about the Roaring Forties. But an unexpected discovery was how quickly the wind direction can swing through 180 degrees and turn a tailwind into a head-on struggle.

But no amount of thigh pumping made me regret for a second where I was. I was on the first of three days cycling the 150km Otago Central Rail Trail through New Zealand's South Island. I had been involved with Sustrans in the early days of the UK's National Cycle Network, and I wanted to experience the pioneer of New Zealand's equivalent 23 Great Trails.

It wasn't just the idea of the stunning landscapes; a new generation of visionaries had been determined not to waste the asset of what had been the lifeline of remote communities. They could see that this magnificently engineered narrow ribbon through breathtaking scenery could again sustain communities and prevent people having to desert the place they loved.

I met one of those visionaries, Daphne Hull, in a café in Clyde before I set off. She told me that in many ways the trail owes its success to the determination of strong-minded rural women, and her words stayed with me as I met some of them.

Clyde's many historic stone and wooden buildings would provide a perfect set for a film about the 1860s gold rush which brought many of them into being. I collected my bike from Trail Journeys on the site of the old railway station and headed east.

The flat 8km to Alexandra through orchards and vineyards are perfect for getting acquainted with the bike and the trail's features. I stopped at the first of the corrugated-iron gangers' huts that punctuate the route, providing shelter and outstanding information boards about the flora and fauna, civil engineering structures and local history.

Skirting Alex, the trail crosses the Galloway Flat beside the Manuherikia River, willows bordering the sheep station land which once filled whole trains of double-deck sheep vans. Appropriately I was ready for lunch as I forged past Tucker Hill, so named because the miners won only enough gold in this area to pay for their tucker.

Chatto Creek Tavern opened its doors in 1886 and its first patrons would have been astounded to see today's menu of dishes such as salmon ballotine and blue cod. Customers for such fare are recent, as proprietor Lesley Middlemas told me; Chatto Creek was dying after the last train whistle was heard in 1990 and she had little doubt the pub owed its survival to the trail.

I wasn't back in the saddle for many minutes before sensing the beginning of the climb up to Tiger Hill which became as steep as 1 in 50 – hardly taxing on a bike, but quite enough to exert the fireman on a steam locomotive. The weather had been dry so the views over the Dunstan Range wore a mantle of umber relieved by the summer green of trees and the ubiquitous gorse – one of the natural curses of New Zealand. Introduced from Scotland in the 1830s to hedge livestock, it is almost impossible to eradicate.

At Omakau I made a detour to see the historic jewel of Ophir, just off the trail. This gold-rush town had been bypassed by the railway to save a bridge across the Manuherikia River, but its proximity to the trail and its many old buildings have revived the fortunes of the single-street town, with New Zealand's oldest post office, built in 1886.

I continued to my first overnight stop across flattish dairy-farming country. Named after the Berwickshire town, Lauder was a typical Otago settlement of a dozen or two scattered single-storey houses with red and green corrugated-iron roofs. The converted Lauder Store where I stayed was made of the dried mud brick common throughout Central Otago because of the sparsity of trees and cost of stone. Across the road was the Lauder Hotel, which served locally reared venison.

Setting off next morning I began the climb towards the summit of the line near Wedderburn. Crack willows lined the river below, shimmering as their contrasting leaf surfaces of dark and light green caught the wind. A curved viaduct carries the trail over the final crossing of the Manuherikia River before the line joins the Ida Burn and climbs through two tunnels in Poolburn Gorge.

The exit from the second tunnel provided an extraordinary transition from the stark schist cuttings of the gorge to a panorama over the pasture land of the Ida Valley, riven by ribbons of tree-lined water courses, and far across the broad valley a gentle range of hills with trees filling the declivities. I could see why Peter Jackson had chosen the valley for scenes set in Rohan in *The Lord of the Rings*.

Legs tiring from the steady climb, I happily obeyed the recommendation of an information board and paused to admire the monumental masonry piers of Poolburn Viaduct, its stones hewn from local outcrops. One of a number of long, straight stretches brought me to one of the 'mustn't miss' sights just off the trail, the Hayes Engineering Works. This miraculous time warp is the workshop of belt-shaft-driven machines, looking as though the workmen had just downed tools for tea.

Approaching the summit of the line, the last thing I expected was an invitation to morning tea. But a board beside the trail suggested I stop for a cuppa at the next gangers' hut. The only catch was a questionnaire to find out all the predictable things to inform a survey of the trail's use. The last one indicated that the trail injected NZ$4.7 million into the Central Otago economy each year.

That set me thinking as I pedalled on towards the summit; I remembered Daphne Hull's words about the initial opposition to the idea by farmers, but it was their wives and women in the communities who could see the benefits of bringing new visitors to the area and putting spare rooms to work as B&Bs. The enlightened Department of Conservation set up the trust and saw the whole 150km reopened by 2000.

After such a long climb, it was a relief to let gravity take over, assuming the wind didn't have other ideas. Beyond a lovely cutting of pines, I stopped at Wedderburn Cottages to talk to Stuart Duncan who has created a café and exhibition about the railway at his wooden cottages overlooking rolling hills. I learned that the Otago Central Railway was begun in 1879 from Dunedin to transport supplies to the gold-rush settlements but it was not until 1907 that it was finally opened to Clyde.

I stopped for a late lunch at Ranfurly, the largest town of the Maniototo Plains with some fine 1930s Art Deco buildings thanks to suspicious fires destroying their predecessors. The station building is one of the few still standing and is now the tourist information office.

After the only crossing on the trail of the Taieri River, which the railway follows to the sea, I reached one of those delightful places that one is almost surprised to find in such empty country. Screened by a crescent of pines at the back and overlooking a gentle bowl of country, Kokonga Lodge is home to Malcolm Edwards and Dorothy Piper; he creates colour in the garden, she on canvas, and both on the plate with outstanding dishes using produce from the garden.

Rather reluctantly, on day three I left the idyllic lodge for the final 44km to Middlemarch. Deep rock cuttings filled with pine cones alternated with embankments giving views over crumpled hills as the trail wound round the contours. I found sanctuary from a shower in Hyde's Otago Central Hotel – 'Stop and eat or we'll both starve to death' warned its trailside board. Near the hotel is a World War I memorial with twelve names; Hyde barely had twelve houses.

Squalls occasionally forced me to slow for fear of becoming airborne, so I could well understand why the station building at Ngapuna had to be wired to iron posts to stop it blowing away. Rounding the final curve, I could see journey's end at Middlemarch far in the distance at the end of the longest straight on the trail.

Any sense of disappointment at coming to the end of such a fascinating journey was mitigated by the only practical way of leaving Middlemarch – by the Taieri Gorge Railway. So spectacular is this railway that when the Otago Central closed in 1990, Dunedin City

Council bought the line to Middlemarch to reopen it with vintage carriages as a tourist attraction. The train to Dunedin threads the astoundingly dramatic gorge with frequent tunnels, great viaducts and deep rock cuttings. Even after the scenic delights of the Otago, the Taieri Gorge Railway seemed the perfect coda to a pioneering vision of green tourism.

THE NEW SRI LANKAN HIKING TRAIL THAT LEADS TO THE HEART OF THE HILL COUNTRY

National Geographic Traveller (UK),
Indian Ocean supplement, September 2023
Jessica Vincent explores Sri Lanka's quiet central highlands on the Pekoe Trail.

When I reach Galaha in Sri Lanka's central highlands, the sun is high in the sky and the streets are clouded with dust. Tuk-tuks rattle around women in red saris flecked with gold, and narrowly miss the one-eyed dog sleeping in the road. Amid the honking and coconut selling, I hear a familiar sound – Beethoven's *Für Elise* – moving closer, crackling from a tuk-tuk selling fish buns, and bringing with it the smell of freshly baked bread.

This is where, 12 miles south of Kandy, my journey along the new Pekoe Trail – Sri Lanka's first long-distance hiking route – begins. Its name refers to the high-grade black tea made from young leaves, a speciality of the country's central highlands. Spanning 185 miles from Kandy to Nuwara Eliya in the heart of the hill country, it links, with US and EU funding, an existing network of footpaths created when the British established a tea-growing industry here during colonial rule in the 19th century.

At that time thousands of stone and dirt roads were cut into the forest to transport plantation workers and cargo between tea fields, factories and the newly built railway line, so that hardwood boxes branded 'Ceylon Tea' could travel to Colombo's harbour for export to Britain. It's hoped that the new trail, which passes through dozens of remote villages and tea estates, will encourage visitors away from the country's well-trodden Cultural Triangle and into Sri Lanka's less visited interior. Many of its twenty-two stages are now open, with the remaining ones due to follow by December.

Rather than completing the whole route, I plan to experience it in manageable sections. With my guide, Ramli Raban, we head 9 miles southeast to Loolecondera, where Scottish planter James Taylor established Sri Lanka's first tea estate, via the market town of Deltota. Passing a Hindu temple painted in pastel yellows and blues, we swap Galaha's tarmacked road for a dirt track lined with pepper plants and papaya trees.

The footpath crosses the Deltotte Tea Estate, where rows of parakeet-green tea bushes – each exactly a metre apart and pruned to waist height – carpet the undulating hills. Women walk silently between the bushes, plucking young tea buds at lightning speed and depositing them into tarpaulin sacks. We accompany them to a weighing station, a wooden shelter where their sacks are hung from hooks to assess their morning's work. The assistant superintendent, a man in knee-high socks and side-slicked hair, scribbles the weight in his notepad. The day's quota is 20kg per picker, says Ramli, which will earn the women around 600 Sri Lankan rupees – or around £1.50.

'Many of my school friends work on these tea estates,' says Ramli, who grew up in the highland capital Kandy, which was Sri Lanka's last independent kingdom before the British took control in 1815. 'It's a hard life. The day starts at five a.m. and you have to walk long distances to pick leaves – we're talking ten miles before breakfast.'

Ramli explains how years ago he trained as a chef and later achieved his dream of opening a burger restaurant in Colombo, but the city's Easter bombings forced him to close his business in the capital and return to Kandy in 2019. 'Three of my friends died,' says Ramli, as we climb through a field of pine trees, golden sap seeping from their blackened bark. 'I was in Colombo when it happened. It was terrifying. Then Covid hit, followed by food and fuel shortages. So I decided to start afresh and train as a guide.'

Becoming a guide when Sri Lanka had already lost the majority of its tourists seems like a risky career move, I say. Ramli has guided only a handful of guests all year, but he's hopeful things will change.

'No matter how hard the situation gets, tourism will bounce back. And when it does, I want to show people the real Sri Lanka,' he says. 'With the Pekoe Trail, you see Sri Lanka on a grassroots level. This isn't like the tour buses – there's no script for me to follow.'

For the next two nights my base is the village of Ambadandegama – four hours' drive south of Loolecondera near Ella – from where I plan to hike a further section of the trail. I stay at Amba Estate, an organic farm and guesthouse that's producing hand-rolled teas for restaurants such as Copenhagen's Noma.

'We don't use terms like "tea plucker" or "superintendent" here,' says Neethanjana Senadheera, the estate's production manager and tea taster. Born and raised in Ambadandegama, he began working here after writing his master's thesis on Sri Lanka's tea industry. 'It's colonial language,' he says. 'At Amba, pluckers are tea artisans, and we call each other brother and sister.'

Focusing on small-scale, high-quality production, Amba pays these artisans up to six times more than the average tea plantation. Whereas a tea artisan's working day usually ends at the weighing station, Amba's staff are involved in the whole process from drying and rolling to tasting and packaging.

In the small production room, leaves dry on wooden racks and women hand-roll tea in muslin cloths. 'Some estates are still run like colonial plantations,' says Neethanjana. 'Tea workers are treated as the lowest of society in Sri Lanka. But at Amba, there's pride in making Sri Lankan tea.'

The next morning I meet guide Thilantha Abeysinghe. We plan to spend two days travelling through hill country from Lipton's Seat viewpoint – where Scottish tea baron Sir Thomas Lipton is said to have kept an eye over his empire – to Demodara train station.

The views are mesmerising. Morning mist clings to layers of forested hills. Below me, the tea fields are a sea of electric green, but in a valley to my right a patch of virgin forest bursts with pockets of orange, yellow and red. We pass Hindu shrines and Buddhist temples draped in colourful silks. All around, the air ripples with the song of flycatchers; a serpent eagle perches on a nearby eucalyptus tree.

'Many Sri Lankans take these landscapes for granted,' says Thilantha, a former banker and chef. 'Those with enough money to go on holiday go to the beach resorts. They don't walk these trails; they think walking is something you do out of necessity.'

He explains that while the trail seems to be popular with foreign visitors, its impact could stretch further: 'On the Pekoe Trail, you're given the chance to understand people who live and look differently to you. That's important not just for tourists, but for Sri Lankans too.'

In the shade of an empty tea-weighing station, he magics up two china cups and a flask of hot ginger tea from his backpack. Coconut *sambal* and still warm chapatis appear next, served on a palm leaf. As I take my first bite, the winds carry a hollow rumble to our ears from the valley floor. It's the Muslim call to prayer, Thilantha tells me, mixing with Hindu drums, Christian bells and Buddhist chanting. Even this far from any town or city, there's a lot to learn about Sri Lanka's cultural identity.

'We'll spend many more hours together,' says Thilantha. He's packing up the tea and *sambal* ready to walk again. 'We started not knowing each other, but by the time we finish the trail, we'll be good friends. You'll see.'

A DAY WITH THE TEA GOD

Chau-Jean Lin returns to her roots in Songboling in Taiwan to discover the history and traditions of making the island's renowned oolong tea.

'The flavour unlocks in your hands.' Mr Chen Ai-Bing is talking about tea making, but he might as well be talking about the surrounding tea fields he farms. Taipei has Taiwan's (once the world's) tallest building; Kaohsiung has the music; but Songboling – once famed for freedom, pineapples and home of the tea god – has the best brew. He tells me this while standing next to his small tea factory from the 1980s. His fingers roll freshly cut tea leaves like cigarettes. We speak in the local dialect of Taiwanese. He says, 'What I love about this village are the people, fresh mountain air, and its history.'

Getting a taste of Songboling's history could not be easier. With a direct flight from the UK to Taipei, China Airlines departs five times a week from London Heathrow, bringing you to an island famous for its stunning views, tea, and street food. A two-and-a-half-hour trip from Taipei on the Taiwan High Speed Rail and taxi, Songboling is home to a tea trail and a pilgrimage destination for tea lovers – the village produces the most tea per annum of any place in Taiwan. Nearby, where the annual October Nantou Global Tea Expo is held, a patchwork of makers, farmers, and tea masters demonstrate their craft and sell local goods. Beyond pedestrian experiences, a series of cycling festivals runs through the autumn starting from Sun Moon Lake to the Jiji Railway Cycling Festival.

I arrived mid-morning at Shoutian Temple, home of Xuantian Shangdi, a Taoist tea deity with powers to command poisonous snakes in tea fields. Walking about, I was surprised to see the filter on the joss paper furnace, its new columns, and the etchings of tea processing along its façade – all rebuilt after the 921 Earthquake in 1999. Inside, it was a smoky, surreal, meditative dream. The smell of incense filled the air, sweat dripped from my forehead, and the people around me – locals and tourists alike – bowed three times to the sound of 18th-century gongs. I could only imagine what it might have been like for my ancestors who visited every lunar month.

That sense of history and spirit in the temple infuses every corner of the village. During lunchtime, I explored the winding streets nearby: a marketplace with a kaleidoscope of parked cars and aging street vendors. Freshly cut pineapple; tea overspilling from large sacks; rice crackers used for offerings. It was difficult to resist the freshly squeezed sugarcane juice and the local tempura, a relic of Japanese colonisation. Not much had changed here since the 1980s, except that the signs were now in English, Mandarin, and Indonesian.

I escaped the summer afternoon heat in the Songboling Visitor Center down the road: a relatively new concrete complex, tucked away among tea fields that had been growing for generations, open to the public every day. In a span of two hours, I'd plucked tea leaves from the garden, pan-fried tea in a traditional way, and had a tea leaf facial.

With a freshly brewed cup of oolong tea in hand, I was ready to go back to my roots and become a tea farmer.

At the end of the day, I found my way back to the temple's car park. As electric cars hummed in the background, I took a trail, abandoned at the mountain's edge, to an overlook scattered with selfie sticks. Surrounding the temple, a breathtaking scene of verdant green landscape gave way to the earthquake's legacy: concrete block houses. It was like viewing the Highlands from Loch Lomond – but on a tropical island. I could only imagine what settlers here had to do to cross the Qingshui and Zhoushoui rivers as I stood above them.

As I left, I bumped into a four-year-old: a pink digital camera adorned her neck, heart-shaped sunglasses covered her eyes. Not taking notice, her parents were indulging in selfies. 'I want to go back to give offerings,' I overheard her say. That spirit to be part of the history was the essence of Songboling.

Turning back, I stopped and looked out over the fields. Two farmers were harvesting tea; the sun was setting, and the sound of their machines buzzed harmoniously with the cicadas. Somewhere in the distance, my ancestors were making and sipping tea – unlocking its flavour and brewing up the history of the village.

LATECOMERS TO THE NEW YEAR SHOW

The *Sunday Telegraph*, 16 December 1999
In Hanoi, Kate Wickers banishes bad spirits and
welcomes in the New Year.

A child, no more than four years old, lit a match and held it against the red touchpaper of a string of firecrackers longer than he was tall. He watched in delight as his writhing toy spat and crackled, popped and banged. He kept a tight hold of the string, waiting until a split second before the final explosion at his small fingertips before letting go. In Vietnam there is no such thing as public safety warnings and Tết Nguyên Đán (Tết), the Vietnamese New Year, makes Guy Fawkes Night look as sober as a Sunday school picnic.

This said, Vietnam is one country that won't be in the throes of millennium mania next Friday night. Despite the adoption of the Gregorian calendar in other parts of southeast Asia, it has not been widely accepted in this largely rural country whose farmers prefer instead to celebrate the onset of spring. Clinging tenaciously to their ancient traditions, the Vietnamese will let off a few fireworks as a polite recognition of the Gregorian New Year, but their hearts and souls will be withheld for Tết on 5 February.

I was in Hanoi for this most important festival, a time for family reunions, the settlement of debts and the resolution of quarrels. In the important pre-Tết ceremony, Le Tao Quan, the three Spirits of the Hearth, who live in the kitchen of every home, ascend to heaven to give their annual report to the Jade Emperor. Outside every home a *cây nêu* (bamboo stripped of its leaves, wrapped in red paper, and decorated with clay bells) had been placed to protect against evil spirits.

I picked my way along the busy roads, past piles of firecrackers for sale, most made in the village of Dong Ky, infamous for producing the world's loudest. Not only do they create those that can last for up to one hour, but also monstrous 30ft beasts that take ten strong men to lift, which I'd seen strung from top floor windows of apartment buildings.

In the Tết flower market, at the centre of Hanoi's oldest quarter, careful, last-minute selections of *cây đào* (peach blossom) were being made. The blossom is a symbol of wealth and prosperity, and it's believed that the longer into the New Year it blooms, the greater your good fortune will be. I bought a small branch for my hotel room and continued to Dong Xuan market, in search of *mứt*, a favourite sweet treat during Tết, which is a delicious mix of candied coconut, ginger, tomato and carrot.

There was mayhem on the already chaotic streets as locals made their way home for the start of the festivities. Rickshaws and bikes cut a zigzag path through the jam of pollution-churning buses, and I spotted a man cycling with fifteen live ducks and chickens, indignantly quacking and clucking, hanging from his handlebars. Curbside, stalls selling *bánh chưng*, a cake made of sticky rice, pork fat, spices and beans, wrapped in four layers of banana leaves, were doing a roaring trade. This is the Vietnamese equivalent of Christmas cake – a stodgy victual that everyone buys, which hangs around the house for weeks after the holiday.

By early evening, wisps of smoke hung in the air and a snow of red paper had begun to fall as fireworks were ignited. I made my way back to the shelter of The Orchid Hotel, jumping at every explosion. The noise escalated steadily in the following hours, until it was impossible to have a conversation without shouting. It reached its climax at midnight in an ear-splitting medley of drums, gongs and firecrackers as the old year was ushered out and the Spirits of the Hearth welcomed back. At this moment all the hardships of the previous year are left behind and the simple goal is to make as much noise as possible to ward off any lingering bad spirits.

I couldn't let the occasion pass without contributing to the bedlam. So, thinking of money I was owed and a friend who had let me down, I borrowed a gong to bash – hard. I also ignited a few small firecrackers but found it difficult to shrug off years of November 5th conditioning. Putting match to paper, I stood sensibly back, much to the crowd's amusement.

On New Year's Day I strolled past Ho Chi Minh's Mausoleum, where Uncle Ho, the founder of the Vietnamese Communist Party and president of the Democratic Republic of Vietnam from 1946 to 1969, lies in state. He wasn't receiving many visitors that day as the Vietnamese believe that the first person you see on the morning of the New Year will determine your luck for the rest. A corpse, even if greatly loved and beautifully embalmed, would not be considered auspicious. Other people to avoid are the recently bereaved and those that have lost their jobs. Instead, the Vietnamese extend invitations to their richest, most successful, relations. Families in their finery also go in droves to Hoàn Kiếm Lake, a tranquil body of water at the heart of Hanoi, to have their prosperity captured by professional photographers, who set up studios by the water.

I left Hanoi just as normal life was resuming. The garish red and gold banners that wished all a Happy New Year had been taken down; new feuds were beginning, and money was, once again, being borrowed. My branch of *cây đào*, which I'd stood in a tooth mug, still flourished as a reassuring sign that my good fortune would last long into the New Year.

A Fright on the Bare Mountain by Clive Tully

CENTRAL AMERICA, CARIBBEAN & SOUTH AMERICA

A 21ST-CENTURY WILD GOOSE CHASE IN ARGENTINA IN 2008

James Lowen looks for a bird that might be extinct.

'What bird do I most want to see in Argentina?' ponders Mark. He pauses, stroking stubble. '*El ganso de monte,*' he concludes, 'Orinoco goose. A chestnut shelduck with jet-black wings. Gorgeous. Close to global extinction. But there's a catch.' Another pause; another reflective stroke. With his swarthy build and deep-set eyes, this cockney-turned-South American-gaucho could play himself in a Guy Ritchie gangster flick.

'There's no recent records from Argentina. But it's gotta be there, somewhere. I reckon the way to see it is to float down a remote river on a raft. Fancy joinin' me?'

I decline. It's July 2006 and I've recently moved to South America's second largest country, with three-plus years to explore its wilderness wonders. This is needle-in-a-giant-haystack territory. No way are we going to find it. And the prospect of drowning on a wild goose chase doesn't appeal.

Fast-forward two years, to mid-2008. The phone rings. It's the cockney cowboy. The telephone reverberates with his adrenalin. 'Orinoco goose. Some geezers have found it. Rio Bermejo, Salta

province. We don't need the raft trick. I'm goin'. You comin'?'
This time, I need no asking.

Two days later, Mark and I fly from Buenos Aires to Salta to join Germán. Wild-eyed and wild-haired, Germán vies with Mark for the dubious accolade of Argentina's top twitcher. We embrace, share a yerba maté tea from a cow-horn gourd and drive four hours to a dusty town marking the biogeographical frontier with the Chaco's dense, desiccated scrubland.

Germán makes phone calls. He tracks down who discovered the geese, and where. We arrange a midnight rendezvous with the finders in a backstreet bar. We arrive early, tense. The night is sultry. Even the walls are sweating. We down a Quilmes beer, to keep cool. We wait. We neck another Quilmes, to keep calm. We wait.

Just as I am losing the will to live, in walk two national park rangers, in uniform. Marcelo and Maximo are tired, but excited. They have good news! They found two hundred Orinoco geese a month back! A hitherto unknown population! But there's also bad news. Marcelo last saw the geese a fortnight back. The flock has flown.

We pore over what passes for a map. Salta's Chaco comprises Argentina's outback. Discernible details are scarce. Marcelo indicates the floodplain where he found the geese. Similar habitat extends for 100 miles either side. 'That's some haystack.' Mark grimaces. We discuss options. We could drive the few roads. We could rent a boat.

'Or,' exclaims Germán, 'we could hire a plane, fly the length of the river, spot geese from the air, then drive in!' It's a bonkers idea. But also a very good one. Despite the hour, we phone a pilot contact: Argentine aviators rarely sleep. Two thousand pesos – three hundred quid – will buy us three hours' flight time. 'It's a deal, *pibe*,' Maximo agrees.

Inevitably, there's a catch. We are five; the plane seats three. We draw straws. Marcelo, Mark and I form the lucky few. The others are gutted.

Seven hours later, the tiny, rickety aircraft stutters upwards. I have never flown in so petite a plane. I have never felt so unsafe. The engine roar is deafening; the engine judder debilitating. We are trying to spot a bird from 100m above ground while travelling at 110 miles per hour. The odds favour the haystack.

River, floodplain and winged shapes whirr by. We fly 100 miles upstream but find no geese. Any further and we will run out of fuel. We retreat, disconsolate. But still scan below. Ten minutes from the airfield I glimpse jet-black wings; I clock chestnut.

'*Aca! Aca!*' I yell. The pilot loops back. 'There! There!' I scream. '*Ganso de monte*!' We all see them. I grab a photo. Mark captures the location on his GPS. Exhausted but elated, we land. We share the tale with the ground crew, slurp another maté. But can we find the site from the ground? Can we get there?

We relocate to an internet café: in 2008, in remote parts of Argentina, such locations were the only way to get online. We load Google Earth and enter the co-ordinates from Mark's GPS. In the absence of Wi-Fi, Google's world expands frustratingly slowly in front of our eyes, as South America painstakingly morphs into Argentina, then into Salta, then ultimately into the Río Bermejo.

Electronically, we explore the terrain. A dirt track pierces the scrubland to within 6 miles. We can surely walk from there, following the GPS. It looks like ground access will be feasible. Everyone brightens up. We celebrate with Quilmes.

We set off at dawn. The 4WD bounces along ever-shrinking lanes into ever-wilder bush. As the thickets encroach, drivability dissipates. From here we must hike. Twisting round thorns, we emerge at the Bermejo's parched plain. As the sun intensifies, we navigate by GPS. Five miles and closing. Four, three, two, one. Will the *gansos* be there? We flip between fatigue and frenzy. Mark's GPS suggests we are just 100m away. A bend in the river blocks our view. We turn the corner.

Barely 50m ahead, a pair of Orinoco geese slumbers. We cannot believe our eyes. The chestnut beauties awake, preen and graze.

Thanks to modern transport, satellite technology and the internet, our 21st-century wild goose chase has worked. Who needs a raft?

THE WORLD'S BEST FOOD

FT Weekend, 25 June 2005
*Louise Simpson discovers the secrets
behind the Bajan national dish.*

A queue is forming outside a mint-green wooden shack near The Boatyard in Barbados' capital, Bridgetown. It's Saturday morning and the locals have come to collect their take-aways from Mrs Simmonds, a renowned pudding-and-souse maker. As she busies herself in the kitchen, I see the front room has been transformed into a makeshift barber's shop with her husband giving one of his neighbours a close shave.

Mrs Simmonds comes to the door with my portion of pudding and souse with breadfruit and I hand over B$2 (about 60p). I lean against the wall outside in the sunshine and open the polystyrene container. Beads of sweat pour on to my temples as I taste the hot-pepper punch of the pickle against the grainy sweet-potato pudding and tender pieces of pork souse. In the admiring words of the young boy next to me: 'Her pudding 'n souse too sweet, it is.'

After a month in Barbados, I have just discovered this national dish and one of the island's best-kept secrets. Tourist restaurants serve a wealth of red snapper, dolphin fish, marlin and shark, but little pork and no pudding and pork souse.

The only local speciality highlighted on most menus is flying fish. This exotic-sounding fish even appears on the Bajan (Barbadian) coat of arms. In reality it no longer inhabits the waters around Barbados and is imported from Trinidad. Compared with the sweet and fiery flavour of other local dishes, flying fish is a tame token effort. Is pudding and souse too adventurous for the tourist palate? Or are restaurants pandering to diners' expectations that desert island dining is all about fish?

Bajans eat fish, but they love chicken and pork – especially with rocket-fire seasonings using Scotch bonnet pepper, cloves and allspice. Bajan cuisine dates back to colonial plantations when food was designed to fuel the heavy manual labour of workers in the fields. African and English influences combined with native Amerindian cooking to create filling and economic food. Dishes were made from the odds and ends of meat left over after the plantation owners had taken their pick of the better cuts of meat. The spicy seasonings originated from the need to preserve the meat. Pig tails, cow heels and chicken feet were served with rice, pasta or potatoes, as well as locally grown starches such as sweet potatoes, chewy breadfruit and richly flavoured *eddoes*.

One starchy dish with African origins is *cou-cou*, made from ground cornmeal, okras and water. It's cooked slowly until all the liquid is absorbed. The key lies in stirring with a large *cou-cou* stick. The ability to 'turn a mellow *cou-cou*' is symbolic of domestic bliss – or quite literally a woman's ability in bed. Such culinary secrets have been passed down for centuries from mother to daughter and no self-respecting Bajan woman owns a cookbook.

Each day of the week is allocated a special dish. While fish and *cou-cou* are relegated to midweek, weekends are for roast chicken with peas (usually beans), rice and macaroni cheese or pork chops and crackling. Despite the competition, pudding and souse remains the favourite Saturday dish. For those too busy to make their own, most villages have a self-appointed pudding-and-souse specialist who cooks up a huge quantity to sell to neighbours on Fridays and Saturdays. One such guru, Yvonne, has agreed to show me how she makes it. Laden down with a pig's head and trotters bought from the local abattoir, I arrive at her wooden chattel house in a sleepy village near Six Roads. We sit on her terrace drinking mauby – a dark brown syrup drink made from tree bark – as Yvonne explains the basics.

The traditional preparation of pudding and souse is not for the faint-hearted. The sweet potato pudding is darkened with pig's blood and stuffed into pig's intestine, while the souse is made from pig's head and trotters. Nowadays, a tamer preparation is preferred, with the pudding made in a bowl and darkened with food colouring. Although pig's head and trotters are still often used, some households use pork chops as a tasty alternative, which may be more appealing for the squeamish European palate.

As we cook, several friends arrive in a white minibus, curious to meet the pale, blond journalist. The sun is falling and the whistling frogs are starting up. We crouch on the terrace steps with glasses of rum, looking out over the fields beyond the hut and waiting for the pudding to finish cooking and cool. An hour later, it's ready and we tuck in. The flavoursome trio of the pork, the sweet potato pudding and the breadfruit mingle with the pickle that prickles and soothes at the same time. Bajan author Austin Clarke's words spring to mind: 'Gimme Saturdays seven days of the week! Saturday [is] the day for making black pudding-and-souse, the best food in the world.'

A NEW DAWN FOR
THE GARIFUNA PEOPLE

Wanderlust, October/November 2023
*When the Garifuna people settled in Belize they carried their
traditions and culture with them. Lynn Houghton discovers a
new trail that explores this heritage through local community.*

'Would you like to try some homemade wine?' asked Pen
Cayetano, an integral part of the Dangriga township
situated on the Caribbean Sea. Tall, gangly and with a fistful of
dreads tightly clenched in a ponytail atop his head, the prolific
painter and musician proffered a glass with the air of a good host.

As introductions to the world of traditional Garifuna music
went, this was certainly a more genteel opening gambit than I'd
anticipated, particularly from a man credited with the creation of
Punta rock. Even now, the 1980s sound of his Original Turtle Shell
Band underscores much of Belize's club-music scene.

I accepted the glass and stepped up to the backyard bandstand,
where I was faced with an imposing set of tall, African-style drums
reminiscent of Cuban congas. They were played in a similar fashion,
and after Pen laid out the basic rhythm, I set my wine to one side
and followed along.

I'd had a drum kit in my youth, so I relished the opportunity to
relive those days. Pen, meanwhile, accompanied himself as he sang
a song of freedom and the transfixing power of the sea. I played
along but mostly just listened, enthralled by the sounds that came
from his hands.

'It was the women who created the Punta beat with the rhythm
of their kitchen utensils,' Pen explained, sketching the origins of
a music unique to the Garifuna people. When I thought about

the enormous pestles and mortars I'd seen pummelling plantains into mash, it was easy to see the connection. As Pen played, my mind drifted along with the music even as I admired his paint-splattered Crocs.

Prior to my drum session, his wife, Ingrid, had ushered me into their studio gallery, showing me some of his early paintings depicting the Garifuna experience, culture and roots. Images of hurricanes and hardships blared from the canvas. But when he beat out his Punta rhythms with the broad slap of his palms, he painted a history of his community every bit as vivid as if he had done so with the stroke of a brush.

It was certainly a story worth hearing. Dangriga in Belize is a major cultural centre for the Garifuna people, known collectively as the Garinagu. They trace their roots to the island of Saint Vincent, and although differing tales of their origins exist, it was here that a group of West Africans and the island's Indigenous Kalinago-Taino (Carib-Arawak) people formed a unique culture and community, bolstered by the steady influx of those escaping slavery. The Garinagu resisted European colonisation until a bloody conflict with the British led to them being exiled to a Honduran island in the late 1700s, from where they spread out along the Caribbean coast. By the time Belize acquired its modern-day name in 1973, they made up around 6% of the country's population.

In 1802, the first Garifuna settlers arrived. This is celebrated on 19 November as Garifuna Settlement Day, when festivities take over this small coastal community. It includes the re-enactment of a coterie of sailors arriving on the beach while others drift up Stann Creek in traditional boats, followed by lots of food and dancing.

I had arrived just as celebrations were being planned for this year's events. But I was also exploring the Garifuna Trail, an exciting new scheme aimed at introducing visitors to local businesses and institutions that promote Garifuna art, food, crafts and dance in the context of the wider community. Pen was just my first stop. So, after wrapping up our session, I took a few photos, wished Pen good day and set off into town.

Dangriga's buildings are mostly decorated in bright hues of yellow and black, the official colours of the Garifuna flag. Some of the older houses – painted orange, indigo blue or cerise – are constructed of wood, so had been treated with a resin to combat the furious wind and rain of hurricane season, the tail end of which fades just as November's celebrations begin. It seemed a fitting symbol for everything this resilient community has had to weather down the centuries.

It was now time to visit local drum maker Daytha Rodriguez. Her 'workshop', I discovered, was the family's front garden, which was populated with logs, equipment, a baby, chickens and dogs.

Daytha and her sister are carrying on a tradition that was passed down from their father, Aston, who arrived by bicycle halfway through our session but didn't take part; he instead took up grandfatherly duties and settled down to play with the littlest child. As training began, Daytha's daughter held up a large, laminated poster that provided a step-by-step illustration of the process of traditional drum making. It felt like I'd been invited into their family.

What I have left unsaid is just how unique this whole business is. Historically, it was only the Garifuna men that took up this craft. Drums are a hugely important part of their culture, and the two sisters were breaking a generations-long mould by being the first women to have taken up the calling. I soon learned that Daytha had shown an early interest in her father's profession. As a child, she had been intrigued that he didn't seem to work every day, and she only grew more curious after he explained this was because he was his own boss. With her brothers uninterested in the family business, Daytha and her sister carried it on instead.

I found it fascinating that not only had Daytha and her family broken with convention, but she was willing to innovate too. She had decided to speed up the process of hollowing out the drums by using a chainsaw, which she ably demonstrated. Aston was initially against this, preferring the old-fashioned way of crafting entirely by hand, but using modern machinery has revolutionised her drum-making business, meaning they can make instruments much faster.

Before long, it was time to depart, but I did so knowing that I was in for a treat. I joined up with tour guide Ian, who delivered us to the popular beachside restaurant Tauni for a taste of traditional Garifuna food.

'Don't be afraid to use your fingers,' he advised as the food arrived, picking at a piece of fish dexterously. We were having *hudutu*, a traditional Garifuna coconut soup. Next to this steaming bowl was a grilled red snapper, ready to be pulled apart and added to the broth, and floating atop the soup was a Habanero chilli – locals typically sprinkle in the seeds to spice things up.

Wiggling my toes in the sand, I scoffed down the accompanying plantain mash and thought back to Pen's story of the origins of Punta music. All the while we were watched over by Bob Marley, Elvis Presley and other legendary figures painted on the walls.

This wasn't my first taste of local cuisine. Earlier in the week I had visited another Garifuna stronghold, the town of Hopkins, to have a cookery lesson with Gloria at Tucina Gloria. We made *hudutu* soup using only traditional utensils and methods. Gloria passed on her secret, 'Be sure to put passion into everything you cook!' Perhaps it was because of the effort that had been involved in making it, I decided that this was one of the most delicious meals I had ever tasted.

Back in Dangriga, we finished lunch and moved on to our final stop, the Gulisi Garifuna Museum, which has a primary school on its grounds that teaches lessons in the Garifuna language. I was met here by Wahrisie Elijio, who was, appropriately, wearing a yellow dress with black trim for the occasion. She gave me a personal tour of the museum, highlighting Garifuna history, music and educational principles. Several displays showed cooking utensils, including *matapi*, which are used to remove toxins from the cassava root before baking bread.

I was fascinated by a timeline in the museum that indicated an alternative history to the one widely told about the origins of the Garifuna. In 1311, it claimed, two expeditions travelled the Atlantic Ocean from West Africa under the orders of King Abubakari II of Mali to what we now know as the Caribbean island of Saint Vincent. There is some controversy about this, but whatever the history, there is no doubting the remarkable culture that it gave rise to.

The most important exhibit in the museum demonstrated the making of drums. It made me think back to Pen and to Daytha, who had carried on this tradition but also shaped it in their own image. It made me realise that you can't turn a living culture into an exhibit, as it's forever evolving, but you can meet and talk to the people who carry it within them: in their art, their food, their clothes, their music. That is the point of the Garifuna Trail, and in doing this, I had experienced a side to Belize every bit as unique as its reefs and Maya ruins.

BREATHLESS IN BOLIVIA

The *Daily Telegraph*, May 2018
*In the high plains of the Altiplano, Nigel Tisdall sleeps
in a hotel made of salt and learns where trains go to die.*

I have just drunk a bottle of tequila, smoked a hundred Woodbines and had my chest filled with quick-setting concrete. Well, that is how it feels when you fly into La Paz, 12,000ft up in the Bolivian Andes.

To get here I had endured a thirteen-hour flight from London to Buenos Aires, then a six-hour wait inside its rain-drenched airport, then a three-hour flight north to Santa Cruz for a crazy race through immigration, then another hour's flight up to the Bolivian capital. All that, just to land in a place that has run out of air. When I finally staggered into my room in the skyscraping Hotel Presidente, I didn't care whether I was going to my bed or my grave.

Next morning I woke with a head like lead, pulled back the curtains and swore. La Paz is one of the most audaciously located cities in the world, and the first view of it, like the altitude, is breathtaking.

The City of Our Lady of Peace was founded in 1548 by Spanish gold diggers who took shelter from the cold Andean winds in a 1,200ft-deep canyon fenced with snowy peaks. Today La Paz is Bolivia's third-largest city, a great bowl of humanity caught between the rocks where many residents commute to work by aerial cable car. More than a million Bolivians live here, and its thin-aired streets are a chaotic stage where office workers, bowler-hatted Aymara and puffing tourists endure their daily dramas against a backdrop of Baroque churches, shiny corporate headquarters and heap upon heap of shanty homes.

La Paz is bursting at the seams. No longer content to climb up the canyon walls, its impoverished suburbs are now spreading across the high plains of the Altiplano to the west. It was this vast and austere plateau that I had come to explore. This is Bolivia's historic heart, the roof of the New World, the eye of the Andes – and the glint in it is Lake Titicaca.

These fabled blue waters lie only 45 miles west of La Paz, but they could be on another planet. Driving up to the Altiplano, I felt a shock similar to emerging onto the open-air roof of a multistorey car park. Up here it is big country. The sky rolls on forever, and the light has a wintry clarity that induces a growing sense of omniscience. Nothing can escape your all-seeing eye – the mud-brick houses, the herds of llamas, the golden totora reeds from which the Uros make curvy canoes that have sailed Titicaca for millennia.

I was hooked. 'Head for Salar de Uyuni,' a friend had advised. So I flew 280 miles south to Potosí, the world's highest city, then caught a bus west. It's a six-hour ride to Uyuni, following a bumpy road that winds down the western slopes of the Cordillera Central, into a wild landscape of khaki hills dotted with llamas and abandoned adobe villages.

At the end of it stands a surreal railway junction town with gleaming Communist-style statues and empty streets as wide as motorways. Uyuni's star tourist sight is a sprawling train cemetery where lines of abandoned steam engines rust in the pitiless sun. Travellers who make it here tend to be committed high plains drifters, wilderness freaks keen to lose themselves in the elemental wonderland of the Salar de Uyuni.

Twenty-five thousand years ago this was a vast lake, but the sun has relentlessly boiled everything down to a sheet of salt flats covering an area almost as big as Northern Ireland. The Salar is Lake Titicaca in the future, a great white plate, flat and stark as an ice rink, clean as snow. Its surface is covered with a bas-relief of hexagons that feel as crisp and sharp as the frosting on a most excellent margarita.

The only thing to do in the Salar is to be in it. Drive across it, walk on it, dream with it. Forty miles west of Uyuni, I checked into a new hotel built entirely from its salt. The architects simply cut blocks out of the ground and piled them up as a child might build a toy house. I dined beside pillars of salt and slept on a bed of salt beneath a cupola made from more than three hundred salt cubes. Every now and again, I pressed a licked finger to the walls to check I wasn't hallucinating.

Uyuni has numerous small adventure companies offering tours by Land Cruiser into the Salar so I signed up for a three-day trip with Empresa Sol de Mañana, which turned out to be a mother-and-son team called Domy and Edwin.

He drove; she cooked; I chose the music. Small and wiry, Domy had a physical and spiritual toughness reflecting her Aymara ancestry. Edwin was chubbier, with the lazy confidence of a young Bolivian raised on American soaps. It was Domy who insisted we stop to make observances to Pachamama, the Earth Mother, and Edwin who had to carry them out. Solemnly he sprinkled each wheel of the 4WD with alcohol and coca leaves. Domy said a few words. Edwin took a sly swig from the bottle. Then we sped off into the wilderness.

I hadn't a clue what to expect. It certainly wasn't Colcha K, a bizarre military post run by Action Man conscripts, where an officer wrote down our names with a yellow crayon. Or the minimalist village of San Juan beyond. The only movement in its dusty streets came from pigs and gaggles of children wearing a school uniform of long white coats. Wandering around, I became convinced I had discovered a secret community of dwarf lab technicians.

San Juan had a church, a football pitch and a small hostel run by Roberto and Ricardo, a pair of dudes whom I never saw sober. They had bottles of stout, a log fire and a stack of Stones, Beatles and Pink Floyd tapes – not what I expected in the Bolivian desert.

At this point the volcanic cabaret began. We left San Juan before dawn, driving across the rocky plains as the sun ignited the peaks of the Andes like an altar boy lighting a row of candles. We had now crossed the width of the Altiplano and were heading into the mountains to find seven lakes renowned for the hues of their mineral- and algae-rich waters.

Out here God works with a limited palette. Laguna Colorada, the largest, is like a blood-red gash on a mustard canvas. Others have waters that are Arctic-blue, pencil-grey, pea-green. What looks like ice is actually gypsum; what seems a pink cloud turns into hundreds of flamingos. To get near these magnificent birds you have to creep up slowly, as if playing grandmother's footsteps, while at the same time moving fast enough to prevent your boots sinking into crimson mud. Just as you get close, the flamingos gracefully walk away in unison, luring their admirers even farther into the lake. I doubt there is a more romantic way to die.

Next to Laguna Colorada is a small electric power station with a few buildings where we all fell into bed wearing as many clothes as possible. I thought this was the end of our journey, but Domy had a suggestion. 'Do you want to see Laguna Verde?' It would take only another six hours to get there and back…

The last lake in this chain of Andean jewels proved worth the extra effort. Stepping out of the Land Cruiser, I was hit by a whirling scene of bright sunshine, roaring winds and scarlet flamingos. The lake's waters were jade, its shores as frothy as bubble bath. Beside it stood the perfect triangle of the 1,800ft Licancabur volcano, streaked with snow. It was the sort of lonely, holy place where, in Auden's wishful words, we all might 'clear from our heads the masses of impressive rubbish…'

Yet even here, in one of the most remote spots you could possibly fire yourself off to, there was a surprise. A large painted metal sign that exuberantly proclaimed 'Bolivia – Bienvenidos!'. What? I had travelled more than 6,000 miles looking for the end of things, and here was a sign suggesting I was only at the beginning.

Bolivia is like that: it knocks you dead on arrival, then lifts you into the clouds.

WHY I TRAVELLED TO RIO AND FOUND A LASTING LEGACY OF MUSIC AND COMMUNITY

*Shebs Alom traces the steps of a musical icon
in a place he helped put on the map.*

Growing up in the 1990s, I saw Brazil as the powerhouse of international football. When they won the 1994 World Cup, I recall everyone in school celebrating, scoring a goal, just as Bebeto did when he put his arms out, rocking them left to right, now known as the 'baby celebration'. I also grew up wanting to visit the country after Michael Jackson (MJ) went over to film his music video 'They Don't Care About Us'. I was and still am a massive MJ fan. I had the chance to visit back in 2018; here's why it was so memorable.

Rio was on my list of places to travel for two reasons: Christ the Redeemer (I was on a journey at the time, trying to see all the Seven Wonders of the World), and the Dona Marta favela which MJ made famous. His decision to film a music video there was controversial, sparking a debate about the international portrayal of urban poverty.

Ronaldo Cezar Coelho, the state secretary for Industry, Commerce and Tourism at the time, protested that such a video would damage the city's image. He told a local newspaper, 'I don't see why we should have to facilitate films that will contribute nothing to all our efforts to rehabilitate Rio's image'.

Another prominent individual, Cristina Becker of the Rio Convention Bureau, said: 'We've always oriented producers to show the good that Rio has. If Michael Jackson only wants to show the bad side, it's better that he not come.' Even the football legend Pelé went on record saying Jackson's filming would hinder their Olympic bid for 2004.

Fast-forward two decades, after both the 2014 World Cup final and the 2016 Olympics in Rio, the city is no longer so ashamed of its favelas. Thanks to MJ, Dona Marta is now a tourist hotspot.

Elias Dudre and his family have lived in Dona Marta for generations. I was lucky enough to meet Dudre, a local tour guide for the favela, and to be chauffeured around by him in late September 2018. He told me the favela has become internationally known due to MJ's video in 1995. 'Since Michael Jackson came here, many more have come to visit. Madonna, Vin Diesel and Paul Walker, who both filmed *Fast Five* here. Bradley Cooper came with his friends. There are so many other famous celebrities. Not to mention people like you, tourists from all over the world. I am so happy to have my home visited.'

I was delighted to hear this as, over the years, there have been problems relating to gang violence. But as Dudre explained to me, as long as you are taken on an organised tour or with someone known to the favela, you will have no problems.

My only request to Dudre was to show me all the spots Michael Jackson filmed in the video. He said that was not a problem… as long as I would go to his house for tea. Of course, I accepted.

Being shown around the favela, I found it hard to believe how the houses were built on top of one another. The colours of the building's exteriors made them look majestic. I visited local schools and met people who invited me for dinner. I made my way to the alleyways where Michael Jackson danced away and to the place where his statue now stands. There it was, arms out and sporting his iconic sunglasses. It was jaw-dropping. It is situated where you can see the magnificent Christ the Redeemer statue and the spectacular Sugarloaf Mountain on either side of the figure. A mural of MJ next to the statue is pretty impressive as well.

As Dudre explained, 'No matter the troubles here, no-one touches this statue. This is a symbol of greatness given to us by Michael Jackson. People regard this place as wholly sacred ground.' I understood the feeling, particularly as most of his dance sequences were filmed here.

After getting my MJ fix, I headed over to Dudre's house for tea. I felt at home, then he put on the music video 'They Don't Care About Us'.

When it was time for me to leave, I felt sad; this was the highlight of my visit to Rio. I thanked Dudre for showing me around and providing me with hospitality. He had only one request before I left: 'Please tell all your friends and family about Dona Marta and what life we have here. Maybe one day they will visit.' I said that of course I would, and next time I visited, could I stay for dinner? That is the deal, he said.

And those worries that the music video would harm Rio and Brazil's tourism with the poverty on display? It couldn't be further from the truth. Michael Jackson has opened the door to so many visitors from around the world. It's such an awe-inspiring experience to behold. I still have to pinch myself; I got to walk the same path Michael Jackson danced away.

MONTSERRAT, THE EMERALD ISLE
OF THE CARIBBEAN

*Laura McVeigh visits Montserrat in the
Leeward Islands to research her novel.*

It is 2016 and I am working on a novel set on the volcanic Leeward Island of Montserrat in the West Indies. Known as the Emerald Isle of the Caribbean, it is so-called for its historical links to Ireland. It is a lush green place, where St Patrick's Day is a time of full-on celebration, complete with Irish dancing and music. Places have Irish names such as St Patrick's, Kinsale and Cork Hill. Locals are proud of their heritage – Fitzpatricks, Kellys, Sweeneys, Rileys abound. And to this day even the distinctive lilt of Irish-English can be heard mixed with the melodic sounds of Montserrat Creole.

Intrigued by the Irish connection and the island's complex history, I find myself on what feels like the world's tiniest aeroplane (it fits the pilot, me, my young daughter, and two other intrepid travellers), circling over the rugged volcanic terrain and verdant island ridges. From above Montserrat looks 'like Jurassic Park', says my daughter, staring down at the lush hillsides, the jagged peaks and the swirling turquoise waters.

It is a small island, a mere 10 miles long and 7 miles wide, dominated by the Soufrière Hills volcano which has shaped not only the island's geography but its tragic history. The plane rattles as it lands, its wheels bouncing along the tarmac. When the door opens we all exhale a thankful breath and shakily jump down (there are no steps) into a blast of sticky Caribbean heat. We walk into the hangar that serves as the island's airport. A smiling local customs officer stamps our passports with a green shamrock. Above his head hangs a sign saying *Céad Míle Fáilte* ('Welcome' in Irish).

Outside in the humid evening air, one lone taxi hums, its driver (Daley, another nod to Ireland) waiting to take us to Olveston House. The island roads twist and turn, cut into the steep hillside; the verges full of lush tropical vegetation, exuberant hibiscus flowers and darting geckos. In my head a James Bond-style soundtrack is playing as the car sweeps round the hairpin bends, a salty sea breeze whipping through the open window.

In the 1980s and 1990s musicians flocked to the island to record at Air Studios, founded by legendary Beatles music producer George Martin. Paul McCartney, Elton John, Stevie Wonder, The Police and Dire Straits all recorded music in Montserrat, attracted by the privacy and the beauty of the tropical setting.

We arrive at Olveston House, outside Salem, just as night is falling. The colonial-style house, looking out over the misty island peaks and Caribbean Sea, was once George Martin's private residence and a popular island clubhouse of sorts for the musicians. Nowadays it is a welcoming, elegant guesthouse and restaurant, retaining its original charm and history. A white wooden balcony replete with wicker chairs surrounds the villa, set in lush tropical gardens.

A band plays in the gardens, the trees strung with warm twinkling bulbs. Tea lights glimmer on the table of the open-air terrace restaurant. A party of sorts is in full swing.

My daughter has fallen asleep on my shoulder in the taxi. The driver helps me lift her up the steps and into the house. We are quietly welcomed and taken to our room. It is modest, a little old-fashioned, but cool with a ceiling fan whirring overhead.

Inside the house lamps glow, and the walls are covered with black-and-white photographs of famous guests from Lou Reed to Eric Clapton, Mick Jagger to Sting. Some pictures capture moments in the recording studio, impromptu jam sessions.

The vibe is more private country villa than hotel. In fact there are only six guest rooms. There's nothing flashy about Olveston; it is all understated and authentic. I don't catch the name of the band, but the singer has a smoky, intimate voice, like Billie Holiday. The night air is full of the heady scent of jasmine, mixed with damp mineral earth, and vanilla-sweet frangipani in the palm-filled gardens. We soon fall asleep, exhausted from the day's travels.

In the morning, we stop on the terrace for breakfast and fuel up with coffee, fresh mango juice, fruit and cheese, while our taxi driver patiently waits. Then, we drive south to what was once the island's capital.

In 1995 the Soufrière Hills volcano started erupting, taking with it much of the southern side of the island. The capital, Plymouth, once a vibrant home to four thousand people and the commercial heart of the island, was devastated, covered in ash and pyroclastic flow. There is a wide exclusion zone in place, but scientific research continues and it is possible to see the Buried City with a guide. It is a sobering visit – homes with the doors left open, half-submerged buildings, cars in the empty streets covered in ash, an eerie stillness over everything – heartbreaking to witness so much loss and disruption of life trapped in time.

Banks of cloud wreathe the top of the Soufrière Hills as we leave behind the poignant exclusion zone and travel the hairpin bends back towards the north of the island. I want to take in the lush vegetation, the island's diverse flora and study its rainforest reserve, home to rich wildlife, including the endangered Montserrat oriole. We arrive at the Botanical Gardens. Like the Soufrière Hills, the gardens feature large in my novel, and I want to discover them up close. The gardens are testament to the dedication of the islanders to protect this remarkable landscape of rainforest, mangrove and tropical planting, a sign of life renewing and starting over.

We explore the island trails of the Centre Hills forest reserve, which lead us through pockets of ancient rainforest, bamboo groves, mossy, rocky paths, deep with ferns, cool mountain gullies and freshwater springs called *ghauts* – it's said if you drink from one, you'll return to the island. There are iridescent-hued blue mahoe trees, and trumpet trees that make my daughter laugh with their trumpet-shaped flowers. Mango, guava and papaya trees surround old, abandoned plantation houses. Higher up, ficus and silk cotton trees with their twisting roots thrive. A thick, heavy mist still lingers, turning the forest paths mysterious and other-worldly.

We make our way back to Salem, stopping at a roadside stall to buy sweet, smoky roast corn and a fresh coconut to drink, sliced open for us.

I feel steeped in the magic of the island, a wild yet welcoming place, little visited by tourists, cast somewhat adrift by its British caretakers. A different kind of Emerald Isle.

The novel has burst into life, fuelled by the sounds and sensations of the island visit. I want to stay longer, explore more, but my daughter falls ill with a high fever. I panic, knowing that the tiny plane is our only way to get her quickly to medical care on neighbouring Antigua. We are in luck, booking the last two free seats of the day, and carrying her against my shoulder, I wave goodbye to the still-smiling customs officer on our way out.

'*Go n-éirí an t-ádh leat!*' I call out in Irish. 'May luck be with you!' I wish him, as we board the plane one last time.

BARRY'S FLYING VISIT

Beastly Journeys, an anthology of travel tales, June 2018
*Adrian Phillips picks up a parasite during
his short stay in Ecuador.*

When did Barry first enter my life? Well, he may have been with our group when Fredy led us into the swamp on the hunt for anacondas. Or when we took that night walk through the grasping foliage and Fredy had to rescue us from the herd of wild pigs. I couldn't say for sure.

But we came together at some point during that rainforest expedition, and for a while we were inseparable. We remained together on the river journey back out of the jungle and on the flight home to the UK. I took him on walks around my local haunts and on evenings out in town.

And then, on a Saturday morning, as I sat dreaming in a chair, Barry poked his head out of my leg.

I should clarify: this wasn't like a scene in *Alien* when a slimy, toothy thing bursts from the body of an unsuspecting astronaut, and everyone's popcorn goes flying. Barry's emergence was a graceful flick, quickly out and in, so fast that I assumed it was a trick of the light. But, no, there he came again, a tentacle worming from the centre of an inflamed insect bite on my thigh. It was ghoulishly fascinating.

I knew Barry must be a rainforest parasite. Fredy entertained us over dinner with stories of parasitic larvae. He even described his favoured method of extraction. 'You need to make a special noise until the worm pops up,' he had advised, 'and then spit tobacco juice on it. The worm gets drunk' – he had rolled his eyes like an inebriated worm – 'and you can grab it!'

Unfortunately, I didn't have any tobacco juice to hand now, and – even if I had – I couldn't remember the special noise. And so I phoned the travel pharmacy on the high street. 'Good morning, I wonder whether you can help. I recently returned from Ecuador and I've noticed something moving in my leg.' 'Sorry? I thought you said *moving* in your *leg*.'

It became quickly evident that the removal of worms from legs wasn't an area of expertise for the lady at the travel pharmacy on the high street. 'Yes, there's something moving in my leg. It's white.' 'Ah, right. Hmmm. Would you hold the line?'

There followed some urgent, muffled conversation with a fellow expert at the travel pharmacy on the high street. A minute later, she was back. 'Hello? I've consulted my colleague, and we both feel you should go to the hospital immediately.' 'You don't have an ointment or something?' 'Errm, no.'

'And it's probably best not just to leave it?' 'No, probably best not.' 'Righto, thanks anyway.' 'No problem at all. Bye bye!' Then, in the space between receiver leaving her ear and hitting the cradle, I heard her say 'That's *disgus—*' My sense was that she was addressing her colleague rather than me.

It was on the drive to hospital that I christened my parasite 'Barry'. It felt right to give him a name, seeing as we were existing so intimately. But, more than that, I was beginning to feel a certain affection for the tiny chap. He'd come a long way. I admired his pluck.

After registering at the front desk of Northwick Park Hospital, I wedged myself between an old lady with her arm in a sling and a man with a grubby T-shirt riding high up his stomach.

'Don't expect to be seen quickly, dear,' said the old woman conversationally. 'I've been here two hours now, and...' '*Adrian? Adrian Phillips?*' said a nurse called Bob with a clipboard. 'Come with me, please.'

News of the case of the bloke with something living in his leg had obviously spread quickly among the hospital staff. Barry had star factor, and you don't keep a star waiting among the common herd.

My working theory was that Barry was a sand flea or 'jigger'. Jiggers lurk about in sandy soil until an unsuspecting host comes along. They then hop on, burrow head first beneath the skin, and generally set about making themselves at home, feeding on blood and posting their bodily excretions out of the hole.

I lay on the cubicle bed in my boxer shorts as Bob peered at my leg. The area in question certainly resembled images of sand flea infestations I'd found online: a reddish lump – or, to use the correct term, a 'warble' – with a dot of deepest black at its centre that would occasionally contract or dilate as the creature fidgeted inside. There were some nagging doubts, though, not least the absence of any reference to a white tentacle. But Bob had no time for nagging doubts and so, after watching a short video of a tribesman cutting a jigger out of his own toe with a thorn, he gathered his instruments and got to work.

Initially, Bob favoured the waiting game. He sat staring at the warble, a pair of tweezers poised in front of his face in anticipation of Barry's appearance; he reminded me of a heron about to strike. Barry, however, had become uncharacteristically shy. And Bob wasn't the patient type. After a while, he started pecking lightly at the hole with the tweezers, perhaps hoping Barry would pop up to see what all the commotion was about.

As it became clear that waiting and pecking weren't working, Bob elected for more forceful action. 'This might sting a bit,' he warned, as he injected anaesthetic around the lump, and began squeezing it between his thumbs. My eyes watered and the warble grew redder, the skin webbed with broken veins as Bob squeezed harder and harder. Still no Barry.

Bob considered things for a moment before producing an oversized needle with a hook at the end. He crouched over my leg, digging and squeezing as I winced at the ceiling. The hole was widening, filling with blood that he dabbed away with a scrap of white muslin. He continued for fifteen minutes in this way, working with the relish of the merchant of Venice claiming his pound of flesh, until the cloth was mottled red. Finally, he stopped and gazed down dumbly at his handiwork; the tip of his little finger could have fitted inside the wound he'd created. 'I don't think it's coming out,' he admitted weakly, his face pale, and retreated to confess to his boss.

My visit next day to the Hospital for Tropical Diseases came with a couple of bombshells. First, I discovered that – even with tobacco juice in short supply – Bob's approach was not recommended best practice for the treatment of parasites. 'A botfly larva should be teased out carefully!' exclaimed a horrified consultant called Lucy. And therein lay the second bombshell. Barry was a botfly not a jigger.

Lucy showed me a photo of a botfly larva, plump and anaemic, with hairs on its segmented body and a breathing tube protruding from its backside, which is what I had thought was its head squirming out of my thigh.

When a botfly egg comes into contact with skin, the larva hatches and eats its way into the host with sharp black fangs, gorging and growing to over an inch in length before exiting a few weeks later to complete its transformation into a fly. It's an animal that only a parent could love.

But you had to admit that 'Barry the botfly' was pleasingly alliterative, I thought, smiling to myself. It seemed meant to be.

I only hoped Barry could forgive me for mistaking his arse for his face.

'They've almost certainly killed it,' said Lucy, bringing me back abruptly to the matter in hand. 'We can't leave the body in there. You'll need an operation.'

No trace of Barry was ever found. The official verdict was that he'd been squished between Bob's thumbs and his juices absorbed by my body. But I prefer to believe he somehow made his escape when Bob's back was turned, ghosting from my life just as he'd ghosted into it. He certainly left his mark. The surgeon at University College London Hospital cut out an area two inches long and an inch wide in his search for any pieces of Barry, and the wound was left to heal naturally rather than stitched because of the risk of infection. It's an impressive scar. I'll show you some time.

A couple of months later, I met Fredy in a pub on the Strand. His rainforest tourism project had been shortlisted for an award by the British Guild of Travel Writers, and he'd flown across to attend a swanky champagne ceremony. I'd never seen anyone so out of place in a suit. Of course, I couldn't wait to tell him about Barry, and he listened to my story with chin propped in his leathered hand and brow furrowed in concentration. When I'd finished, he was silent for a while. And then, with a knowing shake of the head, he said, 'You really should have tried the special noise.'

FEARLESS BUT FRAGILE

City AM, 15 April 2012
Ben Westwood is mesmerised by the wildlife of
the Galápagos Islands, but chastened by the
archipelago's environmental challenges.

'How's the snorkelling?' I ask Christina as she emerges from the turquoise waters of Playa Cabo del Horno on the

Galápagos island of San Cristóbal. 'Quite good,' she replies with a shrug. 'I saw a sea turtle and a sea lion.'

Christina, a rather po-faced Dane who's been on the Galápagos a few weeks, is clearly not easily impressed, but I've just arrived, so I take the bit between my teeth and dive in. Sure enough, a 4ft sea turtle swims right past me followed by a baby. Spellbound, I follow them for a few minutes, receiving a nonchalant glance from the adult before it shakes me off by diving down to the murky depths and out of sight. If turtles could blow raspberries, I'm sure she was blowing one. The sea lion is nowhere to be seen, but I find her a little later, lounging on the beach drying off. As I click away with the camera, she opens her eyes lazily and lifts her head up as if to strike a pose, emitting a loud snort before returning to her snooze.

In the next few days, I discovered that Christina was right. By Galápagos standards, this was only a 'quite good' wildlife experience. The islands that captivated Charles Darwin in the 1830s, inspiring him to develop his famous theory of evolution, have been captivating visitors ever since. It's easy to see why; there was so much on offer that I didn't know which way to turn – sea lions, sea turtles, sharks and penguins underwater; iguanas, giant tortoises and blue-footed boobies on land. The miracles of evolution were everywhere.

What really makes these islands special is the attitude of the wildlife, from nonchalant turtles to curious boobies and downright naughty sea-lion pups. The lack of natural predators on the islands means that the wildlife has no fear of humans whatsoever. I discovered this the next day when I went snorkelling with dozens of sea lions at La Loberia. An enormous 8ft male streaked past me and started getting amorous with his mate. I tried to keep my distance because he was more than a little scary. Keeping my distance from the pups, however, proved impossible because they were so interested in me. They kept rushing towards me, clearly delighting in an impromptu game of peekaboo. After my initial nervousness I relaxed into it and started to play, following them around. This was their playground, after all.

I thought this was as good as it could get but there was more to come. Our next stop was a rock formation off the coast of San Cristóbal called León Dormido (sleeping lion). This is famous as one of the best snorkelling spots in the archipelago and a prime location to see reef sharks and hammerheads.

The snorkelling route was through a channel between two 500ft rock faces. It was an imposing setting and I had to remind myself that the sharks were harmless as I stepped into the dark waters. On our first swim through the channel, I didn't see much, but on the return journey, our guide pulled out a neat trick, banging his fists together underwater. The vibrations served their purpose and dark shapes began slowly rising. Being surrounded by reef sharks was rather different to being surrounded by sea lions, I discovered. The sharks were more interested in plankton than me and there was no peekaboo, but I was definitely OK with that.

Predictably the biggest threat the wildlife faces on the Galápagos is from humans. Any visitor cannot help but feel a certain amount of guilt that these islands have been so affected by tourism and accompanying immigration. Development has accelerated rapidly in recent years and the local population is still rising to some 33,000 residents. The biggest problems are too much traffic, a lack of adequate sewage treatment, and invasive species – everything from the pigs, dogs and rats that eat eggs, baby lizards and birds, to fruit trees which displace the endemic cacti that are the staple of giant tortoises. More than fifty Galápagos species are currently considered critically endangered, including giant tortoises, waved albatross, mangrove finches and pink iguanas.

Fortunately, organisations like the UK's Galapagos Conservation Trust are doing vital work to improve the archipelago's ecosystem. One of the trust's biggest current projects is to eradicate invasive species from the southern island of Floreana, and there have already been successes removing feral dogs, pigs and goats. Livestock are now fenced in, whereas previously they could roam free to wreak havoc. The latest project involves a huge operation to lay bait for mice and rats, while simultaneously capturing birds to protect them from eating the bait. The next step on Floreana is to reintroduce species including giant tortoises, Galápagos racer snakes and birds including vermilion flycatchers, mockingbirds and Darwin's finches.

Despite all the challenges, it's comforting to know that only 3% of Galápagos land is populated and one hundred Galápagos visitor sites comprise less than 1% of the total landmass. Half of this land is formed by the island of Isabela, and on the largest island in the archipelago I took a boat trip to see one of the smallest attractions – Galápagos penguins. At only 35cm tall, these endearing birds are one of the smallest penguins in the world and the only species in the northern hemisphere.

On my way back, I encountered a family of marine iguanas sunning themselves on the walkway. Some scurried away while others eyed me disdainfully. These amazing creatures are the only seafaring lizards in the world, living proof of evolution because they lived originally on land before adapting over time to find food in the ocean.

Isabela has six active volcanoes and some of the most dramatic landscapes in the Galápagos. The most popular hike is to Sierra Negra, the second largest crater in the world. The views were spectacular, as was the descent through yellow hills into the pungent sulphur mines. On the path back, we came across a tiny illegal immigrant in the shape of a field mouse. He sat there without a care in the world and even had the audacity to start climbing over my boots; he'd obviously adopted the friendly local attitude to humans. Rather like us, he meant no harm even though he had no business being there.

A visit to the Galápagos is both inspiring and chastening. Although the natural harmony has been disturbed, the archipelago is still a wonder to experience and local and international organisations are working hard to restore the balance of this fragile ecosystem. It will take time, though; evolution is, after all, a slow process.

FROM JAMAICA WITH LOVE

The *Daily Telegraph Travel*, 16 November 2014
*Jonathan Thompson discovers that it
all began with a naked girl on a beach.*

Peering down from the clifftop as she emerged from the waves into a pristine white bay, Ian Fleming's friend Ivar Bryce knew he'd found the spot. 'Tie it up tomorrow,' he said to the Jamaican fixer with him. 'Ian will adore this place.'

Bryce had first introduced Fleming to Jamaica three years earlier, during a wartime naval conference in Kingston. As their return flight took off, Fleming slammed his briefcase shut and turned to his friend. 'Ivar, I've made a great decision,' he said. 'When we've won this blasted war, I'm going to live in Jamaica. Just live in Jamaica and lap it up, and swim in the sea and write books.' Those books, of course, would become his bestselling James Bond novels.

But first that home would become Goldeneye – built on that clifftop overlooking the pristine white bay. This year (2014) marks the 50th anniversary of Fleming's death, but the house he built – rather like the super-spy he built there – is still going strong. Pre-production is well underway on Bond's latest movie outing, his 24th no less, but the little estate where he was conceived continues to grow too. And now a significant new book, *Goldeneye: Where Bond Was Born: Ian Fleming's Jamaica*, by historian Matthew Parker, looks to analyse the close links between the two.

'Would the books have been born if I had not been living in the gorgeous vacuum of a Jamaican holiday?' wrote Fleming. 'I doubt it.' But Parker goes further, arguing that Fleming's love for Jamaica was so great that it is stamped throughout Bond's DNA.

At the heart of this love affair, of course, was Goldeneye, midway along Jamaica's north coast, next to the pretty little banana port of Oracabessa. Fleming designed the house himself, religiously travelling here for two months every winter between 1946 and his death in 1964. A sleek, U-shaped bungalow with glassless windows looking out across the Caribbean, Fleming named it Goldeneye after a wartime plan he'd helped devise for the protection of Gibraltar, but also as a nod (or wink) to Oracabessa itself, which translates as 'Golden Head'.

Now, as then, Goldeneye is a wonderful spot, with a quaint sunken garden on the cliff edge (where Fleming would take his breakfast every morning), and thirty-two steps leading down to his private beach. Naked girl or not, Bryce was right: Fleming *did* adore this place. But what he loved most of all was the reef, just 20 yards from the shore, which teemed with 'colour and danger'. As Parker explains, this reef fuelled countless Bond scenes, from the dramatic underwater action of *Thunderball* to character descriptions in many of the other novels. In *Casino Royale*, for example, the villainous Le Chiffre watches Bond during the pivotal card game 'like an octopus under a rock'.

On one occasion during a Jamaican sojourn, Fleming – an employee of the *Sunday Times* during his 'real life' in London – dropped a dead donkey off the reef, to see what would happen. The resulting sound when a huge shark arrived and tore into the carcass, 'a terrible snuffling grunt', was then used to describe the similar demise of Mr Big in *Live and Let Die*.

Sadly, the reef is not as vibrant as it once was, but in recent years local charities including the Oracabessa Fish Sanctuary have been making major inroads into returning it to its former glory (including an impressive 1,300% increase in marine life since May 2011). As a result, snorkelling among the kaleidoscopic schools of angel, doctor and parrot fish here, as Fleming himself did on a daily basis, is a major treat. It's hard not to hum John Barry's famous Bond theme while gliding up and down the coral, or cast a wary glance over one's shoulder for any harpoon-wielding henchmen.

Today Goldeneye is a luxury boutique hotel, with eighteen well-appointed cottages scattered tastefully to the west of the main rocky promontory. The gazebo Fleming constructed later in life, to write undisturbed by his family is now a fine dining restaurant; to the west, salt- and freshwater infinity pools flank Bizot, a breezy beach bar.

When Fleming lived and wrote here, impressively churning out a Bond novel every winter from his redwood desk, he was also part of what was dubbed Jamaica's 'Gold Coast glitterati'. Contemporaries with homes here included Ivor Novello, Errol Flynn, Lord Beaverbrook and, above all, Fleming's closest friend on the island, Noël Coward.

Nicknamed 'The Master', Coward was inevitably at the centre of any hijinks within the group and a frequent visitor to Goldeneye after building two properties himself nearby: 'Blue Harbour' along the coast and 'Firefly' in the lush, jungle-bedecked hills above.

Today, Firefly and Goldeneye are both owned by legendary Island Records music producer Chris Blackwell, and guests at the latter are welcome to explore the former – which remains exactly as Coward left it on his death in 1973, and boasts some of the most spectacular views in the Caribbean.

Fleming and Coward particularly loved rafting on Jamaica's Rio Grande river – an activity started by Errol Flynn, who noticed locals shipping bananas from the highlands down to Port Antonio this way and asked for a ride. Soon, all the Gold Coast glitterati were doing the same, taking around four hours to descend the Rio Grande, often with elaborate picnics. On one occasion, Fleming's wife Ann was riding alongside Evelyn Waugh and a 'stupendous' lunch of 'wine packed in biscuit tins, cold roast fowls and legions of boiled eggs' when their bamboo raft overturned. Waugh – in blue silk pyjamas and a pink-ribboned panama hat – was forced to swim for the shore, much to the amusement of Fleming and Coward.

Rafting the Rio Grande – which Fleming described as 'an enchantingly languid… elegant and delicately romantic adventure' – remains excellent fun today (although the cold roast fowls are harder to come by). Fleming's favourite boatman, Red Grant, is long gone, but his name lives on in villainy as the main protagonist in the fifth Bond novel (and second film) *From Russia with Love*.

Jamaica's north coast is peppered with other landmarks from the 007 books and films – particularly the three stories set on the island: *Dr No, Live and Let Die*, and *The Man with the Golden Gun*. A twenty-minute boat ride from Goldeneye is Laughing Waters beach, where Ursula Andress emerged from the surf during the first movie, doing her best impersonation of Botticelli's Venus.

Nearby is cascading Dunn's River Falls, now one of the most popular tourist destinations in the Caribbean, where Sean Connery's Bond and Andress took a dip in the waterfall, and hundreds of visitors now do the same every day. Just off the coast at pretty Port Maria (where Fleming and Ann were married in 1952), sits Cabarita Island – the prototype for Mr Big's 'Island of Surprises' in *Live and Let Die*. Meanwhile, the gates of 'Swamp Safari' still say 'Trespassers Will Be Eaten', exactly as they did when Roger Moore's 007 escaped gun-wielding goons by leaping on the backs of crocodiles to safety.

Lit in the afternoon by a warm apricot glow, Jamaica's Gold Coast was an enchanted oasis for Ian Fleming: a place of recovery, sanctuary and creativity while London shivered itself through winter and 'people streamed miserably to work, their legs whipped by the wet hems of their mackintoshes'. The great storytellers, the Cowards and the Flemings, may be gone, but everything that inspired the Master and Commander remains. Goldeneye, Bond and the magical corner of the Caribbean that created them both live on. Here amid the 'peace and silence and cutoffness' that Fleming so adored, is the perfect place to escape when the world is not enough.

MY SAINT LUCIA: POET DEREK WALCOTT

The Observer, **January 2010**
Antonia Windsor interviewed Nobel laureate Derek Walcott about his Saint Lucia island home. This was published on his eightieth birthday in 2010 and Walcott died in 2017.

My heart has been pounding more than once this holiday: as I zip-wired through the rainforest, and hiked up the steep rocky path of one of the world's largest volcanic plugs. But now the racing heartbeat has nothing to do with exercise. I am sitting in a parked car on a dirt path. Below me is a cluster of buildings above a brilliant blue Caribbean Sea. This is Derek Walcott's Saint Lucian home and I am plucking up the courage to walk down.

The Nobel laureate is considered the Caribbean's foremost poet and playwright, and has put his island on the literary map in work that explores the impact of Caribbean colonisation, giving voice to the West Indian people – and celebrating their culture and landscapes. Next Saturday is his eightieth birthday and he will be playing host to other literary greats including Irish poet Seamus Heaney and African playwright Wole Soyinka. I intend to get a preview of what Walcott is planning for his guests, and his recommendations for what to see and do in Saint Lucia.

This hilly volcanic island belongs to Walcott in the way Gabriel García Márquez possesses South America or Salman Rushdie's thumbprint is on India. In his 1973 verse autobiography *Another Life*, he tells of the vocation he felt to 'name' Saint Lucia – this 'virginal, unpainted world' that was missing from the history books, where there were 'forests of history thickening with amnesia'. His birthplace has been the backdrop to many of his works, most notably his 1990 epic poem *Omeros*, in which he reimagines Homer's *Odyssey* as the tale of two Saint Lucian fishermen.

Walcott is wary of journalists and had initially barked at me on the phone. However, when he realises it is his island I want to talk to him about, he becomes an affable host, offering me rum punch and inviting me to join him and his partner Sigrid for a swim and lunch.

Later, we pack deckchairs into the boot of a jeep and Walcott climbs into the back, grumbling as his partner Sigrid drives over rough ground on a short cut to the beach. 'Derek's son Peter calls this bit Serengeti,' she jokes, and there is a whiff of Africa about the place: a couple of horses stand like wary antelope under a calabash tree. Many of the roads were like this when Walcott was growing up.

'We didn't travel much,' he says. 'We went to Soufrière, where the Pitons [the island's twin peaks] are, but the road from the capital, Castries, was torturous, so we went by boat. It's a terrific journey.' His grey-blue eyes dance at the thought. 'That's what I'll be doing with Wole and Seamus. It's a hell of a trip, coming in under the Pitons.'

Walcott also plans to take his guests to a favourite restaurant, Dasheene, at the Ladera resort above Soufrière: 'I know the chef there, and the view's incredible.' 'It's my favourite place,' says Sigrid. 'We stayed there a few nights when Derek was working on the film version of his play *Ti-Jean and His Brothers*.'

I go there the following night. Chef Orlando Satchell, British of Caribbean parentage, cooks a menu that combines fresh produce, traditional recipes and international know-how. Dishes include fried green tomato and plantain tart with goat cheese salad and guava balsamic, and chicken stuffed with plantain mousse served with a sweet potato dauphinoise.

I stay a night at this retreat, where the rooms have just three walls, and each has its own plunge pool, a playground for bugs and birds, which you can shoo with your complimentary water pistol if they get too close to your biscuits. From here, you can take a guided hike up Gros Piton, which Walcott often refers to in his work ('In the mist of the sea there is a horned island/with deep green harbours'). It is a steep climb, and will make you pant, but the views over the lush rainforest interior with its white sand-fringed edges are worth the effort.

Walcott now lives just outside the northern town of Gros Islet, where he set much of *Omeros*. 'They have the jump-up on a Friday night,' Sigrid says as we drive. 'It's a big street party, with stalls of barbecued food and lots of music and dancing.' I've been to a similar Saturday night in Dennery, on the east coast, where Walcott used to visit an aunt as a boy. I remark on the suggestive dancing. 'Of course the dances are sexual,' says Walcott. 'That's what's great about them – but there is wit in the movement: it is a parody of the act.'

In daylight it's hard to imagine such raucous partying; the village seems a world away from the tourist developments at nearby Rodney Bay. Men swig from bottles of Piton beer on the first-floor verandas of wooden buildings that tell of the island's colonial past. The French claimed Saint Lucia in 1635, with the British hot on their heels. The island changed hands between the two powers fourteen times before the British finally wrested control in 1814, running it as a colony until it won independence in 1979. Walcott's house overlooks Pigeon Island, an outcrop that was once a fortress and is now a national park. He stages a harrowing scene in *Omeros* here, imagining slave ancestors building the fort for the British Admiral Rodney, and recommends a visit.

Any other suggestions? 'The riding here is great. Have you been riding?'

There are stables in Gros Islet, and a couple of days later I take a gentle trek to a little beach at Cas en Bas. Here, the guide removes the saddle and coaxes my horse into the sea. I feel like I'm in a seventies B-movie, sitting in my bikini on the damp flank of a black horse in an eau-de-nil sea. I can't quite imagine Heaney and Soyinka riding bareback with Walcott, but you never know.

He recommends the Royal by Rex at Rodney Bay. Walcott likes it because it is one of the few hotels that isn't all-inclusive, allowing him to dine at his favourite places on what he terms 'restaurant row', just behind the hotel.

'There's a very good Chinese – Memories of Hong Kong – and a fine Indian.'

Walcott believes all-inclusive holidays are bad for local businesses, and this isn't the only gripe he has with the tourist industry: 'All the building that is going up is absentee-ownership. It's another plantation culture.'

Today, we are having lunch at home. Walcott sits at the wooden table on the veranda with a big bowl of mashed avocado and starts mixing in capers and cassava flour. It's his own recipe. Sigrid brings out spiced beef stew, braised purple cabbage, boiled breadfruit, rice and peas – and it's all delicious.

This is my second taste of traditional island food. My first was at a gem of a restaurant near Laborie in the south of the island called Debbie's Place, where with every main course Debbie brings dish after dish of side orders. Go for lunch, preferably having skipped dinner the night before, and you can enjoy the backyard atmosphere all afternoon.

'Isn't this just marvellous?' Walcott says suddenly. And I look out at a scene that might have been enhanced by Photoshop: the blues of pool, sea and sky, the whites of sunloungers, egrets and scudding clouds, all framed by the varying greens of lawn, palms and the 'twin-humped promontory' of Pigeon Island.

It's easy to understand why Saint Lucia is the palette Walcott always returns to.

End note: The Rex Resort is now the Royalton Saint Lucia, an all-inclusive hotel.

NORTH AMERICA

BROKEBANKER MOUNTAIN

TNT Magazine, **April 2005**
Sarah Tucker discovers that Canada's cowboy country is a
life-changing pocket of peace among the Rockies...
Which might explain all the ex-London bankers.

'We get lots of stressed-out types here,' says Mac McKenny, a silver-haired John Wayne type – same walk, same handsome, chiselled looks, with a charismatic glint to match – who has been running the Homeplace Ranch for more than forty years.

'Real city slickers. They turn up burnt out, uptight and unsmiling. But, by the end of the first day, they're grinning from ear to ear, at peace with the world, a bit saddle-sore, but much happier with life and themselves. It's good to watch.'

It might be 6am, but here at Homeplace, a working horse and guest ranch in Alberta, Canada's high cattle country – 31 miles southwest of Calgary – the early hour doesn't seem so bad. After all, the area was called Paradise by the Native Americans, before wagons brought new settlers to the untamed land in the mid-1800s. Here in the foothills of the Rocky Mountains, at an elevation of 4,900ft, the air is that bit fresher, the colours somehow sharper. *Brokeback Mountain* was filmed in Alberta, so imagine the movie's sweeping vistas and you're almost there.

Looking out of my cabin window, I watch the horses, perhaps twenty of them, slowly walking out through the forest trees and into the fields, against the dramatic backdrop of the Rockies. Each animal walks in silence, as though drawn by invisible threads, to the ranch house where the wranglers have started preparing the saddles for the day.

Once zipped into my fleece – one made in Canada, because they understand cold in this country – I take a walk around the ranch with Mac. After starting out as a successful advertising executive, Mac turned his back on the rat race and bought the ranch. He continues to ride and lead groups even though he is now in his seventies.

'I prefer the company of horses to people sometimes,' he says as we groom a horse called Dave. 'At least you know why they bite you.'

The simple life in his own private idyll has given Mac plenty of time to philosophise. 'The secret to happiness is to have something to do, have someone to love and have something to look forward to,' he says. He's keen to share the knowledge: a plaque on the stable door is engraved with this piece of wisdom.

It's not just the guests who have found peace in Mac's slice of paradise. Jane, a ranch staff member who cleans rooms and helps with meals, was an accountant in London as recently as last year. 'I got fed up of London,' she tells me. 'I would have a hundred pounds in my pocket on Saturday morning and by midday it had gone, and I didn't know what I'd spent it on. Here, money has little meaning. It's all about the quality of life, and I had none at home.'

Ed and Mike, the wranglers who care for the horses, are both ex-London bankers. 'I wouldn't go back there for all the money in the world,' says Mike, who used to work at Deutsche Bank.

Together with being the perfect escape from the frenetic pace of big-city life, Homeplace is also a great place to start for those who have always fancied riding through rolling hills but have little experience with horses.

I meet up with a group of five others, all ages, all abilities, who tuck into their homemade fry-up of eggs, bacon and beans before the day's ride. We've all been tested for our abilities on our horse in advance – there's a wooden horse in the yard that Mac nicknames Woody, and he and his wranglers watch how each one of us gets on and off. 'We can tell what you can do by how you sit,' he explains.

Mac also has a list of dos and don'ts to make sure the horses are handled with care. 'Don't shout round the horses, they will kick and bite. Don't go straight up to a horse and pat it on the nose, approach it gently from the side and talk softly. Always be aware in what order your horse should go on the trail. They know where they should go, but do you? If you don't and try to lead them when you shouldn't, chaos will break loose. Horses know their place.'

Anything else? 'Don't pull the reins too tight. In Europe you pull the reins too tight. The horse knows where you want it to go. You don't need to shout, just whisper to it.'

Mac tells me that he has three priorities in his ranch: the safety of the guests, the safety of the horses, and that the guests enjoy themselves. In the thirty years since he opened his ranch to the public, he seems to have got his priorities right – more than 80% of his guests are returners.

He chooses a horse called Favour for me. She's a strong beast, but will do as she's told, if she is told in a strong voice. Favour also has no stirrups, so the only thing that keeps the saddle on is my gripping like crazy with my thighs.

Things go well to start. Favour does me a favour by not being nervous, jittery or aggressive, and I'm overwhelmed by the beauty of the surroundings, spotting wild deer, hawks and falcons hovering overhead. It goes some way towards taking the edge off the ever-present threat of grizzly bears that wander the forests around the ranch and have been known to raid the larder.

Of course, I forget to grip and gradually ever so slowly I slide down the side of Favour – as if I will just keep going and do the complete circle, coming up the other side. The horse stops, and could have kicked and killed me, but as Mac says, 'She's a good horse. She realised she's cleverer than you are.' Thanks, Mac.

TRACKING POLAR BEARS AND PIONEERS

Wanderlust, Spring 2010
Anthony Lambert visits the pioneer Western settlement
on Hudson Bay in search of polar bears
and the legacy of its founders.

'Are you sure you want to get out?' asked Mark Ingebrigtson laconically as I was about to leave his car to photograph huskies at Bird Cove. I hadn't spotted the dozing bear just yards away, its clotted-cream-coloured coat blending seamlessly with the spume along the shore and the light covering of snow on the pale grey rocks. Like all the polar bears I was to see over the following week, it was indifferent to our presence.

I had arrived in Churchill on the southwestern corner of Hudson Bay by train from Manitoba's capital, Winnipeg. There is no better introduction to the vast, sparsely populated tracts of forest and muskeg that follow the fertile strip of prairie when heading north. It's a slow journey, entailing two nights in a sleeping car, and the reason is evident as the train crawls past some upturned freight cars in the boggy ground beside the line.

The swampy ground is colonised by willow and black spruce, leaving the drier ground to white spruce and poplars. Beaver trails weave through the rushes to open pools and the tangle of a dam. A narrow gap between the trees indicates a trap line, worked by residents of the tiny community that huddles round a clapboard church in a forest clearing. The trees shrink and shorten as the train eases north, and the tripod telegraph poles testify to the ferocity of the winds that tear across this flat land.

The gentle progress was welcome: sleep came more easily, and the convivial crew and passengers made for leisurely mealtimes in the dining car, listening to Ute from Bremen talk about her fascination for deserts and her camel treks with the Tuareg. Or Simon and Nan who in 1978 had bought a $500 Mini in Sydney, driven it across the Nullarbor Plain and then through southeast Asia, Pakistan, Afghanistan and on through Europe to Britain.

The train arrived in Churchill at dawn, the strengthening grey light revealing a town of snow-covered low-rise buildings on a grid of broad streets. Towering over them is the immense bulk of the grain terminal, from which the first cargo of prairie wheat was shipped in 1931 after completion of the railway. Churchill has had to reinvent itself over the centuries, from its birth as a centre of the fur trade, through the Cold War years when the area was home to thousands of military personnel testing equipment in extreme conditions, to today's incarnation as 'polar bear capital of the world'.

To give me an introduction to the area, Mark Ingebrigtson drove me round the few roads before they petered out – there is no road access to Churchill. A few miles out of town and blowing up a cloud of snow in our wake, we passed the long-abandoned, gaunt military blocks and reached Bird Cove where a musher keeps his dogs and I had my first unforgettable sight of a polar bear in the wild.

The almost hourly importance of weather is impressed on visitors when they call at the Parks Canada office in the restored railway station. Heritage Presenter Duane Collins has the ability to deliver such lugubrious forecasts as 'bucketloads of misery coming sideways from the sky' in such a way that laughter is the only response. Parks Canada arranges talks in the lecture theatre almost every day, and it was an evening talk about the impact of scurvy on the first explorers of Hudson Bay that encouraged me to visit Churchill's oldest structure and one of Canada's most extraordinary places.

Situated on an isolated peninsula, Prince of Wales Fort was built by the Hudson's Bay Company (HBC) between 1732 and 1771 with stone walls 37–42ft thick. The storeroom, workshop and accommodation blocks survive to first-floor level in a central area sunk below the artillery platforms. While ice is forming at the onset of winter it can be reached only by air, so Duane Collins and I hitched a lift with Chuck Burke who had flown helicopters for the UN in Somalia.

From the air, the sea is a grey-brown with scummy foam rippling along the rocky shoreline. We circled the fort a couple of times to check for bears. Duane had cartridges as well as cracker shells for his gun, since the good bear cover around the fort could result in an uncomfortably close meeting.

The emotions of newly arrived HBC men must have been in turmoil as they stood before the gated entrance and regarded their new home. A more desolate and inhospitable spot is hard to imagine. Even the man who recommended the fort be built here, Captain James Knight, wrote of the site in 1717 that he had 'never See such A Miserable Place in all my life'.

Yet its bleakness and the challenges those early settlers faced make it a fascinating place to visit and wonder at the endurance of early HBC recruits, mostly from London and the Orkneys. In winter they had to contend with cold so intense that a man woke to find his hair frozen to the wall, and when officers tried to commemorate the coronation of George II 'good port wine froze in the Glass as soon as pour'd out of the bottle'. And that was inside. In summer they were plagued by black fly and mosquitoes whose bites could soon reduce the face to 'nothing in the World but knotts & bumps'.

The almost square fort with arrowhead-shaped bastions is all the more incongruous for being unmistakably influenced by the great French military engineer Vauban, making it one of the most advanced forts in North America. Yet it was surrendered to three French warships in 1782 without a shot being fired, when the governor, Samuel Hearne, recognised that resistance was futile: none of the fort's thirty-nine men had been trained to fire the fort's forty-two cannon, each of which required a crew of ten to twelve men. Most of the guns can still be seen at the fort.

Curiously the early journals and diaries of the company men seldom mention white bears as they called them. Yet today visitors in October and November are almost guaranteed to see the polar bears that wait for the ice to form so that they can resume hunting for ringed seals, their primary food source. The bears congregate around Churchill because they know this is the first part of the bay to freeze up.

Most visitors see polar bears from specially built tundra buggies resembling something out of *Star Wars*. Dwarfing buses, they are built on airport fire-tender chassis and have seats for up to forty people, with a propane gas heater, toilet and open rear viewing platform. Their vast tyres weave through an almost flat landscape of innumerable small lakes fringed with willow. The short growing season and brutal climate mean that even small trees can be over 120 years old.

I spent a day on the tundra with natural scientist David Hatch, who has been coming to Churchill for forty-two years and leads parties in search of bears each winter. It wasn't long before we had our first sighting, of a huge recumbent bear in a typical posture of head resting on a paw while David quietly shared his knowledge with me.

The slow deliberate movements of the bear and its languid yawns made it hard to visualise him moving at 50 kilometres per hour in pursuit of the quarry. They can surprise a resting seal by climbing onto the ice floe or waiting patiently by an air hole gnawed by the seal. A mother with two cubs may wait beside three adjacent holes, the young cubs fidgeting around their holes and unintentionally sending the seal to the quiet hole beside which the mother is waiting motionless. The bear will sink its teeth into the seal's head and lift it out through the strength of its powerful neck and shoulders.

Another person who first visited Churchill decades ago and fell in love with the austere beauty of the place is Bill Calnan from New Jersey. We met at St Paul's Anglican church where he gives weekly talks. A natural raconteur, Bill entertained the audience with stories of the search for a Northwest Passage, leading up to a *coup de théâtre* when he switched on a light behind a beautiful stained-glass window, sent in a barrel of molasses to the HBC church at York Factory by Lady Franklin in memory of her husband, Sir John Franklin, and his lost expedition of 1847. In 1967 the window was airlifted from the abandoned York Factory and placed in St Paul's.

My last night was Halloween, and bear patrols were mounted at strategic points around the town to safeguard trick-or-treaters, though the –25°C plus wind chill deterred all but the hardiest. Bears that wander through town have to be sedated and taken to a hangar-like compound managed by Manitoba Conservation.

On my last morning I watched a sedated bear being placed in a burlap bag for a lift by helicopter up Hudson Bay to Seal River. Once there, a biologist would wait near the bear until the sedative had worn off to make sure there was no ill effect. A large crowd had gathered to watch the lift. As a symbol of the impact of climate change took to the sky and whirled into the grey sky, many must have been wondering how long these creatures have left in their extraordinary wilderness.

THE LEVIATHANS OF SAN IGNACIO

Sunday Times Magazine, September 1990
Brian Jackman has a desert encounter down Mexico way.

Already we had spotted the far-off plumes of spouting grey whales. Like us, many were heading for their winter home in Laguna San Ignacio. The entrance is a sailor's nightmare of pounding surf and treacherous shoals, but once inside, its waters spread and flatten out, spilling inland for 25km towards the sombre volcanic peaks of the Santa Clara mountains.

The lagoon is a magical place of tidal channels and shining sandbanks, an oasis of marine life in the Mexican desert. Here live not only the grey whales but also dolphins, sea lions and a whole host of seabirds.

Here we anchored as the breeze died, and the lagoon became a burnished mirror. But out in the surf where the sun was setting, a whale breached six times in succession, flinging its huge body halfway clear of the water before falling back in a crash of spray. And as we watched, we could hear the luxurious sighs of other whales as they surfaced and could see their white spouts rising and falling in the windless air.

Next morning I went beachcombing along the edge of the lagoon. The desert air was cold and clean, but the sun was shining, and I walked for miles, barefoot in the creaming tide. An osprey flew overhead, clutching a fish in its talons, and a solitary coyote trotted away into the sandhills. On that lonely shore, among the smooth driftwood and bleached bones of long-dead whales, his and mine were the only footprints.

Back on board there was much jubilation. One of the skiffs had gone out with Greg, a laid-back Californian crewman, and had even managed to touch a whale. They were ecstatic. Even the laconic Greg was grinning under his sombrero.

At dusk the moon rose, ripe and orange over the Vizcaino desert. It was the time of the spring tides, and the water ran past our bows like a river, pulling the anchor chain until it was as taut as an iron bar. The whales had been late arriving this year but now more were coming in with every tide.

For three days we stayed at that enchanted anchorage, and all the time the whales grew increasingly more tolerant, regularly allowing us within a skiff's length. When they spouted, a fine spray drifted over us, misting the lenses of my binoculars. And when they 'spy-hopped', standing on their tails to get a better look at us, it was impossible not to feel one's senses reaching out to them.

Who, watching those strange, monolithic snouts rising so trustingly into the air, could fail to be profoundly moved, knowing how cruelly we have persecuted these huge, innocent creatures down the centuries?

The voyage, begun in a spirit of adventure and curiosity, had ended as a kind of pilgrimage. Like penitents seeking absolution from the sins of our fathers, we had sought and found forgiveness among the leviathans of San Ignacio.

DEFINITELY MOBY

Sunday Herald Magazine, November 2000
*A slightly queasy Simon Heathcote tracks a
boyhood obsession from London's Natural History
Museum to the biggest mouth in Monterey.*

A diverse, if slightly desultory-looking, crowd gathers at the back of Randy's Fishing Trips awaiting the imminent arrival of a date with destiny. A Hindu woman, eyes battened down by too much kohl, an Englishman, a Scot and a handful of Americans avoid each other's gaze; all eyes are on a brown baby pelican, an unwitting cynosure, being fed anchovies by a teenager in high heels in a daily ritual that fixes trippers as they loll awkwardly, hoping for the next boat.

Sanctuary comes in late and starts offloading its passengers. Heidi, the former captain but happily demoted for the day as partner Steph takes over the wheelhouse, gives the pep talk. There is a lot said about seasickness; a recent bowl of clam chowder now seems foolhardy.

Two hours earlier, at Monterey's tourism office, the chance of sighting any whales had looked slim. October is the end of season, they said, and any trips would have left by 9am. A compensatory clam chowder seems no bad thing, but the news on Fisherman's Wharf is hopeful: a number of boats are out and will be going out again.

Thirty years earlier, in unflattering grey flannels, I had craned my neck to gawp at a model of the largest creature on earth, suspended from the ceiling of London's Natural History Museum. The blue whale held endless fascination due to its sheer size and power, gentle intelligence and unwitting defiance of current politically correct 'small is beautiful' musings.

Balaenoptera musculus once grew to 110ft and is the largest mammal mankind has ever seen, but the chances of spotting one are remote. Whalers slaughtered the biggest, leaving a decimated population of 80-footers. Around five to ten thousand remain, but innate shyness and awareness of man's predation combine to keep this great creature mostly out of sight.

But not today. Not far out to sea, we are told, a blue whale was briefly spotted during the previous three-hour cruise and Heidi and Steph – a lean, moustachioed former private eye and leg amputee – are eager to get back out. We are lucky and we know it. Monterey Bay is more likely to yield orcas, humpbacks or minkes at this time of year in what is America's largest marine sanctuary in an underwater fissure the size of the Grand Canyon.

As we pile down the wharf's wooden steps and on to Monterey's only non-fishing, non-smoking whale-watching boat, the port's resident pelicans watch in silence. Mute sentinels flown in from prehistory. In the near distance, a small army of barking sea lions hangs around hopefully at the base of the Monterey Fishing Company, or on the lone rocks that *Sanctuary* circumnavigates on her passage from the harbour to the open sea.

Six of us race for the best views, lunging, politely, for the makeshift fibreglass seats outside the wheelhouse and already pulling on coats to beat the coming spray. Unusually, it is the Germans who wind up sitting on the deck. But no-one's complaining, for there is little to complain about. On a cloudless autumn day, California's central coast is easy on the eye.

Monterey has too much false front for some. Fisherman's Wharf is the place for tacky souvenirs and good eating. *Sanctuary* leaves it all behind and, as the land recedes, the vista of the Pacific widens to embrace sun, sea and sky. On the way out to the deep waters, we pass Lover's Point. It is, says Steph, great on a moonlit night with a bottle of wine and a lover, or two bottles of wine and someone you just met.

Cannery Row, once the sardine capital of the world and famous thanks to the novel of the same name by John Steinbeck, comes up on the port side looking redundant and sad. As we leave the last rocky outcrop, the swell of the water becomes more violent, showering us with spray and the bonhomie of shared experience. Some of us even let out the odd yelp. It seems the right thing to do, a communal language of awe on what should be the memory of a lifetime. But spontaneity breaks through any remaining reserve when, standing above the wheelhouse, Heidi screams out the first sighting.

There, almost straight in front of us, and a quarter of a mile in the distance, a misty plume of water and air rises from the surface of the water. My stomach turns; the hunt is on.

Ahead of us, *Magnum Force* is nearer the whale but with a name like that perhaps shouldn't be. Even Clint Eastwood, who lives a stone's throw away in Carmel, might have misgivings about this great peaceful leviathan being tracked by a boat named after violence. *Sanctuary* slows, keeping a respectful distance. Whales should never be approached head-on or too close.

Meanwhile, this 80-footer descends into the depths of the canyon in search of krill and we wait, like Dreyfuss, Shaw and Scheider in some scene from *Jaws*, to see what it will do next. Years ago, blue whales numbered around 200,000 here, but despite whaling laws, numbers have never recovered. Nowadays, they usually roam in pairs, toothless warriors, filtering four tons of small crustaceans daily to feed a 2,000lb heart.

Time ticks on. Eleven minutes go by before Heidi screams again, pointing 100m out as *Balaenoptera musculus* betrays itself with a luminous blue-green shimmer beneath the waves. The whale teases us with an extended glimpse of its liver-coloured back and a disproportionately small dorsal fin, then dives again.

Sanctuary turns full circle as our experienced skippers accurately predict the location of the next sighting. Thirteen minutes pass as our quarry pops up on the port side, tantalisingly close. A second dive still fails to show us its gigantic tail. *Magnum Force* heads in, leaving the ocean free of objects, the mighty blue whale comes up for another brief sojourn and a flash of cameras, then dives once more, soon to head for the warmer climes of Costa Rica for the winter. All that is left is a footprint of smooth water that sits oddly, like a skin of cold coffee, on the sea.

Finally, *Sanctuary* heads home and a fond fatigue washes away years of worry. If only for a while.

In the coming months, migrating grey whales will dodge whalers in their journey from Alaska to the lagoons of Baja, California and our blue whale will be long gone. A line of five pelicans, awkward and ugly on land, passes us with a grace that would have seemed impossible just hours earlier.

Highway 1, the Pacific Coast road, is mile after mile of undulating blacktop from San Francisco to Los Angeles. We picked it up after joining the SR-17 from Los Gatos, near San Jose, and enjoyed the snaking climb that skirted redwood country. It is a fine journey for a driver new to the US, covering an array of terrain over the course of ninety minutes and allowing an unhurried look into an unchanged world. As giant trees gave way to plains and dunes, Steinbeck's description of an unforgiving life on the land appeared before our eyes.

First came the fields and row after row of artichokes; then came the workers, bent over the plants, indigent labour trying to make it in a country that held out vast opportunity. Add an old bus, something out of the sixties, and we're straight into *The Grapes of Wrath*.

But as the half-moon bay of Monterey comes into view, deeply held impressions of a land and its people are surrendered for the sheer magnificence of the Pacific and a world that seems a million miles away from life on terra firma.

It is not hard to see why Steinbeck, a local boy, loved this place despite his depiction of the harshness meted out to some. As we drive back to the city, I think about the blue whale and a part of me shrinks behind the wheel of the rented Suzuki, a small boy from another life lucky enough to see a dream come true.

For at last, he can lower his head in the knowledge that, unlike in the museum, whales do not come down from out of the sky.

ANGOLA PRISON RODEO: WHEN CONVICTS BECOME COWBOYS

The *Daily Telegraph*, 25 May 2016
*Twice a year, inmates of Louisiana's maximum-security
Angola prison stage a public rodeo within the compound.
Nigel Tisdall went along.*

It's not on every holiday that you get to shake hands with a murderer.

'I made a mistake and it cost me,' thirty-seven-year-old 'BK' admits as I examine some silver jewellery he has made for sale. Surrounding us are rows of stalls piled high with 'hobby craft' – good-quality bags, toys, clothing and furniture made by the inmates at Angola, the largest maximum-security prison in the United States.

A hundred miles northwest of New Orleans, the Louisiana State Penitentiary is so-called because it stands on the site of a plantation once worked by enslaved people from West Africa. Now it is home to five thousand male offenders, three-quarters of whom are on a life sentence. Their crimes may have been violent, but the mood inside seems surprisingly benign, with neat white fences and green lawns basking in the Southern sunshine. Take away the razor wire and the watchtowers and the cops on quad bikes, and you could be visiting a manicured country club.

Twice a year Angola swings open its security gates and invites the general public to come on down and enjoy some 'extreme rodeo'. Most of the prisoners who take part have never been on a horse, yet now they will try to ride irate bulls and bucking broncos, catch wild mustangs and play poker while being charged by ferocious horned cattle. 'It's an awesome sight,' a biker from Kent tells me, 'providing you like seeing people hurt.'

The craft stalls are a sideshow to what began in 1965 as internal recreation. Now the Angola Prison Rodeo is an important rehabilitation tool that draws thousands of shoppers and spectators. The standard of the handiwork on sale is impressive, and the prices reasonable. Beautifully turned bowls made from pecan and persimmon wood sit beside shiny leather saddles and ornate rocking horses. You can buy souvenir T-shirts that quip 'Angola – A Gated Community', and fill up at inmate-run food stalls at which you can buy delicacies such as catfish and chips.

Up on stage a six-piece prison band belts out gospel and R&B numbers with verve. It seems monstrous that the twists of life have left so many talented people lost behind bars until they die.

The age range at Angola is from seventeen to ninety-two. Only a few prisoners who are over thirty-five and have achieved 'trustee status' for ten years are allowed to sell direct to the public. The one unsettling part is a section of stalls where the vendors are fenced off so you have to make purchases by passing notes through the wire. 'That part's for sex offenders and the like,' a member of staff explains. I buy a faux alligator-skin belt for a few bucks, hoping it will help.

There is a party atmosphere up in the wooden seats of the rodeo arena, which can hold 10,500 spectators and was built by the inmates. Participating prisoners wear black-and-white-striped shirts and jeans as they face up to snorting bulls and wild horses. Ambulances with open doors are lined up by the ringside – and they're needed. These lifers have little to lose, and they make determined efforts to stay in the saddle and avoid the stampeding hooves.

It sounds like something more suited to Rome's Colosseum, but the show is organised by professionals and highly entertaining. As the programme explains, it's all about 'enabling positive behaviour changes'.

Today there are only three nasty-looking injuries, and then we all get to drive away and continue our lives. BK, meanwhile, will return to the dormitory he shares with ninety-four men, and his job as a filing clerk that pays $2.20 (£1.69) an hour. Around 2050, perhaps, he will enter the inmate-run hospice, and then take up his place in Angola's Point Lookout Cemetery.

It has been an absorbing, if thought-provoking, only-in-America day out. Covering 18,000 acres, the penitentiary feels like a mini nation. It has extensive farmland worked by shire horses that are bred here, and a nine-hole golf course where a round costs ten bucks. Outside the prison gates, an engrossing museum tells the history of Angola, including the many ingenious methods used in attempts to escape from the 'Alcatraz of the South'.

The surrounding parish of West Feliciana could not feel more free and easy. It is known as 'English plantation country', having been settled by east-coast Episcopalians after the American Revolution. The landscape is scenic and orderly, with well-kept Baptist churches and jokey mailboxes at the end of drives.

St Francisville, its peaceful capital, sits close to the Mississippi River and makes a good base from which to visit the many fine plantation houses nearby, including Rosedown, with its magnificent allée of oak trees bearded with Spanish moss, and Oakley, where the naturalist John James Audubon painted thirty-two of his famous *Birds of America* series. All is calm – until October, when a window briefly opens on to another world, and you can admire a few brave, trapped men going all out for a wild moment of 'guts and glory'.

THE PERILOUS PATH TO AMERICAN INDEPENDENCE

Yorkshire Post, 19 April 2025

Lindsay Sutton discovers that the path to independence was more complicated... and interesting... than we realise.

It's a massive understatement to say that the American city of Boston has a deep heritage and a fascinating history. For a start, Boston played a pivotal role in the American War of Independence – and looking back, the ironies surrounding that role are real food for thought.

The biggest irony is that Donald Trump's recently imposed taxes on British imports come exactly 250 years on from the British doing pretty much the same thing to their American colonists. Just as President Trump's actions have triggered a political backlash, so the suddenly imposed British taxes triggered the American War of Independence, with the Boston neighbourhoods at the heart of the action.

This very day – 19 April, back in 1775 – saw the first showdown between British troops and local militiamen in the little town of Lexington, just 20 miles inland from Boston. With taxes slapped on imported tea, newspapers and other everyday goods and services, feelings ran high in Britain's North American colonies, with Bostonians leading the way.

Everyone tends to focus on that famous American Declaration of Independence in Philadelphia – made a year later, on 4 July 1776. But the battles that put the British on the back foot early on in the American Revolution took place in Boston, higher up the northeast coast. As Boston folk are quick to tell you: 'We did the heavy lifting; Philly did the paperwork.'

Today, liberal-minded Bostonians take the high ground, and welcome British visitors with open arms. As do folk in the charming and historic nearby towns of Lexington and Concord. That's where the action began, when the first gunshot rang out on Lexington Common – 'the shot heard round the world', as they say in these parts. Here there's a statue of a defiant local militiaman ready to take on the British troops. Who shot first is still unknown, but when those five colonists died in the showdown, the battle for independence was on.

You can drive along the exact same route followed by the British Redcoats who marched out from Boston on a mission to find hidden armaments being stockpiled for use in any forthcoming battles against the British authorities.

Down the road in Concord, visitors can walk across the bridge that crosses the local stream where the second confrontation occurred. When the British decided to retreat back to Boston, the local farmers and volunteers harried them all the way, ultimately fighting a tooth-and-nail battle at north Boston's Bunker Hill, where a huge obelisk memorial now marks the spot. The British Redcoats won the day, but at huge cost in deaths and casualties.

Less than a year on, the British evacuated from Boston to Nova Scotia up the coast when they realised that George Washington's rebel army had hauled thirty cannons to the commanding Dorchester Heights above the harbour. Round one to the Americans, but there would be five more years of warfare throughout the colonies, with Boston now out of the frame.

Before heading back to Boston ourselves, my wife and I stayed at the Inn at Hastings Park in Lexington, a four-star hotel that is central to the neighbouring American Revolution sites. The feeling of charm and well-being is in stark contrast to the reception the British troops received back in 1775.

Incidentally, in nearby Concord, you can visit the home of Louisa May Alcott, and you can still sit at the exact spot where she wrote *Little Women* back in 1868. Her life-enhancing book is still a classic – in written form, on stage, or on film.

For those with a love of history, not to mention seafood, Boston is a great city to visit. It's fantastic to look out from your bedroom window in the swish Newbury Hotel on to the historic Boston Common and Public Gardens right in the heart of the city. The 500-acre green space, complete with beautiful lakes and tree-lined public walkways, has its own historic significance. It's the oldest public park in America, and back in the 16th century, when the God-fearing British Puritans founded the Massachusetts Bay Colony, there were whipping posts, stocks, and even hanging gibbets to implement their form of justice.

Boston has so much to offer. On the history front, there's the famous Freedom Trail, a walking route that can be followed independently or led by guides in 17th-century dress. Departing from the edge of Boston Common, the guided tour takes in ten places of significance. From churches, graveyards, old meeting houses, to the site of the Boston Massacre where those five colonists were shot by Redcoats. Most walks end at Faneuil Hall, a vibrant marketplace in central Boston.

From there, individuals can follow the red line on the pavement to further-flung places, such as the home of revolutionary hero Paul Revere, whose midnight horse ride from Boston to Lexington raised the alarm that the British were coming.

A key way to unwind and take in the sea air is to do the one-hour Boston City Harbour Cruise, viewing the city from offshore. Then there's the Harvard Museum of Natural History, and you might wish to book a separate tour round the historic university site. I earned a tick for Yorkshire when asked to name the eight American presidents who went there. They knew the game was up when I threw in Rutherford B Hayes.

There's a lot to do in Boston, from the View Boston Observation Deck, giving you an overview of the city, to the Franklin Park Zoo; from the New England Aquarium to the Museum of Science.

Finally make sure that your Boston visit includes sampling the clam chowder, preferably at the Union Oyster House just a block from Faneuil Hall. The creamy soup includes diced potatoes, salt pork and onions. The restaurant is owned by former military general Joe Mitano, who makes you very welcome. Oh, and it's said to be the oldest restaurant in New England. There's history again.

LAND OF HOPE AND STORIES/ A STATE OF MIND

BA High Life, October 2019
Jonathan Thompson discovers Molossia, the world's smallest republic hidden in the Nevada desert.

Clearing his throat, the president steps forward. The crowd falls silent as sunlight dances across the deep rows of medals on his military uniform. A gush of static from a hidden loudspeaker and then an officious female voice: 'Ladies and gentlemen, please be upstanding for the national anthem of Molossia.'

Today is the biggest event in the calendar of the world's smallest republic: Founders Day. From the rear of the crowd, I can see the wire fences marking both the country's eastern *and* western borders. Molossia's northern limits are visible too: customs and passport buildings denoting the sole entry point from the outside world. Only the country's southern border is obscured, lurking beyond distant rocks and desert scrub, but it's of little consequence. All four sides of this tiny nation border the same foreign power: the United States of America.

Molossia, a self-declared micronation, is encircled by the US as Monaco is by France or, more precisely, as Vatican City is comprehensively and completely landlocked by Italy. The only significant difference between this North American republic and its more revered European counterparts is, as His Excellency President Kevin Baugh is at pains to point out, the weather.

'Molossia is like Camelot,' says Baugh, inscrutable behind his dictator-chic mirrored aviators. 'It only ever rains at night here. The problem is that crappy American weather sometimes blows across the border.'

Today's festivities are designed to mark the 42nd anniversary of Molossian independence from the US. With just 1.3 acres of territory, it's a Lilliputian dot in the middle of the Nevada desert – but its thirty-four citizens have all the basics they need, from a bank and post office to a bar and grill.

As President Baugh delivers his Founders Day speech, hands moving with all the enthusiasm and vigour of a magician selling a trick, I scrutinise the rapturous audience. Most of the thirty or so attendees are foreigners from the US, but others have travelled from as far afield as London and Bahrain. All have fresh Molossian stamps in their passports, and all have agreed to abide by the nation's laws during their afternoon visit. Smoking, for instance, is banned throughout the country, along with catfish, spinach and onions.

'All our citizens are very, very happy,' says Baugh. 'I guess you could call me an uber-benevolent dictator. I just want them all to live fulfilling lives. But at the end of the day I *am* still a dictator, and there are some things – like spinach – which I just cannot abide.'

The official address over, some of the guests drift off down Main Street, to where Molossia's charismatic first lady, Adrianne Baugh, is overseeing a Founders Day barbecue (no onions on the burgers, naturally). Others accept the president's invitation to head south and stroll the Trans-Molossian Trail ('Just watch out for snakes: we have all kinds of critters in the southern half of the country!'). Satisfied, the president smooths his carefully pressed uniform, ushering me into a comfortable government office to discuss his nation's history.

Molossia came into existence in 1977 after the then teenaged Baugh watched *The Mouse that Roared*. Starring Peter Sellers, the film deals with a tiny European nation that goes to war with the US, and wins.

'I was very taken with this idea of a tiny country doing this cool thing; this mouse that roared,' says Baugh. 'I wanted to be that mouse. I read up on micronations and made the first step – declaring independence. After that, I just kept researching and expanding the concept. Molossia began as an extension of a kid declaring their bedroom an independent country so they didn't have to pick up their socks. But it kept going – and the idea kept growing. As soon as I bought land here in Nevada in the 1990s, I raised the flag and started turning the idea into reality.'

Molossia has come a long way since then, as has Baugh – who remains not just the keeper of the flame, but the fuel and bellows for it too. Over the last two decades, he's created everything from a working currency (the valora) to an official measurement system, based on the length of his hand. 'I don't know how they'll measure things after I die.' He shrugs. 'The first lady is sixteen years younger than me, so when she takes over the presidency, she'll probably need to keep one of my hands in a jar.'

Molossia also adopts a decidedly hands-off approach to the global superpower on its doorstep. The president himself served across the border for many years as a sergeant in the US Army – and diplomatic relations under the last administration were polite if distant.

'Barack Obama sent me a card every December, in which he wrote: "Dear Mr President, Merry Christmas from Mr President."' Baugh smiles. 'We haven't heard from the White House since he left, but they're aware of our existence of course. We don't give them any trouble and they leave us alone. While we don't contribute US taxes, we do provide foreign aid to our neighbour – which happens to be exactly the same amount.'

While Washington DC is currently cool on the Molossian issue, the same cannot be said of the US media. CNN and Fox both filmed segments here recently, while NBC's *Today* show broadcast a live episode from Main Street. A Hollywood movie about the micronation, produced by and starring Jack Black, is also reportedly in the works.

'We're a tiny nation and we acknowledge our limitations, but we want to build the best little country we can,' says Baugh. 'It's about talking to people, having fun and imagining a better future.'

You may say Baugh's a dreamer, but he's not the only one. There are dozens of self-declared micronations around the world, from Westarctica – a slice of the Seventh Continent managed from Los Angeles – to Sealand, the controversial nation on an oil rig off the British coast. Up to fifty of these countries send representatives to the biennial MicroCon – a United Nations for micronations – which Baugh helped to found.

While many of these geopolitical idiosyncrasies are notoriously private, Molossia actively welcomes visitors. Each year, hundreds of tourists visit this little state for scheduled monthly tours, most making the short international drive from hotels in Dayton, Reno or Carson City.

Among today's crowd is Kelli Justus, a thirty-nine-year-old from Las Vegas, who's been looking forward to her Founders Day visit for months. 'This has to be one of the wildest places on earth,' says Justus. 'I loved going through passport control and I love the energy and passion of His Excellency, as well as his commitment to the environment by banning plastic bags and incandescent light bulbs, and his belief in rights for pets. I wish more world leaders were like him.'

Others, however, were less reverential. 'To me, this is the ultimate dad joke,' says road-tripper Elizabeth Petroff, thirty-two, from Kingsman, Arizona. 'But it's going to look awesome on social media.'

Baugh, for his part, welcomes all comers to his Nevadan Never-Never Land, however outlandish their reactions – or choice of attire. 'We've had all sorts of folks on our tours, and they often like to dress up,' he says. 'Recently we had a group of "furries" in full animal costumes, while a few years ago there was a squad of guys in historically accurate East German military uniforms. Then there was the woman who drove here from across state wearing nothing but body paint…'

Baugh takes it all in his stride, of course; Molossia is officially open to all and tolerant of everyone (the name itself is derived from the Hawaiian word *maluhia*, meaning harmony in the world). But there is one rule on which the president will not compromise.

'I get so many requests for citizenship, you wouldn't believe,' he says. 'I've had more than five thousand now, mainly from the Middle East and Africa, but I won't budge. Molossia is a family nation, and all its citizens are related to me by blood or marriage, whether they live here or are expats across the border in the United States.'

So what's Baugh's ultimate goal? Any territorial expansion is entirely dependent upon whether his neighbour Dwayne is willing to sell him any land. And, for a nation whose primary international export is rubbish once a week on Tuesdays, what hope does Molossia have?

'It's really about the idea,' says Baugh, finally removing his mirrored sunglasses and becoming Kevin from Dayton again. 'It's about how a single concept can evolve; can give people a little hope in the future and maybe some stories to tell. It's about keeping a spark in the world and busting out of cubicle life.'

Kevin blinks at me: diminutive, polite and kind. The Stuart Little of the world's dictators. The Molossian mouse that roared.

LIBERTY BELLE,
NEW YORK'S LADY-IN-WAITING

British Caledonian Airways Let's Go Magazine,
March/April 1986
Peter Jolly sets the scene for one of
America's biggest spectaculars in 1986.

She's French, wears green make-up, is vain enough to accept a facelift for her 100th birthday, influential enough to invite a president to the party, loved enough to inspire a nation to collect $230 million for a present and marketable enough to make her a sponsor's dream. It was on a summer's day in 1885 that this lady arrived in America from her native land to take up citizenship. For nearly a century she has stood on an island site in New York Harbor, her torch shining out both as a symbol of freedom and a welcome to the millions who followed.

In July she will again be welcoming the masses but on this occasion they will be converging on the harbour to join the celebrations to mark the opening by President Reagan of the renovated lady – after a year off duty, the Statue of Liberty will be back in business.

The opening and closing ceremonies of the 1984 Olympic Games in Los Angeles made a tremendous impact but New Yorkers, borrowing a famous phrase, say 'You ain't seen nothing yet'. They predict the party will be the biggest bash given in the Big Apple since the nation's Bicentennial in 1976.

A little more subdued, but no less enthusiastic, is Lee A Iacocca, chairman of the Statue of Liberty Island Centennial Commission, who says 'the ideals of liberty represented by the statue have a universal meaning and this will be an event heard and seen around the world'.

As America's best-known businessman – he saved the Chrysler Corporation from bankruptcy – Mr Iacocca describes his work for the commission as a labour of love. His Italian parents, like so many other immigrants, arrived in the New World full of ambition and hope. Certainly that ambition was fulfilled by their son – *Time* magazine said of him: 'when he talks, America listens.'

The New York Convention and Visitors Bureau plans to squeeze every ounce of publicity out of the reopening on 3 July of the city's number one attraction which draws nearly two million visitors annually.

That's not to say the Americans have been unaware of what has been happening to their favourite lady. The bureau's president,

Charles Gillett, says 80% of the installation funds raised in the USA one hundred years ago were contributions of less than a dollar, many of them from schoolchildren. 'Funds for the restoration work will likewise come from millions of American citizens,' said Mr Gillett.

The Statue of Liberty was originally conceived in 1856 as part of a monument to Franco-American friendship – an alliance that flowered during both the American and French Revolutions.

Designer Frédéric Auguste Bartholdi, working with a plaster model 4ft high, drew up plans for the 1,520ft figure, which would be raised on a 150ft pedestal. Work began in 1875 and was completed in 1884, when it was formally handed over to the United States in Paris.

An abandoned fort on Bedloe's Island in New York Harbor was chosen for the site, and the statue, formally called 'Liberty Enlightening the World', was dedicated by President Grover Cleveland on 28 October 1886. President Eisenhower approved the changing of the island's name to Liberty in 1957.

What needed to be done to restore the statue? A survey revealed that the ironwork was severely corroded and there was also severe deterioration of the 200,000lb of copper sheeting that forms the statue's outer covering. Lady Liberty's right arm and the upheld torch have been dismantled and totally re-engineered.

The work includes building a new torch and strengthening the crown's seven spikes – 9ft long and weighing 150lb – which represent the seven seas and seven continents. One of the spikes is being shortened by a foot. It was so close to the lady's arm that it had worn a hole in the statue's copper skin.

There has been a special clean-up for the bronze plaque carrying a copy of Emma Lazarus' poem, 'The New Colossus', inspired by Lady Liberty:

Give me your tired, your poor,
Your huddled masses yearning to be free,
The wretched refuse of your teeming shore,
Send these, the homeless, tempest-tost to me,
I left my lamp beside the golden door.

Work has been in progress since spring 1985, with crews working twenty-four hours a day, six days a week, to complete the massive project. And the work has not been confined to Liberty Island.

Across on Ellis Island, for so long a ghost town of rotting piers and crumbling buildings, they are restoring the Great Hall to its 1907 appearance – the peak year for immigration. During its time as an immigration station from 1892 to 1954, Ellis Island processed some seventeen million new citizens.

With their flair for the big occasion on Liberty Weekend the Americans have turned to top television producer David L Wolper of the Olympic Games, *Roots* and *The Thorn Birds* fame, to mastermind the weekend's events. TV rights have been sold for a reported $10 million, while big firms with their sponsorships are making it a hugely commercial event.

Mr Wolper's first set piece will be the actual unveiling of the statue when President Reagan, on board the aircraft carrier *John F Kennedy*, pushes a button to start a string of light from the ship to travel across the water and light the darkened statue, section by section.

Not to be left out of the fun, Ellis Island will be the scene of the swearing-in of five thousand new American citizens. Simultaneously throughout the United States, linked by satellite, another twenty thousand Americans will be sworn in. It will be an emotional occasion throughout America.

Visitors are promised one extravaganza after another and none more spectacular than Operation Sail when New York Harbor plays host to the largest flotilla of sailing ships to assemble in modern history – more than three hundred vessels. They will sail past the statue to salute her centenary and unveiling.

The harbour will also be the scene of another record-breaker, this time the world's largest fireworks display, complete with a background of American music, while a live concert in Liberty State Park will ring to the sounds of Sousa, Berlin, Rodgers and many others. Major international performers will join the New York Philharmonic in a concert in Central Park to an expected audience of 250,000. Sport has not been forgotten and the Statue of Liberty Mile will be run by the ten best men and women milers in the world.

As a final salute to Lady Liberty an Olympics-style closing ceremony will feature a cast of fifteen thousand and a line-up of show business personalities including Frank Sinatra, Kenny Rogers and Lionel Richie.

As New Yorkers await the invasion by yet more masses, and thousands of official and not-so-official mini statues arrive in the shops, some people have already gone home with their little chunk of history – they have bought parts of the statue that have been replaced.

PHILADELPHIA – COME FOR AMERICA'S 2026 ANNIVERSARY, STAY FOR THE BONUSES

Mary Go Round America, June 2025
*Mary Moore Mason discovers much to enjoy
in one of America's founding cities.*

Cinemagoers owe a debt to Philadelphia. The seventy-two steps of the Museum of Art are as famous as – and certainly far more widely recognisable than – those in *Battleship Potemkin*. If true film buffs may think of the baby's pram, tumbling down the latter, many more will instantly recognise the flight Sylvester Stallone raced up in *Rocky*, which I climbed, somewhat breathlessly, in his footsteps. The 1976 story of underdog boxer Rocky Balboa put the city on America's top movie map. You can take a photo of the famous Rocky statue at the base of the museum.

And much earlier, in 1940, there was *The Philadelphia Story*, with Katharine Hepburn's Tracy Lord surely based on the blue bloods of Bucks County, family seat of William Penn. You can imagine some sniffy drawing room conversations when she migrated to Rhode Island in the later musical version, *High Society*.

London-born William Penn, of course, was the Quaker founder of Pennsylvania and 'The City of Brotherly Love'. His 37ft-tall bronze statue crowns the tower of majestic 548ft-tall City Hall, America's largest municipal building. You can soar by lift up to its glassed-in observation deck to enjoy 360-degree views of the city and even get a peek of the man himself through openings in the ceiling.

If there is only one thing most of us know about Philadelphia, America's sixth most populous city, it's that the city's stately Independence Hall, now a UNESCO World Heritage Site, was where American patriots signed their Declaration of Independence against their mother country on 4 July 1776. It was the launch of a major new country into the world order.

But there is much more to reward the visitor here as the city prepares for its 250th anniversary in 2026. For one thing there is the Benjamin Franklin Museum and The Franklin Institute, its formation inspired by that most colourful and multifaceted Founding Fathers creativity as a scientist and inventor.

This is also a city of great art galleries, starting with the Philadelphia Museum of Art which has some of the greatest treasures in the country, including works by Renoir, Rubens and Van Gogh. The nearby Rodin Museum displays more of the famous French sculptor's work than any museum or gallery outside Paris.

Don't miss the Barnes Foundation, founded by the eponymous eccentric pharmaceutical tycoon Albert C Barnes, which includes, at last count, eighty-one Renoirs, sixty-nine Cézannes, fifty-nine Matisses and forty-six Picassos.

The Academy of Fine Arts is reputedly America's oldest art museum, the training ground for many famous American artists, and the showcase for a vast array of 19th- and 20th-century American art. And there's one more celebration of American art to savour.

Along the Benjamin Franklin Parkway, a new gallery and garden is devoted to Alexander Calder, one of America's most famous 20th-century artists, particularly known for his mobiles and sculptures.

Philly's artistic treasures are not limited to museums, as I discovered on a dedicated minibus tour of some of the city's four thousand outdoor artworks. The mural programme began many decades ago as part of an anti-graffiti campaign, explains famous muralist Meg Saligman, one of the pioneers.

For close to thirty years she has created more than forty public artworks. Murals depict the multistorey, fantastical *Common Treads* featuring the female students from a local school; a portrait by Kurt Twitchell depicts local basketball hero Dr J (Julius Erving), not in sporting gear but in a business suit. Saligman's latest, quite different creation will be unveiled in 2026, in a six-storey 19th-century former bank building. Titled *The Ministry of Awe*, it will consist of a 'multisensory experience of paintings, sculpture, performance, interactive soundscapes and (quirky) rituals of invented bureaucracy'.

Want to see more than half of Albert Einstein's brain and the world's tallest skeleton (7ft 6in)? Visit the Mutter Museum. The cell where notorious gangster Al Capone was imprisoned for seven months in relatively opulent comfort? Join a tour of long-since closed Eastern State Penitentiary, which in the 19th century was lauded for its justice reforms.

The city may be best known for its cheesesteaks, hoagie sandwiches and giant pretzels, but Philly has a wealth of James Beard Award winners and Michelin-starred restaurants and in 2025 was included, for the first time, in the *MICHELIN Guide Northeast Cities* edition.

Check out one of the numerous restaurants owned by Stephen Starr, a James Beard Award winner, such as Japanese-themed POD and Mexican-themed El Vez and LMNO. And then there's my favourite, Buddakan, for delicious Asian food and a 10ft-tall seated Buddha. There are more surprises at Reading Terminal Market – one of America's oldest and largest public markets. Among its eighty-some vendors are the special Pennsylvania Dutch treats created by the Amish.

On to America's 250th independence celebrations in 2026. Make sure to drop by the National Constitution Center, noting that the vital Constitution, of such significance in these turbulent political times, was also signed in Independence Hall but eleven years later. And who can leave Philadelphia without seeing the nearby iconic Liberty Bell?

Finally to the Museum of the American Revolution, where the displays, dioramas and films bring the eighteen-year struggle of the United States to become an independent nation vividly to life.

CHARLESTON – SOUTH CAROLINA'S SOUTHERN BELLE

Essentially America, Spring/Summer 2016
Mary Moore Mason imagines Charleston as a character in Gone with the Wind... Scarlett O'Hara... beautiful, strong-willed, entrepreneurial and a survivor.

Left 'too poor to paint and too proud to whitewash' by the ravages of the American Civil War – which began on 12 April 1861 when hot-headed local Confederates fired on Union-held Fort Sumter on an island in its harbour – Charleston was forced to retain its wealth of beautiful antebellum buildings rather than replacing them, as did many other cities, with the elaborate Victorian-era structures of the late 19th century. And after being hit by a major earthquake in 1886, which damaged nearly two thousand buildings, she structurally strengthened them against such a future occurrence, again making the best of a bad thing. (Visions of a penniless Scarlett resplendent in a gown made of her velvet curtains spring to mind.) In so doing, Charleston, along with her Southern soul sisters, Savannah and New Orleans, became one of the three major Graces of Southern architectural heritage… a place that everyone fascinated by the Old South should visit.

Set on a peninsula between the Ashley and Cooper rivers – both flowing into a large harbour and then the Atlantic – the small, compact city of about 130,000 residents can easily be explored by foot, pedicab, and harbour boat tours, some stopping at Fort Sumter. My personal preference is via a horse-drawn carriage propelled by a driver who is full of local lore.

Along the city's quiet streets, shaded by huge, Spanish-moss-veiled oak trees and sweetly scented magnolias, are the grand townhouses of the cotton and rice barons whose fortune came from plantations outside town. Other structures include the parade of pastel-coloured cottages, known as Rainbow Row, which reputedly featured in *Porgy*, local author Dubose Heyward's saga of local African American life. It was the inspiration for George Gershwin's bittersweet opera *Porgy and Bess*. Even today, local African American women sell their traditional and valued sweetgrass baskets on street corners and in colourful Old City Market, fronted by the Confederate Museum.

The Charleston Museum claims to be the oldest in America and the Gibbes Museum of Art to contain one of the finest collections of American art in the southeast. The Old Slave Mart Museum explores the harrowing story of the slave trade that enriched many of the area's plantations prior to the Civil War.

For many, the historic lifestyle of Charleston is best seen in its elegant homes. Go from the pre-Revolutionary War cottage of local cabinet maker Thomas Elfe and the Heyward-Washington House – one-time residence of a signer of the Declaration of Independence – to the Aiken-Rhett House (c. 1818), the city's most intact antebellum urban villa, the Edmonston-Alston House, with its views of the harbour from three piazzas, and the Nathaniel Russell House, completed in 1808 and renowned for its magnificent, free-flying staircase.

Among the city's oldest buildings are the early 18th-century Powder House and the Old Exchange and Provost Dungeon, where American patriots were held prisoners during the American War of Independence. The city is home to the oldest municipal college in America, the College of Charleston, founded in 1770, and the impressive Citadel Military College, sometimes referred to as 'The West Point of the South'.

The city's low-rise skyline is dramatised by the spires of numerous historic churches. Among them are the oldest Episcopal and Roman Catholic churches in the Carolinas, the oldest Baptist church in the South, the South's mother Lutheran church, the fourth-oldest synagogue in the USA, a late 18th-century church built for both enslaved and freed African Americans, and early 19th-century churches built by Scottish and French Huguenot immigrants.

Children are catered for by the South Carolina Aquarium, the Children's Museum of the Lowcountry, and Charles Towne Landing, a family attraction on the site of the first (1670) English settlement in South Carolina. Located about five minutes' drive from downtown on Old Towne Road, it includes an animal forest, the replica of a 17th-century sailing ship and living-history displays with characters in period costume.

Theatre lovers should check out the Dock Street Theatre, built in Georgian style on the site of one of America's first (1736) theatres and the hub of the annual summer Spoleto Festival USA. Shoppers will find it hard to tear themselves away from King Street, with its elegant shops and galleries selling everything from jewellery to artwork – some by South Carolina artists.

Head north for the Riverfront Park and the Old Charleston Navy Base, home to the Confederates' *H L Hunley*, the first submarine to sink an enemy warship. Raised from local waters in 2000, it can be visited on Saturdays.

Continue by the bridge across the Cooper River and you have several choices: the Patriot Point Naval & Maritime Museum – where you can clamber aboard the World War II USS *Yorktown* aircraft carrier; the charming town of Mount Pleasant; and Boone Hall Plantation, rebuilt in antebellum style but retaining the original slave cabins. Sullivan's Island has beaches and American Revolutionary War-era Fort Moultrie.

However, the main excursion point for many visitors is across the Ashley River and along the River Road to more plantations. Magnolia Plantation & Gardens boasts America's oldest gardens (c. 1680) and a pre-Revolutionary War home; Middleton Place Museum, in a handsome 1755 structure, and surrounded by 65 acres of the oldest landscaped gardens in America, has an unusual, butterfly-shaped lake. Drayton Hall, America's oldest unrestored plantation, has a particularly poignant history. It is said that it only escaped demolition by rampaging Union troops because the mistress of the house (another Scarlett) put up notices around the plantation's perimeters claiming (falsely) that everyone within its boundaries was suffering from the plague.

And, as I am mentioning Scarlett again, Charlestonians seem to have taken to heart her fervent vow when suffering near starvation during the Civil War: 'As God is my witness, I'll never be hungry again!' There appear to be more excellent restaurants per capita here than in most US cities. Many focus on South Carolina Lowcountry specialities like she-crab soup, shrimp and grits, crab cakes, cornbread, tomato pie, oyster pie and okra soup, but don't miss out on delicious desserts such as mud (chocolate) and pecan pies and memorable cocktails. And if you want to see where it all comes from, visit the Saturday Farmers' Market in pretty Marion Square.

WAGONS ROLL...
EVERY DAY AT SAM SHARP

The *Daily Telegraph*, 6 October 2007
Peter Hughes finds the discipline of a coach tour the
perfect way to tame America's Wild West.

In three days' time I will be spotting prairie dogs from the windows of an American tour bus. At the moment I am spotting luggage labels in Heathrow's Terminal 4.

The ones I am looking for are bright red, orange and blue. They're easy to find but I am studying them like tarot cards: they hold clues to my future. These gaudy little baggage tags identify the total strangers who will be my intimate companions for the next fifteen days.

Soon I can recognise a fellow traveller unaided. We are all 'of a certain age', the men in windcheaters and stout shoes, the women with their hair cut manageably short for travelling. We are 'silver travellers', 'denture venturers', members of a superannuated jet set, our pockets packed with 'grey pounds'. We are a coach party.

More than that we are a British coach party. The tags are there strictly so the airport reps can find us, not as a pretext for socialising. An American group, who would themselves be labelled with name badges, would know each other by nickname before they reached the departure gate. We confine our labels to our luggage where they generate little force fields to repel any embarrassingly premature introductions.

They were still working when we arrived in Denver. At the airport we had our first stray. Mr B, a man travelling on his own, went missing in the 30 yards between entering the concourse and the group rendezvous. Public address announcements were made;

Sherry, the tour manager, scurried through the terminal like a hound without a scent. The rest of us stood awkwardly in couples as if we had just been evacuated from a perilous building and were waiting to be allowed back in.

Mr B was retrieved and we boarded the bus – bus, note, not coach: coaches in America teach sport. In two weeks' time it would deliver us to Phoenix Airport. In the meantime it would take us through the American West, into six states, eight national parks and to four national monuments, memorials or historic sites. It would also deposit us at eleven different hotels.

Sherry had picked up the microphone to welcome us to America. If previous tours were anything to go by we might have trouble with the bath taps. 'Some push, some pull and some have little things that turn in the middle. They are designed to confuse you,' she said. Sherry Lehman is well versed in the preoccupations of British tour groups. She speaks the language too. With her it is 'queues' and 'loos', not 'lines' and 'johns'.

Sherry has been a bus tour manager for fifteen years. Before that she was an airline flight attendant who once flew GIs to the Vietnam War – a lord, well, lady of the aisles in the air and on land. She must be in her sixties but with Sherry it's not a question you ask. She has a cackling laugh, mischievous grin, gleaming bob of silver hair and scuttles through the day with the momentum of a bowling ball. Problems disperse like skittles; unco-operative clients get tactful short shrift too. On one tour she presented a persistent latecomer with a watch. The bus was Sherry's stage, each day another part of her repertoire. She was on tour as much as we were.

Towards the end of our two weeks her customary sangfroid momentarily slipped. A hotel was slow in handling our luggage and Sherry was flustered when she came on to the bus.

'There's the old Spencer Tracy line: "Never let 'em see you sweat." And this morning I let you see me sweat,' she said. Her frustration was understandable because the business of checking in and out of hotels was normally as efficient as a production line. Room keys were distributed as soon as we arrived and luggage delivered within minutes. Not once did we have to fill in a registration form.

As we set off, Sherry moved adroitly to the subject of the restroom at the back of the bus. Bodily functions are a crucial part of coach touring. The door is never locked, she assured us. 'But how do I put this without being rude? We are going into the hinterland where there are not too many dump stations.'

We left Denver and drove north into a land of rock and pine. It was Western scenery, mapped with Western names – canyons, creeks and gulches, Wyoming and Cheyenne.

We diverted to our first national park, Rocky Mountain, on the highest major highway in the States. Trail Ridge Road climbs way above the treeline to a tundra plateau, cropped threadbare by the wind. At more than 12,000ft you are eye level with great peaks of whittled granite, their sheltered eastern flanks wrapped in the ermine of snow. The Native Americans called them the 'mountains of never summer'.

You cover a lot of ground on a bus tour – 3,124 miles on ours: there was a competition at the end to guess. Stan won. He was only 2 miles out. He was one of the quieter passengers. 'Who's Stan?' someone asked.

We followed straight roads across the Great Plains, an ocean of grassland the colour of lichen, and bending roads through the Black Hills of South Dakota, dark with forests of ponderosa pine. There were curiosities: at Fort Laramie, the restored garrison on the Oregon Trail, each dining table is set with a 19th-century bottle of Lea & Perrins Worcestershire Sauce.

There were monstrosities. The figure of the Sioux chief, Crazy Horse, being sculpted with dynamite on a South Dakota mountaintop is a piece of monumental kitsch in the making. It will be big enough to contain the heads of all four presidents at nearby Mount Rushmore.

We saw wolves, in captivity, at Yellowstone National Park, although they have been re-established there in the wild; we saw condors soaring above the Grand Canyon. We gorged ourselves on the unending and ever-changing red rock landscape. For days the journey ran through the big-screen scenery of an extended movie set.

Five days out and our labels' polarity is reversed. Now they are little magnets, emblems of our bonding. The process has been helped by our changing bus seats: every day we move two rows clockwise and have new companions across the aisle. There are shared adventures like the power cut in Yellowstone, which blacked out all the restaurants, the invariable queues for breakfast and our forays into supermarkets the size of small municipalities to buy our occasional picnics. The tour doesn't include meals.

Each morning we inquire about Caroline's back and Dave's swollen toe and exchange boasts of the grotesque size of our steaks the night before. Not Sam and Gill, though; they are vegetarian. But they say they have eaten better than they expected. In Moab, Utah, the competition was for who had found the worst restaurant.

We are a group. We are happy to be shown places rather than have to find them for ourselves; happy to be taken rather than go. We go with the flow. We take pride in being on time, in having our wake-up call at 6am; our bags outside our rooms at 7 and being on the bus by 8.

It snowed in Yellowstone and the bison looked grumpier than ever. By the time we got to Phoenix we'd be wilting in temperatures of 43°C. We drove through the alpine valley of the Snake River and then a succession of little Mormon farming settlements, each with its population recorded on its sign: Etna (pop 200) and Thayne (341), Grover (120) and Smoot (100). 'Don't blink towns,' Sherry called them.

When we left Yellowstone people said they had enjoyed it, but where was the 'wow' factor? No-one said that about Bryce Canyon. Bryce looks as if it has been uncovered, a gargantuan cave where the roof has been removed to expose a deep valley bristling with stalagmites. Except these are sandstone, not limestone, turrets and spires, tinted with every shade from the red spectrum.

David, from Yorkshire, not easily impressed by anything to which you can't pin a white rose, gazed at the 'grottoes', vast niches bitten into the canyon wall. 'It's like entering a cathedral,' he allowed. 'Rievaulx Abbey or somewhere.'

After a day gazing at pristine wilderness you can begin to take it for granted and forget there is anything else. Reality slaps as soon as you exit the park gate. Within yards you are immersed in the h3uckstering neon and gimcrack architecture of small-town America.

At Phoenix Airport Sherry gave us maps on which she had marked the route to remind us where we'd been. It was a gesture of typical generosity, although the itinerary was only the half of it. Group we may have been, but actually the journey had been different for each of us.

FACE THE MUSIC

Sunday World, 21 October 2023
From blue skies to blue grass, America's bustling Mecca of music hits all the right notes for Isabel Conway.

'What do you get when you play country music backwards?' asks the dude up at the bar in Tootsie's, the iconic Nashville honky-tonk where many a future star has been discovered. He's thinking hard, stroking his stubbly face after wiping beer foam off it. Pushing back a battered Stetson he chuckles, 'You get your girl back, your dog back, your pick-up truck back and you stop drinking.' The dude didn't invent the joke but he wants to share it and I can see why.

Country lyrics are the home of *The Bottle Let Me Down*, *I Fall to Pieces*, *Don't Take the Girl* and umpteen other odes to misery and loss. *I'll Never Get Out Of This World Alive*, ironically, was Hank Williams' last hit record before he popped his braided boots. Be it a man (usually it's the male species) separated from a woman by forces beyond his control, work, or the call of the road, maudlin ballads and tear-jerkers, songs of forgiveness and redemption still draw in country music fans. Nowhere more so than in Nashville where musical energy literally bounces off the walls of dozens of bars, half of them reputedly owned by successful country music stars along downtown Broadway.

The capital of Tennessee has always been a magnet for singer-songwriters, from Elvis to Johnny Cash, Dolly Parton to Taylor Swift. Take Tootsie's, for example. Its three floors each point toward a grand stage, upon which different musicians play each night. A young band named Running for Congress are bringing down the house the afternoon I drop by.

Nashville's connection to music is unequalled. Live music is written, recorded and performed 24/7 in the city that 'music calls home', boasting over 180 music venues, ranging from huge stadiums where Taylor Swift and Ed Sheeran pack in 100,000-plus fans, to more intimate concert halls and small clubs featuring nearly every genre of music.

These world-famous honky-tonks offer free live music 365 days a year, so little wonder that Nashville is one of the top ten American vacation destinations and bachelorette grand central. On almost any day the music venues in the city are packed with crowds, spilling on to the sideways, decked out in Stetsons and cowboy boots. Party buses are filled with beer-swigging groups of guys on tour and pedal bars are weighed down by singing bachelorettes.

On my first visit to Music City I'm serenaded from the nineteenth floor in the Omni hotel by Kenny Rogers singing *She Believes in Me*. *The Gambler* starts as the lift zooms down to ground zero. Hall of Fame songwriter Don Schlitz was only twenty-three years of age, struggling like so many other wannabes who flock to Nashville, when he wrote *The Gambler* while working the graveyard shift as a computer operator. The song would change his life, giving him an indelible place in pop culture. When *The Gambler* was originally offered to Johnny Cash he disliked it, but Kenny Rogers jumped in fast and the rest, as they say, is part of this city's rags-to-riches history.

Nashville abounds with museums and we take a whistle-stop tour of some of the best of them. My favourite is RCA Studio B on Music Row away from the oven-high heat of street. Later we troop over to explore numerous galleries in the Country Music Hall of Fame then historic Ryman Auditorium and the recently opened National Museum of African American Music.

Known as 'the home of a thousand hits' in the city's historic Music Row district, RCA Studio B can be visited on the same ticket as the Country Music Hall of Fame. Breakthrough artists, from Elvis to Dolly Parton and from Jim Reeves and Patsy Cline to Roy Orbison, who defined the city's music industry, recorded hits inside the first purpose-built recording studio in Nashville back in 1957.

RCA Studio B walls used to be covered in purple shag carpet to improve the sound quality. Young hopefuls would loiter outside, singing their hearts out in hopes of discovery. Elvis Presley recorded *Are You Lonesome Tonight* in the pitch-dark, a tiny red light in a corner adding to the emotional impact of the song.

Our guide Brad tells how Dolly Parton wrote thousands of songs recorded by other singers, but she held on to the publishing rights for famous hits, earning about $30 million for her iconic song *I Will Always Love You* that she refused to allow the King of Rock 'n' Roll himself to record despite entreaties to do so.

The world-renowned Ryman Auditorium, one of the most famous concert venues in America, is another must visit; it's the original home of *Grand Ole Opry*, the radio show that ignited the careers of hundreds of country stars back in the dark ages.

Generations of artists, from country legends to the newest ones on the scene, performed at the Opry, which has since moved off to an out-of-town performance hub next to Opryland, a vast hotel and leisure complex. The Ryman is open for daily tours where visitors can stand on its famous stage in front of the microphone where Bruce Springsteen, Paul Simon, the Foo Fighters, James Brown, Diana Ross and most recently Ed Sheeran have performed.

The National Museum of African American Music that opened in 2021 is the only museum dedicated to preserving and celebrating music created, influenced and inspired by African Americans, throughout history, from jazz to hip-hop and beyond. Visitors go on a technically brilliant interactive journey, given a wristband that allows them to download activities as they go, create their favourite playlist (emailed to you afterwards), sing with a gospel choir and boogie with the greats of soul.

Beyond music, Nashville has plenty to offer in terms of food and drink. Vintage John Wayne movies play on a screen in Four Walls cocktail bar at The Joseph hotel whose 'Knock on my Door' and 'A Fistful of Dollars' are among the myriad cocktail offerings. Our barman, sporting grey plaits and forehead band, was a dead ringer for a young Willie Nelson. A wannabee C & W star or undiscovered songwriter perchance? 'Naw,' he shakes his plaits, 'I used to sell solar panels.' After encountering yet another giant stack of pancakes drizzled in syrup – normal American breakfast – it was a joy to sample brunch at Chauhan Ale & Masala House founded by celebrity chef Manee Chauhan that combined southern staples with delicious adapted Indian dishes.

If you fancy kicking back in Taylor Swift's favourite pew at Fox Bar and Cocktail Club in East Nashville ask Alex to mix you Taylor's favourite cocktail: 'Thai Mule' with a vodka base, Thai basil, ginger, honey, and lemon stock. Noko, the go-to restaurant of the district, is Asian-inspired, offering Japanese sharing plates, smoked *gochujang* hot wings and massive beef ribs, roasted over a wood fire. Assembly Food Hall, downtown, is an affordable fast-food emporium (in this surprisingly pricey town), featuring established Nashville eateries and a variety of tastes in a communal dining space. At legendary Party Fowl, home of 'Nashville Hot', patrons almost need the fire brigade to help dowse the flames after trying its ultra-hot chicken. The fishbowl-sized slushy cocktails help to quell the heat. Another southern food Mecca, using locally sourced ingredients, Farm House raises the taste-buds barometer that bit higher offering the best in farm-to-table fare.

UNFORGETTABLE EXPERIENCES

LIVE YOUR OWN LIFE-AFFIRMING STORY WITH BGTW MEMBERS' FAVOURITES.

BY RAIL & SEA

RIDE AFRICA'S REHABILITATED RAILS
In Angola, on the Benguela Railway
(experienced by Ian Packham)

Although it no longer reaches the laid-back Atlantic city of Benguela, the railway that has borne its name since 1905 is not only a vital transport link as Angola's longest train line, but also a celebration of travel in its rawest form. Following total rehabilitation, completed in 2015 after a generation of disruption, trains once again run on sections of the Benguela Railway three times per week in either direction. Join it on its journey between Huambo and Luena via Cuíto, and you'll experience the thrill of traversing a country that seems endless in extent, while stopping at small village stations where everything from home-grown potatoes to pieces of fried chicken are thrust up to the high carriage windows for sale, gaining an unrivalled slice of local life both inside and outside your carriage in the process. 🌐 portal.cfb.ao

ISLAND-HOP TO OFF-GRID BAMBOO HUTS
In the Philippines, with the 'Lost Boys'
(experienced by Vicky Philpott)

The white-sand beaches of El Nido and Coron may have called me, but it was the off-grid sailing adventure between them where the most memorable adventure lay. On board a traditional *paraw* sailboat with its perfectly balanced colourful bamboo outriggers, we island-hopped barefoot from one remote paradise to the next – snorkelling in coral reefs, fishing off the side, and jumping off the boat. Each time we came ashore, our crew, affectionately known as the 'Lost Boys', introduced us to island locals like old friends. We went along as they bought the *pinatuyong isda* (dried fish) and juicy mangoes we'd be eating that day. Without internet you'll be fully present – taking in the shimmering sea and dramatic limestone cliffs. Over four unforgettable nights, we prepared traditional meals communally (including the live killing, butchering, spit-roasting, and eating of a pig), gathered around crackling campfires, and slept under the stars in hand-built bamboo huts. You'll find it hard to believe you've been together for such a short time. ⊕ taophilippines.com

TRUNDLE INTO WINE TASTING
In Vipava, Slovenia, with Jani Peljhan's wine train
(experienced by Daniel James Clarke)

Slovenia's criminally underrated Vipavska Dolina (Vipava Valley) is an unapologetically green land of sustainable, small-batch, family-style wine producers. Spend a few days here flitting between ancient underground stone cellars to taste indigenous grapes such as Zelen, and you'll stumble away with a bunch of wholesome memories. For a quicker intro, join local Jani and his team on the monthly wine train. Departing from Habsburg-era Nova Gorica station, the 1970s carriages trundle along picturesque rails soundtracked by live Slovenian accordion music. On board, you'll sample five wines, meet the producer (each journey spotlights a different wine cellar), and pause for a tour of Roman-founded Ajdovščina. My highlight? The unexpected two-hour stop at a swoon-worthy winery for hearty soups and endless sips of organic and orange wines overlooking the vines. ⊕ vinskivlak.si

FOOD & FESTIVALS

TAKE A CULTURAL COOKING CLASS
In Lake Atitlán, Guatemala, with Anita from Mayan Kitchen
(experienced by Katja Gaskell)

Local food markets are one of my first ports of call when travelling. Lively and colourful, they offer a fascinating glimpse into everyday life, but without a guide it can be easy to miss the good bits. Fortunately we had Anita from Mayan Kitchen with us. Anita has been running cooking classes from her home overlooking Lake Atitlán for some fifteen years. The four-hour experience starts with shopping in San Pedro La Laguna market, after which you head to Anita's rooftop kitchen and learn to create a typical Guatemalan meal.

Menus vary according to what's in season, but ours consisted of a traditional *hilacha* stew, accompanied by *tamales* and *tortas de papa* (potato pancakes), followed by a plateful of delicious *rellenos de platano*, plantain balls stuffed with chocolate. The highlight of the experience, however, is Anita and her stories. You will leave not only with a full stomach but with a far deeper understanding of Guatemala. 🌐 mayankitchencookingclass.com

HAVE A PINT AT AFRICA'S HIGHEST PUB
In Lesotho, with Roof of Africa Tours
(experienced by Julia Hammond)

In Lesotho, nicknamed the Mountain Kingdom, nowhere is less than 1,400m above sea level. In fact, as you lean on the bar of the highest pub in Africa at Sani Top, you'll be at 2,874m. The most exhilarating way to reach it is by driving up the infamous Sani Pass, which snakes up no man's land between the South African border post and its Lesotho counterpart. It's a rough gravel road known for its switchbacks and precipitous drop-offs. You'll need a 4WD;

be grateful that someone else is driving it. If the mist descends, all you'll see is what's directly ahead, but on a clear day, the landscape beneath the pub's terrace creates a remarkable setting. Tuck into a plate of Basotho lamb stew as you sip a pint of Maluti lager and drink in the view. ⊕ **roofofafricatours.com**

DANCE WITH 'DEVILS'
In Mallorca, Spain, with the local dimonis
(experienced by Mark Julian Edwards)
Join Felanitx's annual (28 August) Sant Agustí Festival, a typical *Correfoc* – a Catalan feature of town festivals, where people dressed up as devils run through the streets, setting off fireworks – and you'll experience another side of Mallorca. I'll never forget hearing the whistles and loud bangs, smelling the gunpowder, and listening to chanting accompanied by beating *ximbombas* (drums) around bonfire pits. But the most dramatic moment came when I saw a *dimoni*: a bloodied devil. Adorned with horns, a scary face mask and gruesome chains, he was a sight to behold.

I followed this man as he approached children and adults alike, catching them off guard and shocking them. It turned out he is a schoolteacher at the very traditional Sant Françesc Catholic School. 'Being part of the Devil's Association (Dimonis de Sa Cova des Fossar) is by far the most exciting thing I do. It is all about keeping traditions alive,' Miquel Cabrer told me before declaring how much fun he had 'scaring the hell out of people'. ⊕ **felanitx.org**

FLOAT INTO MARDI GRAS' SPIRIT AND SOUL
In New Orleans, USA, with the Orpheus Krewe
(experienced by Jane Wilson)
Watch out for flying coloured beads, frisbees and doubloons heading straight for you during New Orleans' Mardi Gras. Catch

them or dodge them if you want to survive! Over forty-seven days before Easter and during seventy parades, crowds line the streets in outfits that would win most fancy dress contests, including mine. Fortunate to have a top-deck perspective (some krewes sell spots on their floats), I was harnessed in place on a float, looking jolly in a vivid yellow costume and mask for the five-hour parade. And what a spectacle I witnessed.

The line-up of floats, all bedecked in elaborate designs, was like a beauty pageant of wagons, each pulled by a tractor. On the ground, children and adults begged for freebies; the carnival spirit was chaotic and colourful, while the sounds of jazz and the legendary vocals of Louis Armstrong, who was born here, seemed to permeate along the route. And in the distance, I could see the elegant architecture of the French Quarter with flamboyantly decorated balconies. I aim a handful of coloured beads to the revellers below, their arms outstretched – I hope they catch them! ⊕ kreweoforpheus.com

HUMAN-POWERED ADVENTURES

TIME-TRAVEL BY BIKE
In Sark, the Channel Islands, with puffins and peace (experienced by Kate Wickers)

L'Etac islet lies off the south side of Sark, and is where, come spring, amid the pink thrift, puffin couples raise one single chick, charmingly known as a puffling. Cycle for five hours on this car-free island, and you'll spot guillemots, gannets, and fulmars circling above local men hand-diving for scallops, and fishermen casting out lobster pots. It's 2025, but it could easily be 1925. There's a charm to Sark that would be easy to label as lost in time, but that wouldn't pay respect to the islanders' conscious decision to keep tight hold of their traditions, such as the home-grown and artisan produce that is left on 'hedge veg' stalls outside their homes (alongside honesty boxes for payment so that they may make a modest profit).

On my cycle route around the island, I collect a delicious bounty to ferry home: a jar of raspberry jam made from the first fruits of the season, walnut fudge (melt in the mouth and creamy), and a small bottle of sloe gin. With bike tethered, I walk through woods to Port du Moulin beach, where I've only winkle-picking gulls for company, and a family content in gathering seaweed to use as garden fertiliser. I paddle in pools surrounded by peppery rock samphire and wild hops; the air thick with their yeasty-garlic aroma. ⊕ avenuecyclessark.com

CANYON IN THE CARIBBEAN
In Dominica, with Benny Bellot from Extreme Dominica
(experienced by Daniel James Clarke)
Relaxing resorts, rum punches and paradisical shorelines – that's the postcard Caribbean. But on Dominica – the Nature Island – you'll find another story; something I quickly learned when donning a hard hat and harness to jump into a moss-clad gorge while my flawless guides Berani and Benny egged me on from the icy jade pool below. Canyoning in Dominica was epic. Over half a day, my fear of heights was washed away by each abseil into crystal-clear pools. Shrouded by the island's mystical mountains and soundtracked by shrieks, birdsong and cascades, Dominica is a different kind of Caribbean. One ripe for adventures, not all-inclusives. ⊕ extremedominica.com

HIKE EUROPE'S HIDDEN CORNER
In Tusheti, Georgia, with Anna and Tato from
The Natural Adventure (experienced by Steph Parker)

Clambering out of the beaten 4WD, I knew my wild journey would prove worthwhile. Standing in a flower-filled meadow, dotted with distinctive, centuries-old clan stone towers and backed by the Caucasus Mountains' soaring peaks, Tusheti is Europe's most remote corner. An eight-hour drive from the Georgian capital, Tbilisi, the journey here is dominated by a high-altitude dirt track, complete with steep, challenging inclines and the infamous Albano Pass – at over 2,800m, this rugged 70km route is one of the highest drivable passes in Europe.

Guided by GPX maps, The Natural Adventure allows travellers to hike this amazing Georgian region independently, while also enjoying the safety of a local on-hand team. With a focus on responsible travel, nights are spent in family-run guesthouses (like my favourite Guesthouse Omalo), where delicious regional food, such as veggie-friendly Khachapuri (think hot cheesy bread) and Lobio (a bean and walnut casserole), is served. Luggage transfer by donkey lightens the daily load. The ideal way to soak in Georgia's incredible 'a guest is a gift from God' hospitality, cultural heritage, and outstanding mountain scenery, trekking in Tusheti affords an intriguing insight into one of Europe's last hidden corners. ⊕ thenaturaladventure.com

SWIM IN A VOLCANIC SINKHOLE
In Samoa, thanks to Salati and Samuga Petelo Fiame
(experienced by Vicky Philpott)

Formed by volcanic activity and fed by the tide, the To-Sua Ocean Trench is one of Samoa's most iconic natural wonders. Surrounded by thick tropical vegetation and carved deep into an ancient lava field, this perfectly symmetrical sinkhole feels less like a wild swimming spot and more like a sacred cavern. As I descended the slippery, steep, hand-hewn wooden ladder, my heart was thumping with the thrill at being in such a cinematic setting. The tidal pool was so clear it mirrored the palm trees and shifting sky above. Reach the platform and you can scramble down the next ladder, or do as I did and make the leap. Once in the water, venture through the naturally formed tunnel you see open up, and you'll find a second hidden chamber where light spills in. For just a few Samoan tālā, you can experience one of the most beautiful places in the South Pacific. ⊕ **tosuaoceantrench.com**

PADDLE IN PENINSULA PARADISE
In Scotland, UK, with Orkney-born adventurer Mike Martin
(experienced by William Gray)
Riven by sea lochs and sprinkled with skerries, Scotland's northwest coast is a kayaker's dream. Arisaig, just south of Skye, lies at the heart of this coastal paradise. From here, paddlers can explore the sheltered Sound of Arisaig and the rugged Ardnamurchan peninsula. Eigg, Muck, Rum and Canna dimple the western horizon, while Loch nan Ceall's entrance boasts a maze of islets and sandy coves lapped by turquoise waters. This calm yet wild expanse is perfect for exploration – but the weather can be fickle and you need to be well prepared. Guided tours offer safe passage, local knowledge and enriching ecological insights.

At low tide, seaweed coats the shores in amber dreadlocks; grey herons stand hunched, motionless, rooted to their reflections. Your guide spends a few minutes teaching simple paddling techniques. Then you're gliding through narrow channels in the labyrinth of islets, the kayaks skimming effortlessly across shallows covered with tangled rafts of bladderwrack. You pause often to

stare into the limpid waters: a mesmerising world of writhing kelp and gently pulsing moon jellyfish. As the tide rises, beaches vanish and channels deepen, reshaping the world around you. Arisaig guards its tidal secrets – retreating like a Scottish Atlantis.
🌐 arisaigseakayakcentre.co.uk

PEER INSIDE AN ACTIVE VOLCANO
In Vanuatu, with White Grass Ocean Resort & Spa
(experienced by Julia Hammond)

'Straight up is fine, but…' said the guide, referring to the ash that was billowing upwards after a loud explosion.

'…if it comes towards us…?'

'You keep watching. And if it looks like a rock's going to hit you, duck.'

We were scrambling up a gritty flank of Mount Yasur. Located on the island of Tanna, it is one of Vanuatu's most accessible active volcanoes – our ute deposited us just shy of the crater rim for the final short ascent on foot. Thunderous booms emanated from the magma chamber; every so often, the cantankerous volcano spat out a red-hot boulder. As darkness fell, scarlet lava fountains illuminated an ink-black sky. Nature's firework display won't fail to impress, though you'll need nerves of steel not to turn and run as the volcano rumbles and shakes beneath your feet.
🌐 whitegrasstanna.com

TREK FOR CHARITY
In Merida, Venezuela, with Charity Challenge
(experienced by Dr Jacqueline Jeynes)

Seeing an advertisement to 'Trek up the Andes in Venezuela and raise funds for the YWCA' sounded like a great challenge, so I signed up. I was a bit nervous at the first group meeting, but there was no need to worry, as we had novice long-distance walkers and experienced global trekkers, including two friends celebrating a sixtieth birthday. Training plans were discussed, and the itinerary was outlined. Fly from London to Caracas via Spain, then aboard the tiniest plane to Merida – even the locals on board didn't look confident! – to start the climb.

Apart from spectacular scenery and lovely people, we watched black condors plodding uphill to launch themselves and fly, relaxed in a natural hot-spring pool with Humboldt Glacier in the distance, and sampled sprout-flavoured ice cream at the biggest ice-cream parlour in the world (then). Training is vital, with well-worn boots, socks inside out, and be prepared to pee behind a shrub! As with any charity trek, we had to raise £2,500 each, but it was well worth it.
🌐 charitychallenge.com

INDIGENOUS CONNECTIONS

(NOT JUST) A WALK IN THE PARK
In Tarntanya (Adelaide), South Australia, with Tiimarai Sanderson-Milera (experienced by Renate Ruge)
Breathing in lemony scents of native grass while ducking under the branches of towering gum trees to find shade, Aboriginal guide Tiimarai Sanderson-Milera points to the holes where witchetty grubs burrow in tree trunks. Sharing insights passed down through generations of his family – First Nations Kaurna people – a ninety-minute guided Botanic Garden Native Plant Trail walk of Adelaide's Botanic Garden with Tiimarai is fascinating.

A world away from city life, what could have been simply a walk in the park is an educational journey. Seeing, touching and tasting, Tiimarai reveals the healing secrets of native plants and teaches us how to find shelter, food and even a way to serve lunch on plates made from paperbark trees. He explains how bottle trees store water, canoes are carved from eucalyptus rostrata red gum trees and shares artful ways of catching wild ducks. Food-wise, we find 'sacred' lotus and macadamias in his 'bush shopping centre' – the whole experience is a peaceful, soul-nourishing way to reconnect with nature. ⊕ kumarninthi.com.au

UNDERSTAND ABORIGINAL DOT ART
In Kuku Yalanji territory (Port Douglas), Australia, with Brian 'Binna' Swindley (experienced by Daniel James Clarke)
The first time I met Binna was to film a mini documentary about Aboriginal art for *Lonely Planet*. We spent a few days together in Tropical North Queensland, where Binna taught me all about his people, the Kuku Yalanji. We strolled along the endless, forest-backed Cooya Beach, tasting 'citrus' ants and learning how to traditionally spear sand crabs, and joined a spirit-cleansing smoking ceremony. My standout memory – and I've been lucky enough to return for a second workshop – was learning how to paint Aboriginal dot art using natural pigments (and their alternative uses) at Janbal Gallery, named for his mother. After a couple of hours, you'll come away with a small canvas featuring cassowary footprints, blue quandong berries, or other locally inspired motifs. But the real highlight is spending time with Binna and learning more about his artistic style and story. ⊕ janbalgallery.com.au

RAFT FIRST NATIONS RIVERS
In Mi'kma'ki (Nova Scotia), Canada, with Indigenous-owned Tidal Bore Rafting (experienced by James Ruddy)
Bursting with old-style charm as well as the world's finest seafood and the friendliest of people who 'jus' love you British', the ocean-kissed

Canadian province of Nova Scotia has it all. My week-long tour on near-empty roads became a surf ride through big waves of the creamiest of fish chowder and the freshest of lobster and shrimp – all enjoyed in an atmosphere of laid-back allure and the white-breaker rhythm of those ever-present seas.

Yet the seas weren't the wildest adventure; that was as we bounced through the world's only tidal-bore raft ride on the wild Shubenacadie River, laughing hysterically. Huge waves – they reach 4m and are produced by the world's highest tides in the nearby Bay of Fundy – propel your expertly driven Zodiac boat like a crazy cork through a charging torrent of iron-brown water rapids for the ride of your life. Oh, and there is also some big-kid mud-sliding fun at the trip's midpoint. Bring your least favourite T-shirt and pants! ⊕ raftingcanada.ca

SCHOOL YOURSELF ON SALMON
In K'emk'emeláy (Vancouver), Canada,
with thousands of salmon (experienced by Alicia Sheber)
A traditional 'First Food' honoured at tribal ceremonies, salmon is at the heart of the Pacific Northwest coast's Indigenous identity. Native American iconography, folklore, and festivals celebrate it as a perennial source of sacred nourishment, associated with abundance, fertility, and rebirth. Fuel your curiosity about the fish's cultural and ecological significance at Vancouver's Capilano Salmon Hatchery, which births one million offspring annually. Splashing alongside schools of spawning salmon is off limits. Still, you can walk *through* the Capilano River via the glass-walled 'Fishway' to be mesmerised by Chinook, steelhead or coho species enthusiastically climbing pool 'ladders' as they jump upstream to spawn at Burrard Inlet, home for thousands of years to Musqueam, Squamish and Tsleil-Waututh Nations.

In co-operation with these three Indigenous communities to ensure equal partnership – plus consultation with Fisheries and Oceans Canada, government bodies and local initiatives – this unusual tourism destination is modernising its 1971 infrastructure with low-carbon, energy-efficient upgrades, enabling long-term adaptability to climate change. Free and open year-round, visits range from fifteen-minute self-guided observatory tours to languid hours of forest bathing, hiking, cycling, picnics, and birdwatching amid the fertile temperate rainforest. September's Coho Festival coincides with the peak spawning season. ⊕ pac.dfo-mpo.gc.ca/index-eng.html

COOK WITH 'THE NEVER CONQUERED'
In Oaxaca, Mexico, with the Mixe Community
(experienced by Teresa Gomez)
Deep in Oaxaca's eastern highlands lies the Sierra Mixe, home to one of Mexico's most fiercely independent Indigenous communities. The Mixes, often referred to as 'the never conquered', have resisted domination by the Aztecs, the Spanish, and even neighbouring Indigenous groups like the Zapotecs. Thanks to this resilience, their ancestral customs have remained remarkably intact. And now they're inviting outsiders to experience them. At the heart of these experiences is *machucado*, a ceremonial dish traditionally prepared only once a year, on 1 August, to mark the end of the harvest. 'We ask the Hunger Spirit not to visit us,' Regina explains, standing in her *cocina de humo*, a traditional smoke kitchen where generations of women have cooked over open flames. Regina, one of the founders of Unión Turística de Nación Mixe, welcomes guests into her home to witness and take part in the ritual throughout the year.

You'll start the day with a shot of sacred mezcal and a whispered blessing in the Mixe language, poured partially onto the earth as an offering. Then the cooking begins: thin strips of wild beef are fire-smoked, while heirloom corn is ground by hand on a *metate* passed down from Regina's great-grandmother. *Memelas* are shaped and cooked, then pounded together and stirred into a sauce of tomato and *chintextle*, a rich, smoky chilli paste unique to the region. Seated in a circle close to the floor, with a spoon and half an avocado for a plate, we ate communally, surrounded by stories, laughter, and the scent of smoke and corn. More than just a meal, *machucado* is a ritual of gratitude, shared memory, and living heritage – an unforgettable way to connect with the soul of the Sierra Mixe. ⊕ raizayuuk.com

GET INTO MĀORI ART DECO
In Ahuriri (Napier), Aotearoa (New Zealand), with Art Deco Trust (experienced by Kate Wickers)
After a devastating earthquake that killed 256 people and flattened Napier in 1931, the town was rebuilt in the exuberant Art Deco style, incorporating Indigenous Māori design among the classic motifs of the era, such as sunbursts, ziggurats, and chevrons. The finest example is the ASB Bank, built in 1932, where the *ngaru*, or curling wave, is carved into the plasterwork, representative of how the Māori people arrived by canoe to Aotearoa. On the façade, the geometric 'tongue' design is inspired by the *whakapohane*, the Māori tradition of displaying the tongue in readiness for battle. The use of Indigenous design in Art Deco isn't new, but, unlike in Napier, little credit was given for design inspiration. ⊕ artdeconapier.com

MEMORABLE STAYS

SLEEP SURROUNDED BY PENGUINS
In the Falkland Islands, with the Pole-Evans family (experienced by Daniel James Clarke)

Reaching 'The Neck' on Saunders Island was an adventure. First, I flew from RAF Brize Norton on the public and personnel Falkland Islands Airbridge via Cape Verde. Then, I transferred to a teeny twin-prop BN-2 Islander. Finally, the Pole-Evans family bounced me an hour away from their farm in a 4WD, depositing me and two others at a silvery, wind-ravaged tombolo. The accommodation? An old military hut with bunks, a walkie-talkie-style radio, and a stove. The panorama? Countless pairs of rockhopper, gentoo and king penguins. Phenomenal. Stay a couple of nights here, embracing the silence, free-roaming sheep and close-up penguin observation, and you'll feel at the end of the world. 🌐 saundersfalklands.com

FEEL AT HOME IN THE HIMALAYAS
In Nepal, with Sita Tilijha at Narchyang Community Homestay (experienced by Becki Enright)

Living in a Nepali family home for two nights will shift your perspective on the country. While avid trekkers land in Nepal's adventure-stacked second city, Pokhara, to trail the mighty Annapurna massif, I spent four hours on car-curling mountain roads northwest towards the remote village of Narchyang. Sita Tilijha, a forty-year-old mother, welcomes international guests into her home and, alongside three other women, opens a door into the rural livelihood of the Pun Indigenous ethnic group.

Huddled around the family table, eating a thali made with home-grown produce, Sita explained how hosting has paved the way for opportunity, empowerment and economic independence in a community where men typically lead and young people leave. Come morning, a local guide will lead you through the thick forest on a steep rock trail used by villagers to reach the older settlement of Upper Narchang, where the snow-capped 8,000m pinnacle of Annapurna I and its jagged neighbours splay across the valley. An alternative viewpoint off the trodden trekking route, where you'll see Nepal differently. 🌐 communityhomestay.com

WILD CAMP IN THE RED SANDS
In the Wahiba Sands, Oman, with your own sense of adventure (experienced by Daniel James Clarke)
Our Oman plan was simple: three friends (well, strangers at that point), two tents, and one 4WD. We didn't have an itinerary, but as wild camping in Oman isn't just legal, but a beloved pastime, we knew we'd work it out. Over ten days, we slept all over, often sharing Khalas dates or dinner with the generously hospitable Omanis we met along the way. The most memorable night was driving deep into the towering golden dunes of the Wahiba (Sharqiya) Sands. Silence. Stillness. Stars so bright I almost cried. The whole night felt like a frigid dream. The next morning, a few wild camels curiously approached, as did a four-wheeler full of Bedouin women who stopped to offer us fresh mint tea before we headed to the nearest wadi for a 'shower'. Sure, you could join one of the organised camps. But if you have mates and are confident navigating in sand, you won't need to drive far to find a secluded desert sleep. 🌐 marktoursoman.com

RETREAT TO AN UNPLUGGED, FUNKY MOUNTAIN
In Jezersko, Slovenia, with Mother Nature
(experienced by Tracey Croke)

There's nothing showy about five-star Vila Planinka. Blink and you'll miss the native-wood alpine retreat tucked away among wild gardens. It's well off Slovenia's relatively less-trodden tourist track (by European standards) for good reason. If you believe that the earth has chakras, then Vila Planinka marks the good vibes spot. Ancient lore says four immune-boosting energy points surface in the forest surrounds where the retreat now sits in the tiny mountain village of Jezersko. More scientifically proven are the reported health benefits of drinking manganese-rich natural spring water found in the surrounding valley.

You can put all claims to the test for yourself over three days of wellness immersion, featuring forest yoga and bathing, a night hike under the stars, and walking and riding on accessible mountain trails right from the door (e-bikes available), plus recovering in their ultra-cool infrared and Finnish bio saunas. Dinner is curated with locally sourced organic ingredients, some foraged by their Michelin-starred chef, who has a choice of over a thousand edible plants found in the surrounding alpine area. Dishes from chef Blaž Derlink's spontaneous menus (think wild bear prosciutto and bee pollen ice cream) are paired with a selection of wines – including 'funky' biodynamics – from some of Slovenia's 28,000 boutique wineries. ⊕ vilaplaninka.com

BUILD (AND BED DOWN IN) AN IGLOO
In Adelboden, Switzerland, with the Alpinschule
(experienced by Anne Gorringe)

Since 2012, one-day winter igloo-building courses have been held on the mountain above the Swiss village of Adelboden, thanks to the members of the Adelboden Alpine School. It's a stunning location and I went along to take part in the World Igloo Building Championships back in 2016, held on Engstligenalp – the largest plateau in the western Swiss Alps. Signing up for a one-day instruction course allows instructors to take you through all the basics to finally completing a finished igloo. Starting from how to mark out the right-sized circle in the snow (which dictates the finished size of your igloo), they show how to cut the icy 'building blocks'. Hot drinks, a saw, plus plenty of encouragement are all provided. Book the two-day workshop, and you can even stay the night. ⊕ alpinschule-adelboden.ch

NATURE & WILDLIFE

GO WILD WITH GORILLAS
In the Virunga Mountains, Rwanda, with trailblazing,
conservation-focused Volcanoes Safaris
(experienced by Kate Wickers)
Of all wildlife encounters, meeting mountain gorillas feels intimate and personal, like visiting long-lost cousins. It's 5am and the sun is just rising as I follow a ranger along a single-file track within Rwanda's Virunga Mountains. It's a heart-pumping experience, caused by a mix of nervous excitement and the steep climb to 762m; the only noise to break the silence is the swish of a machete as a tracker ahead sweeps away nettles, vines, and brambles. First glimpse of the Muhoza gorilla group comes when a juvenile male swings Tarzan-like from a vine, and a female emerges from the ferns with an infant on her back. It peers over its mother's head to lock huge, round brown eyes with mine. 'Oh, I recognise you,' it seems to say – and why wouldn't it when we share 98% of the same DNA?

You'll never feel more alert to your surroundings than when the alpha male stirs, every inch of his 180kg muscley body rippling. Spending an hour among them, observing their meticulous grooming, steady chomping, recreational play and mating habits (so enthusiastically performed, I feel myself blushing), feels like being granted an audience with royalty. If two young juvenile males, all bluff and bluster, tumble towards you in a play fight (and they will), it's best to offer a hasty '*Mm mer*' (gorilla speak for I'm friendly) while reminding yourself to take mental pictures first before reaching for your camera. ⊕ volcanoessafaris.com

FLY ABOVE THE BIG FIVE
In Pilanesberg, South Africa, with photographer Guy Stubbs (experienced by Antonia Windsor)
'Look! By that rock!' The guide excitedly hands me binoculars. There's warmth on the side of my face – not from the sun, which is only just appearing behind the mountains that back Pilanesberg National Park, but from the metre-high flame that's roaring beside me. Because I'm not in a safari jeep as I focus the binoculars on a lion cub licking its belly – I'm in a hot-air balloon. We're drifting hypnotically above the plain in nothing more than an open wicker basket, with swathes of brightly coloured parachute silk billowing above us. The air on the other side of my face feels slightly dewy with the cool of the morning. This is the only hot-air balloon safari to launch from inside a park in South Africa.

It's a once-in-a-lifetime experience and at R6,000 (about £262) for a one-hour flight, it's a relatively affordable way to potentially spot the 'Big Five' among the seven thousand creatures in Pilanesberg. In a hot-air balloon, you don't disturb the animals; you get a bird's-eye view of their behaviour, and it's more peaceful and sustainable than a helicopter. ⊕ pilanesbergnationalparks.com

SEE THE CARIBBEAN'S 'SMALL SIX'

In Saint Lucia with Adams Toussaint, conservationist and former Chief Forestry Officer (experienced by Ian Packham)

A playful take on the African Big Five safari scene I know so well, this two-day tour launched in November 2024 gives you the chance to delve beyond Saint Lucia's admittedly stunning beaches and uncover another side of this tiny Caribbean island – its wildlife. Led by expert local naturalist and conservationist Adams Toussaint, you'll travel to uninhabited islets and along historic forest trails in search of six endemic species sharing Saint Lucia's name.

The list comprises three bird species, including the national bird, the Saint Lucia, which is a parrot, and three reptiles, none of which are found anywhere else on the globe. But as I discovered, as the first journalist to cover the Small Six Safari, Saint Lucia's incredible diversity could easily have seen it named the Diminutive Dozen instead. Having hopefully caught sight of some of the rarest species on our planet, you'll not only have had an incredible experience but come away with a greater understanding of the importance of the island's remaining wild spaces. ⊕ stluciawildlife.com

BE AWED BY ARCTIC LIGHTS

In Abisko, Sweden, at the Aurora Sky Station (experienced by Nigel Tisdall)

The good news about the aurora borealis is that it is always there, up in the heavens, an ethereal, multicoloured light show formed by fast-moving, electrically charged particles emanating from the sun. The bad is that to witness this swirling and spiritually uplifting spectacle, you need clear, dark skies and a bit of luck – and it helps to choose an optimal viewing point. One such sweet spot is the STF Aurora Sky Station in Abisko, Arctic Sweden, which sits right under the auroral zone and is one of the driest places in the country.

Reached by a chairlift that ascends Nuolja mountain to 900m, it is open from mid-November to mid-March, with 9pm to 1am prime time for sightings – try to avoid going when there is a full moon (a rival light source). Nothing is guaranteed, but the Northern Lights have been visible on 70% of the nights that the station is open. The trick is to not fixate on this single goal which might only last a few minutes. Instead, go for an adventurous, activity-filled Arctic holiday flying into Kiruna and staying at several locations – and if those celestial light bulbs flash, well, that's your bonus track. ⊕ auroraskystation.se

WORKSHOPS & TOURS

ENTER A SUBTERRANEAN MINING WORLD
In England, UK, with a practising Freeminer
(experienced by Claire Robinson)

Freeminer is the ancient title given to miners in the Forest of Dean who were granted permission to mine their own coal, iron ochre or stone in the 13th century by King Edward I. There are thought to be around 150 Freeminers still living in the forest today and a handful of small operating collieries. On a forty-five-minute tour into the yawning tunnels that make up Hopewell Colliery Mine in Coleford, a proud and experienced Forest Freeminer will guide you on a descent of 200m below the forest.

It's impossible not to be in awe of the men (and later women) who made this underground landscape their home – I could almost feel ghosts of miners past watching me, knowing I wouldn't have fared long in this colourless environment with only a candle to light the way. On the tour you'll hear fascinating tales about the geology of the forest, the history of Freemining and the skill of this ever-decreasing tradition. And you'll leave with a deep respect for the camaraderie and courage that bonded miners together, boy to man, over the centuries. ⊕ hopewellcolliery.com

POTTER IN THE HIMALAYAS
In Ladakh, India, with the Ganagora family
(experienced by Rashmi Narayan)

'Julley! Welcome to Ladakh – the land of high passes,' is the first greeting I hear from my guide Sonam Namgyal upon arrival in Ladakh in India, up in the Himalayas. After an impressive drive, passing a flock of bharal (blue sheep) along the brackish Zanskar River, we enter Likir, an ethno-tourism village with spectacular views of apricot trees and Buddhist stupas scattered across the peaks. Sonam and I find our way beneath a long willow-woven pergola and meet the Ganagora family, the local potters whose ancestors crafted pots and pans from clay for the royal family of Ladakh, and continue to do so.

Likir is known for its unique pottery, which is a true labour of love. Traditional methods involve grabbing chunks of clay and moulding them into shape, unlike pottery, where the pots are shaped from a clay tank. There's hope in keeping it alive, as the father–son duo has held workshops for children in the village, received support from the National Institute of Design, and hopes to educate tourists by crafting anything that captures their imagination through clay. The one-hour workshop is no ordinary pottery class, as instead of making a small pot, they help me make a *dzo*, a majestic native animal which is a cross between a cow and a yak. 'It's a skill we've learnt from our ancestors, and now, you are a part of us, by making something from our land and taking it home as a unique souvenir,' Rigzin Namgyal, the last of the potters from the family, tells me. ⊙ instagram.com/likir.pottery

AMBLE A GHOUL-STIRRING LITERARY PUB CRAWL
In Dublin, Ireland, with guide and actor Colm Quilligan (experienced by Kate Wickers)

'We are all born mad. Some remain so,' says Estragon in Samuel Beckett's play *Waiting for Godot*, which sums up the existential essence of the drama, and is delivered by actor Colm Quilligan over a pint of Guinness on Dublin's Literary Pub Crawl. Never was there a more fun way to get to grips with the work of the city's famous writers than two hours of songs, quotes, and many an interesting story, while exploring literary pubs, such as M.J. O'Neill's with its atmospheric nooks and crannies. Be warned, though, that with imaginations stirred, it is Bram Stoker's sharp-toothed ghouls that lurk, as Dublin's famous mists prevail. ⊕ dublinpubcrawl.com

STICK YOUR OAR IN
In Venice, Italy, with Jane Carporal of Row Venice (experienced by Sarah Rodrigues)

Venetian gondoliers are almost exclusively men – but all-female regattas date back at least to the 17th century. 'Women rowed out of necessity, as well as for sport,' says founder and president Jane Carporal. 'How else would they get to market from the other islands?' Her not-for-profit, all-female organisation is dedicated to preserving the ancient tradition of Venetian rowing – *voga alla veneta* – and each lesson starts canal-side in the Canareggio, being taught the basics.

When we take to the water, Jane stands at the back of the traditional wooden *batela coda di gambero* to steer while I get the hang of controlling my oar, cradled by the boat's *forcola*. Towards the end of our eighty minutes, we swap places and I stand proudly at the back, navigating around corners and under bridges. You'll never experience Venice in a more empowering and immersive way. ⊕ rowvenice.org

BLADESMITHING WITH A SENSEI
In Kōchi, Japan, with master blacksmith Nobuya Hayashi
(experienced by Daniel James Clarke)

Kōchi Prefecture, on Japan's Shikoku Island, is a world away from Tokyo's teeming streets. It's a place of temple-trekking pilgrims, rivers so blue they anointed a new colour, and where *bonito* (tuna) is still flame-sealed over hay. But don't leave until you've spent a day with Sensei Hayashi at his Kurogane workshop, learning how to forge a knife (swords are sadly out) the traditional way with barrels of flames and plenty of hammering. Producing the elegant utensil is fascinating – think about which inscription you'd like etched on it in advance – but, more so, is chatting with English-speaking Hayashi throughout, gaining the kind of local insights and anecdotes few travellers to Japan ever hear. ⊕ **workshop-kurogane.com**

WALK WITHIN ANCIENT WALLS
In Fez, Morocco, with a local-born guide
(experienced by Kate Wickers)

My guide from Plan-It-Fez was born in the heart of the Medina of Fez, so knows every nook and cranny. 'Don't judge a book by its cover,' he tells me, disappearing into the narrowest of alleyways 'Behind many humble doors in these simple streets, there are beautiful houses with gardens full of flowers.' Occasionally, there's a glimpse into these worlds – a lemon-tree-filled courtyard, an intricately tiled fountain, or a palm-shaded terrace. Within the Medina's UNESCO-protected ancient walls, time stands still: a knife grinder sharpens blades at a rotating stone wheel; a carpenter carves a spoon from aromatic cedar wood; a weaver's bobbin shuttles across an age-old loom; and yarn is dyed by hand in Souk Sabbaghine, the Dyers' Souk, where rainbow streams run to the river. ⊕ **plan-it-fez.com**

UNMASK YOUR TALENT
In Galle, Sri Lanka, with master mask maker
Janaka De Silva (experienced by Juliet Coombe)

Since 2006, Janaka, curator of The Galle Fort Art Gallery, has taught the ancient and deeply therapeutic skills of mask making. During the two-hour workshop, you'll carve a mask from a block of Kaduru wood to create a truly meaningful souvenir. The class includes a brief introduction to the masks' history and traditional painting methods, offering insights into the many different masks in Sri Lankan culture, including Kolam masks (traditional folk-dancing masks) and Sanni masks, used in healing rituals. Children love to paint elephant masks and scary fire-dancing ones.

The class teaches how to expertly correct any mistakes with a yellow cover-up paint, allowing you to rework fine details using a mix of local natural pigments and acrylic. Once finished, your mask is left to dry under the tropical sun while Janaka serves milk tea and shares ancient stories about this exceptional island craft. A true art of living as practised by ancestors for thousands of years, these masks carry a profoundly fascinating cultural significance, having been used to entertain through dramatic folk performances or to exorcise illnesses blamed on malevolent spirits. 🅕 The Galle Fort Art Gallery